Yugoslav-Americans and
National Security during World War II

Yugoslav-Americans and National Security during World War II

LORRAINE M. LEES

UNIVERSITY OF ILLINOIS PRESS

Urbana and Chicago

Library of Congress Cataloging-in-Publication Data
Lees, Lorraine M., 1946–
Yugoslav-Americans and national security during World War II / Lorraine M.
Lees.
p. cm.
Includes bibliographical references and index.
ISBN 978-0-252-03210-3 (cloth : alk. paper)
1. Yugoslav Americans—History—20th century. 2. World War, 1939–1945—United
States. 3. United States—Politics and government—1933–1945. 4. Internal secu-
rity—United States—History—20th century. 5. Subversive activities—United
States—History—20th century.
I. Title.
D769.8.F7Y84   2007
940.53'00899151—dc22   2007011382

To Bill

And to the memory of my immigrant ancestors

Contents

Acknowledgments

When I began this study of ethnicity and national security during World War II, I found that many wartime agencies were involved with foreign nationalities, but no single approach seemed to govern them, and many of the records were classified. Focusing on Yugoslav-Americans allowed me to take advantage of the expertise I had in U.S.-Yugoslav relations and to narrow the field of my inquiry. It also provided me with the best case study of the government's attitude toward the involvement of non-enemy ethnics in the war effort.

Gaining access to the classified material necessary for this study was an obstacle less easily surmounted; it took many years of Freedom of Information Act requests and research trips; I am grateful to Old Dominion University for providing grants to cover the costs and a research leave to complete the manuscript, and to Chandra R. deSilva, Dean of the College of Arts and Letters, for all his support. The interlibrary loan, reference, microfilm, and acquisitions staffs at Old Dominion University also have been invaluable, and I cannot thank them enough. I am indebted as well to the many archivists and librarians I have encountered. I am thankful to John Taylor and the staff at the National Archives and at the Manuscript Division of the Library of Congress, as well as those at the Immigration and Naturalization Service, the Department of Justice, the Immigration History Research Center, and the American Heritage Center. I was especially pleased to work with the wonderful archivists at the Franklin D. Roosevelt Library and the Bancroft Library, for whom no request was ever burdensome. Special thanks must also go to the Princeton University Library, Department of Rare Books and

Special Collections, for permission to quote from the Louis Adamic Papers, and especially to Kim Cranston, who so graciously allowed me to use the papers of his father, Alan Cranston.

My thanks as well to the many friends and colleagues, both in the United States and in the former Yugoslavia, who have played a part in this study. I am also grateful to Laurie Matheson and the University of Illinois Press, who have been very patient and supportive, and to the readers of the manuscript for their valuable comments.

My family, as always, is my greatest source of support. I am grateful to my parents, Caroline and the late James Lees, and most of all, to my husband and fellow historian, William Rodner, who, more than anyone else, has made this study possible.

Last, when I began this project, I hoped only to illuminate the historical connection between ethnicity and national security and to demonstrate the persistence of nativism in American history. I did not anticipate that another outbreak of nativism, occasioned by the events of September 2001, would serve to illustrate my point. While my work will be instructive to anyone wishing to learn from the present and to understand its relevance to the past, I cannot but regret the need for such lessons still to be taught.

Abbreviations

ACS	American Slav Congress
AVNOJ	Anti-Fascist Council for the National Liberation of Yugoslavia
CCAU	Common Council for American Unity
CFU	Croatian Fraternal Union of America
COI	Coordinator of Information
CPI	Committee on Public Information
CPP	Croatian Peasant Party
FARA	Foreign Agents Registration Act
FLD	Foreign Language Division
FLIS	Foreign Language Information Service
FNB	Foreign Nationalities Branch
GID	General Intelligence Division
IDCFNP	Interdepartmental Committee for Foreign Nationality Problems
INS	Immigration and Naturalization Service
IWO	International Workers Order
OC	Office of Censorship
OFF	Office of Facts and Figures
OSS	Office of Strategic Services
OWI	Office of War Information
SNDC	Serbian National Defense Council
SNF	Serb National Federation
SWPU	Special War Policies Unit
UCSSA	United Committee of South-Slavic Americans
UYRF	United Yugoslav Relief Fund
WPB	War Production Board
YGIE	Yugoslav-Government-In-Exile

Yugoslav-Americans and
National Security during World War II

Introduction

   Wars and the events surrounding them have usually produced outbreaks of nativist hysteria in the United States, with the country believing that
ethnic groups, who were presumed to have divided loyalties, represented a
danger to American security. In response, administrations ranging from that
of John Adams in the eighteenth century to George W. Bush in the twenty-
first developed policies aimed at limiting or controlling the political activities
of America's foreign nationalities population.[1] As John Higham observed in
his classic study of nativism, this "intense opposition to an internal minority
on the grounds of its foreign connections," usually focuses on "the loyalty of
some foreign (or allegedly foreign) group" that has failed to assimilate. The
"influence originating abroad" that the nativist perceived as threatening "the
very life of the nation from within . . . is colored and focused by a persistent
conception about what is un-American." More specifically, Alan M. Kraut
has noted that the nativist, mourning a "loss of cultural homogeneity" and
defining America as white, Anglo-Saxon, and Protestant, historically took
action against immigrants who were Catholic, who held radical political
beliefs, or who had a suspect racial heritage.[2]

   By the end of the nineteenth century, the anti-Catholic impulse behind
nativism had weakened, but the anti-radical and racial components remained
alive, feeding on the masses of "new" immigrants arriving from southern and
eastern Europe. Whether being an American meant adhering to "universalis-
tic political and social principles for which the republic stands," or being part
of a community "set apart from others by race, religion, language, national
derivation," or both,[3] the newcomers seemed a poor fit. They represented too

many different nationalities; had too little experience with self-government; and were too closely associated geographically to revolutionary movements. Yet the United States was at peace, and a general feeling of optimism born of the victory over Spain, an expanding economy, and the Progressive movement of the early twentieth century "probably weighed against nativism." Most Progressive reformers had little identification with immigrants, and viewed them, primarily from afar, as "malleable, and still to be molded under the influences of American society." The settlement-house workers, who were motivated by sympathy for the foreign born and were more involved in immigrant lives, tried to provide "a receptive environment for Old World heritages." However, the "immigrant gifts" such Progressives celebrated turned out to be things Americans valued little, such as dances and handcrafts. The American system had already been formed, and the Progressive view of a cosmopolitan American nationality was designed simply to facilitate the immigrants' adjustment to it.[4]

The pressure on immigrants to assimilate grew more intense after the outbreak of World War I. At first, the campaign echoed the softer approach of the settlement house. Philadelphia, at the urging of the Bureau of Naturalization, held a public reception for naturalized citizens in May 1915, with President Woodrow Wilson in attendance. A private group then created a National Americanization Committee, which sponsored similar events under the slogan "Many People, But One Nation" on July 4, designated as "Americanization Day." Within a few months, however, the committee shifted its emphasis to allegiance to the United States, without any acceptance of Old World ties. In 1917, America's entry into the war against Germany, a country that served as the source of so much of America's immigrant population, led to a "free-floating nationalistic anxiety" against "the hyphenated American . . . the immigrant of divided loyalty." The reigning principle of "100% Americanism," promoted by the Committee on Public Information (CPI), embodied "a more widespread concern than Americans had ever before felt over the immigrants' attachment to their adopted country."[5] The CPI and its Division of Work with the Foreign Born attempted to diffuse this fear by sponsoring Fourth of July pageants "with every available nationality conspicuous in its native costumes and its demonstrations of patriotism." However, the CPI also used foreign-language speakers to monitor the foreign-language press for violations of espionage and sedition statutes.[6]

One-third of America's foreign-born population "derived from enemy territory," but the Germans, who in addition to being America's enemy were also presumed to be sympathetic to Bolshevism, bore the brunt of nativist hostility. Immigrants from the Austro-Hungarian Empire saved themselves through their work in defense-related heavy industry and their attachment to democratic sentiments. Although the country's reliance on their labor was "deeply disquieting" to many native-born Americans, the Austro-Hungarians exhibited an admirable support for Wilsonian values. As "subject nationalities" who advocated and worked for the independence of their former homelands, they represented the "kind of hyphenate activity which served to demonstrate the attachment to American war aims of many technically enemy aliens."[7]

*   *   *

By 1917, the threat of Bolshevism had strengthened anti-radical sentiment and given new life to long-standing demands for immigration restriction. The Democrats usually opposed such legislation, and Wilson, though he used the espionage and sedition statutes (enacted during the war) against radicals and socialists opposed to the conflict, continued to veto restrictive measures. However, the revival of anti-radicalism, coupled with new arguments about threats to national defense, enabled Congress to pass over Wilson's veto a bill that instituted a literacy test for immigrants, denied entry to anyone advocating revolution or belonging to an organization that did so, and allowed for the deportation of resident aliens on similar grounds.[8] In the immediate postwar period, anti-radicalism, nourished by the war's patriotic fervor and the fear caused by strikes in industries dominated by the same immigrants who had earlier appeared loyal, redirected "100% Americanism" toward the conviction that "radicalism permeated the foreign-born population."[9] The Red Scare that followed featured raids by Attorney General A. Mitchell Palmer and J. Edgar Hoover, head of the newly formed Radical Division within the Bureau of Investigation, on suspected immigrants, their meeting halls, newspaper offices, and benefit societies.

Although relatively brief, the Red Scare left behind the conviction that the only way to remove the threat of foreign ideologies from America was to eliminate the foreigner who was immune to American ideals. The war had created a demand for unity and homogeneity and destroyed an important prewar idea: "the historic confidence in the capacity of American society to assimilate all men automatically." The Progressive ideal of American nationalism as an "unfinished, steadily improving, cosmopolitan blend" disappeared as the Congress implemented a quota system, designed to keep out the southern and eastern European immigrants who were deemed most likely to be infected with radical views or an inferior heritage. Although John

Higham ended his history of nativism at the point of the restrictionists' victory, he observed that "the new equation between national loyalty and a large measure of political and social conformity" the law mandated "would long outlive the generation that established it."[10]

The immigration restrictions put in place in the 1920s embodied both anti-radical and racial nativism, but the latter underwent some modification in the 1930s as a more pluralist mind set, which supported cultural diversity within a common political framework, gained ground. This pluralist approach allowed immigrants and ethnics "a dual identity," provided they subscribed to a "unifying civic culture."[11] In many ways, the interwar period was not a propitious time for new directions in social thought. Historian Nicholas Montalto points out that by the 1930s, "the collapse of the world economy and the rise of fascism touched the raw nerve of social disunity in the United States," and the drive "to restore social order and wipe out unacceptable cultural differences continued."[12] However, the recognition that culture, not race, was at the root of these differences, and that coercive Americanization campaigns caused more rather than less alienation among immigrants, represented crucial changes in the atmosphere. The work of scientists and anthropologists such as Frank Boas undermined the idea that "more recent immigrants were less assimilable to American standards than earlier ones had been" and helped create an intellectual climate, characteristic of the New Deal, in which "national, racial or ethnic backgrounds did not count for or against people."[13]

Social workers of the 1930s agreed, seeing the idea of the melting pot as one that symbolized dehumanization and exploitation rather than assimilation. The immigrant again became "a contributor to a culture still in process of definition," all of which "bespoke an atmosphere of tolerance."[14] A variety of organizations, including the Service Bureau for Intercultural Education and the Foreign Language Information Service, and immigrant writers such as Louis Adamic, whom Richard Weiss calls "the foremost publicist of immigrant concerns during the Depression years," sought to institutionalize this tolerance by educating the immigrant, especially the second generation, about their group's culture and history, and by interpreting "the Immigrant to America and America to the Immigrant."[15]

Yet the efforts of Adamic and others like him remained essentially assimilationist; the diversity celebrated was cultural rather than political. The rise of fascism and its use of cultural appeals, wrapped within a "Big Lie" of propaganda, soon tested the depths of even this tolerance, as critics of intercultural education came to see diversity as dangerous. As Montalto notes, they asked, "[How could] identification with cultural heritage be separated from allegiance to foreign governments?" Might not this emphasis on ethnic pride be "captured by parasitical elements within the ethnic community or foreign interests hostile [to America]" and thus "lead to a hardening of ethnic and racial divisions and the possible Balkanization of the United States?"[16]

The millions of immigrants still residing in the United States, many of whom were not naturalized, gave form to those fears. The American government had designed the immigration restrictions of the 1920s to insure that if the country were to go to war again, a reduced immigrant population would be in residence. Nonetheless, when America entered World War II, more than "one-fourth (35,000,000) of the . . . inhabitants of the United States . . . either were born abroad or were born in the United States of foreign or mixed parentage."[17] Publicly, the administration of Franklin D. Roosevelt declared its confidence in the loyalty of the foreign nationalities population, while recognizing, as one official involved with foreign nationalities policy later wrote, that ethnics were "disposed by sentiment to concern themselves—often actively, sometimes passionately—with the fate of the lands whose cultures they still share in some degree."[18] Privately, many officials feared that fifth-column activity, or at least manipulation by foreign politicians, was a given in America's ethnic communities. As President Roosevelt asked Federal Bureau of Investigation head J. Edgar Hoover a few months after Pearl Harbor: "Have you pretty well cleaned out the alien waiters in the principal Washington hotels? Altogether too much conversation in the dining rooms!"[19]

When Roosevelt made this request, he already had the precedents and the resources to deal with enemy aliens, ranging from the Enemy Alien Act of 1798, to the internment of Germans during World War I, to the executive orders issued by the president himself in the wake of Pearl Harbor. As soon as the United States entered the war, Roosevelt designated the approximately one million German, Italian, and Japanese aliens residing in the United States to be enemy aliens.[20] More than thirty thousand were interned through an Enemy Alien Internment Program from 1941 until 1946.[21] Within a few months, Roosevelt also allowed the military to exclude both enemy aliens and those of "enemy ancestry" from strategic areas and created an agency to relocate and house the excluded in centers away from the restricted zones.[22] Although all enemy aliens were subject to the exclusion order, its effects fell most heavily on the 120,000 Japanese and Japanese Americans living on the West Coast, who were removed from their homes, relocated, and interned en masse.[23]

But if foreign ancestry in and of itself represented a danger, what of the millions of other ethnics in America with origins in the European countries now represented in the United Nations by resistance movements and governments-in-exile? American officials exhibited an almost equal fear that foreign intrigue in those communities could endanger American security, disrupt the war effort, and involve the United States in ancient political quarrels that would undermine the Grand Alliance. Because of these fears, the Roosevelt administration created several wartime agencies to monitor or manage the political activities of America's at-large foreign nationalities population, and also assigned existing agencies new responsibilities. The strategies each of these agencies developed to deal with foreign nationalities issues often sharply contrasted with the approach to the war taken by the country as a whole. National security, in short, had a decidedly nativist dimension.

*　*　*

This study focuses on the key agencies involved with foreign nationalities and analyzes how they discharged their duties and how they reflected the country's attitude toward the value of ethnicity in a democracy at war. One of the new agencies, the Office of War Information (OWI), originally called the Office of Facts and Figures (OFF), contained a Foreign Language Division that distributed information and propaganda to the foreign-language press and radio for the purpose of promoting unity and building morale. Another wartime creation, the Foreign Nationalities Branch (FNB) of the Office of Strategic Services (OSS), first known as the Coordinator of Information (COI), interviewed exiled European political leaders and members of America's ethnic organizations to gather political intelligence for use in foreign policy and psychological warfare. The Department of Justice, already active in defending the nation's security, administered the Smith Act of 1940, which required the registration and fingerprinting of all resident aliens and made it a crime to advocate or to belong to an organization that advocated the overthrow of the American government. The department also enforced the Voorhis Act, which took effect in 1941 and required the registration of any group seeking to overthrow the American government, and most germane to this study, the amended Foreign Agents Registration Act (FARA) of 1942, which demanded full disclosure and registration by any organization or person operating on behalf of a "foreign principal." The Federal Bureau of Investigation, originally charged by the Roosevelt administration with identifying subversive elements within the population, gathered information to assist the Justice Department in its enforcement of the Smith, Voorhis, and Foreign Agents Registration acts. The bureau also utilized a variety of open and covert methods to insure that ethnics active in fraternal or relief organizations did not constitute a dangerous "fifth column." The Department of State, protective of an area it considered related to foreign policy, maintained a Division of Foreign Activity Correlation under an assistant secretary and attempted to control the other entities involved in ethnic issues by chairing an Interdepartmental Committee for Foreign Nationality Problems.

Each agency understood its own particular task with regard to America's foreign-language population and the European exiles entering the United States, but despite the attempts of several policymakers, the Roosevelt administration failed to develop a single, coherent foreign nationalities policy. The Department of State viewed America's ethnic population as a breeding ground for intrigue and thought it essential to limit, or at least control, the activities of exiles and "free movements" lest they divide or subvert the country's immigrants. Agencies concerned with propaganda and psychological and political warfare, such as the OWI and FNB, saw the foreign nationalities community as a positive resource whose manipulation might give the United States an advantage in the war. The Justice Department, charged with enforcing legislation that, at its most basic level, targeted ethnics as a danger to the country's internal security, found itself divided between the civil libertarian principles of attorneys general Robert H. Jackson and Francis Biddle, and the anti-radical tradition of J. Edgar Hoover's FBI. In the end, the most consistent message conveyed was the Roosevelt administration's willingness to equate ethnicity with disloyalty.

Although virtually every ethnic group in the United States received the attention of the agencies listed, the Yugoslav-American community provided one of the most significant examples of the wartime connection between ethnicity and national security. Still a dominant workforce in heavy industry, immigrants from southern and eastern Europe and their children comprised a majority of the country's at-large foreign nationalities population. Louis Gerson notes that for many, such as the South Slavs who had emigrated before the modern state of Yugoslavia came into being, their "ethnic nationalism and patriotism toward the old country emerged only after their arrival in the United States."[24] The interest-group politics of their new home nurtured these sentiments, as the Republican and Democratic parties routinely courted the ethnic vote by appealing to their "emotional interest in ancestral lands which were or might become affected by both Nazi and fascist ambitions."[25]

The response such appeals could provoke became a concern once the United States entered the war. The Yugoslav community in the United States represented every shade of political opinion, from fascist sympathizers and ethnic monarchists on the right to socialists and communists on the left, with a great measure of intragroup ethnic antagonism. These divisions reflected the history of Yugoslavia, a multi-ethnic state created in 1919, as well as the political and military effects of the war. Throughout the 1920s and 1930s, the more populous Serbs had dominated the Yugoslav government, while the Croats continually demanded either more power within the government or, in extreme cases, their own independent state. This Serb-Croat dispute so consumed the life of the country that, as Balkan historian Barbara Jelavich has noted, "a Yugoslav nationality did not come into existence."[26] When the Axis invaded Yugoslavia in the spring of 1941, they took advantage of these ethnic divisions and partitioned the country. The Yugoslav king and his ministers fled and eventually established a government-in-exile in London. Several Yugoslav officials also took refuge in the United States and Canada.[27]

The Allies recognized the exiled King Peter and his government as the only legitimate rulers of Yugoslavia,[28] but the emergence of rival resistance groups with competing postwar visions complicated the issue of who should hold power when hostilities ended. The Serbs, who controlled the government-in-exile, blamed Croatian treachery for their country's collapse and rejected the restoration of prewar Yugoslavia in favor of a "Greater Serbia." Serb army officers loyal to the exiled king mounted a Chetnik resistance movement in May 1941 under the leadership of Draža Mihailović. A second resistance group, the Communist lead and ethnically diverse Partisans of Josip Broz Tito, who supported the creation of a federated state without the monarchy, began operations a few months later. Eventually, after rumors of Chetnik collaboration with the Axis surfaced, the Allies realized that Mihailović waged parallel wars. He collaborated with the Italians to attack the Partisans while continuing sporadic sabotage against the Germans. The Partisans also engaged the Chetniks, but directed most of their energy against the Axis.[29]

American Serbs, for the most part, supported the Chetniks and the exiled king and used their Serb National Federation (SNF) and its newspaper to publicize their cause. Many Croats and Slovenes favored Tito, despite concerns about his communism, because of his support for an ethnically diverse and federated Yugoslavia. By 1943, Croats and Slovenes had formed a United Committee of South-Slavic Americans (UCSSA) under Louis Adamic to raise funds for the Partisans and to counter the pan-Serb rhetoric of the Serb National Federation. Each group demanded that the United States government assist or recognize only the resistance leader it supported, while the Yugoslav-Government-In-Exile (YGIE) and its influential ambassador,

Konstantin Fotić, did everything possible to foster Mihailović's image as the most gallant defender of Yugoslavia. By contrast, ministers in the Yugoslav Information Center in New York, such as the former governor of Croatia Ivan Šubašić, disagreed with the pan-Serb orientation of the government-in-exile. The center quickly became a focus for pro-Yugoslav opinion, with its staff always at odds with Fotić and thus with its own government.[30]

Early in the war, the FNB identified central and eastern Europe as the areas from which "the most intricate and highly charged political problems of the coming peace arise."[31] Yugoslavia and the Yugoslav-American community reflected these concerns by posing the twin threats of right-wing agitation, represented by the YGIE and their Serbian-American supporters, and left-wing radicalism, represented by the Partisans and their South Slavic American backers. During World War I, the political activities of many of these same ethnic groups had seemed in accord with American policy. In the 1940s, by contrast, the divisions within the Grand Alliance, with the Soviets supporting the Partisans, the British trying to broker a compromise between the two factions, and the Americans reluctant to take sides but wary of Soviet influence, made the ethnics' activities unwelcome.

The level of concern with which American policymakers viewed Yugoslavia is reflected in the archival record. The largest single group of FNB files is on the Yugoslav-American community. The files on Italians and Germans, with ties to the countries with which the United States was at war, are second and third; the material on Poland, the country so closely associated with the collapse of the Grand Alliance, is a distant fourth. The FNB was not alone in its preoccupation with all things Yugoslav. The OWI, and the Departments of State and Justice also attempted, in a variety of ways, to bring the warring factions within the Yugoslav-American community together or at least to limit the attacks by each on the other. Their efforts enjoyed little success, in part because of the suspicions each Yugoslav-American group had about the actual sympathies of American agencies. The State Department, exhibiting two aspects of nativist thought, barely concealed its distaste for any "race group," lest it interfere with the policies of the Grand Alliance, and was also wary of ethnics with communist sympathies. The department maintained relations with the officially recognized but Serb controlled and monarchist YGIE, much to the displeasure of Tito's supporters. The Foreign Language Division of the OWI, under the leadership of Alan Cranston, had close ties to Louis Adamic and other anti-monarchial leaders, which enraged the Serbs.

The FBI surveilled members of each of the factions within the Yugoslav community, but the bureau was especially active in keeping tabs on leftists such as Adamic and the United Committee. The Justice Department spent years attempting to secure the registration, under FARA, of the major organizations representing each of the Yugoslav-American factions. This insistence that the Yugoslav-Americans, by supporting the war effort, had become "agents of a foreign principle," and the outrage and alienation it caused within the ethnic community, ironically served as the only unifying element the government was able to provide. The most constructive work was that of the FNB, which quietly used Adamic and the Yugoslavs, particularly those in the Information Center, to gather important political intelligence for use at home and abroad, and whose director, DeWitt Clinton Poole, seemed to be the only American official genuinely aware of the pain that divided loyalties caused for the ethnics themselves. However, by 1944, Poole became increasingly concerned about the growth of Soviet influence and turned his attention and that of his agency more and more to postwar issues.

*   *   *

The connection between ethnicity and American national security during World War II involved many of the most troublesome issues raised by a democracy's entry into war, and by the nature of the war itself. New Deal liberals who populated many of the country's wartime agencies venerated freedom of speech and free association as pillars of democracy, and many supported the pluralist approach to ethnic issues that had characterized the 1930s. However, the unity necessary for the war effort raised questions about the value and even the safety of continuing to accommodate diversity. Could immigrants who read only the ethnic press be relied upon to draw the right conclusions about American policy and to support the war? How could foreign-language newspapers, which skirted the edge of opposition to the policies of the United Nations, be turned around? Were foreign nationalities groups liable to become the dupes of exiled politicians and attempt to influence American foreign policy in ways that were harmful to the war effort and to the nation's security? Or did they represent a resource that could help wage the war and provide insight into the postwar world that would follow? War bond sales with ethnic themes contributed to the war effort and to the maintenance of domestic morale, but when did the organizations created by foreign nationalities groups to support the war in their former homelands cross the line and become "agents of a foreign principle?" Did the presence of Communists or communist sympathizers within ethnic organizations render them unworthy of support? Could all of these dangers best be met by encouraging or by controlling the political activities of ethnics and immigrants? If the need for security at home compromised the search for security abroad, which should be sacrificed? Were the two even divisible?

This study of America's experience with Yugoslav feuds on American soil during World War II evaluates how American policymakers handled the tension they perceived between ethnicity and national security. The hold that nativism continued to exercise can be seen in the surveillance of foreign nationalities groups such as the Yugoslav-Americans and in the attempts to control the political activities of fraternal organizations and lobbying groups like the Serb National Federation and the United Committee of South Slavic Americans. American officials' conviction that the competition waged by the followers of Mihailović and Tito represented a danger to the administration's foreign policy confirms the tie that existed in their minds between ethnic activities and the country's national security. By concentrating on this group of non-enemy ethnics and the government's attempt to channel and control their political activities, this study demonstrates that the suspicion that ethnicity in and of itself was un-American and a threat to national security was at the heart of the Roosevelt administration's policy toward all ethnics, friendly or enemy. Concern about ethnicity was not a phenomenon unique to the 1940s, but its persistence during a war waged against racial extremism, by liberals dedicated to freedom and tolerance, illustrated that at least part of the country's definition of national security rested firmly on a nativist base.

About Aliens and the Fifth Column

In 1951, former Attorney General Francis Biddle wrote, "Freedom and fear cannot live together in the same community on equal terms." While the "impulse to freedom" was "tolerant" and "rational," that of fear led to "persecution, hatred and violence." Often throughout its history, the United States, Biddle lamented, had sought to protect its own freedom of speech and thought by denying those privileges to others on the grounds that the "expression of opposing views" endangered American democracy.[1] Although Biddle was writing to combat the excesses of the postwar Red Scare, his words are applicable to America in the 1930s and early 1940s. As fascism threatened and then broke the peace, the United States became alarmed at the number of immigrants and aliens present in the country, fearing the effect they might have on internal security. The Roosevelt administration implemented a number of policies in response, ranging from restrictive legislation, to surveillance of ethnic groups, to the creation of agencies designed to boost immigrant morale and participation in the war effort once the country itself had become a belligerent.

* * *

In 1934, President Franklin Roosevelt, concerned about the impact that fascism abroad could have on America's multi-ethnic population, asked Bureau of Investigation head J. Edgar Hoover to furnish him with information on the "influence of foreign totalitarian powers" within the country.[2] By 1936, the information Hoover provided, which demonstrated that both communist and fascist groups existed in the United States, caused Roosevelt to direct the bureau, renamed the Federal Bureau of Investigation the year before, to develop a systematic intelligence program to deal with "subversive activities."[3] However, Hoover could not act on the president's request. During World War I, President Woodrow Wilson had given the Department of State control over espionage and intelligence; other agencies could continue to gather information, but State was to provide "the coordination, evaluation and dissemination of information and overall planning."[4] The Congress had then authorized the secretary of state to "request investigations of foreign directed activities."[5] Before Hoover could comply with Roosevelt's directive, the 1916 statute, under which the attorney general could direct the FBI to undertake such tasks only at the request of the State Department, had to be invoked. When informed of this by Hoover, Roosevelt promptly summoned Secretary of State Cordell Hull, who agreed to make the needed request but to not put it in writing. Hoover later informed the attorney general and military intelligence of the authorization.[6]

Hoover actually needed little encouragement; concern about radicals and immigrants, and the use of administrative tools to alleviate that concern, was virtually second nature to him. Hoover biographer Richard Gid Powers notes that Hoover, a Washington native, had grown up in a white, middle-class world where "immigrants were scarce and self-abasing." In 1917, using family connections, Hoover secured a post in the Justice Department supervising enemy aliens. This placed him at the center of the country's "hysteria over traitors, spies and saboteurs" at a time when the Justice Department was, according to Powers, "committing some of the most egregious violations of civil liberties in American history." Although Hoover was an attorney, his work in the Alien Enemy Bureau, which involved judgments on the loyalty of aliens and their possible internment, "accustomed him to using administrative procedures as a substitute" for legal processes.[7]

As the postwar Red Scare began, Attorney General A. Mitchell Palmer appointed Hoover, the Justice Department's "resident alien expert," to head the Radical Division within the Bureau of Investigation.[8] Renamed the General Intelligence Division (GID) in 1920, it collated "all information about radical activities collected by bureau agents, the State Department's consular service, military and naval intelligence, or the local police or forwarded by patriotic citizens." By 1920, one-third of the bureau's agents were monitoring radicals; the GID had two hundred thousand dossiers on radical activists and files on five hundred foreign-language newspapers that were considered outlets for radical propaganda. As head of the GID, Hoover assisted Attorney General Palmer in his arrests and deportations of supposed alien radicals.[9]

Palmer's excesses and the corruption scandals of the Harding Administration led to a reorganization of the agency in 1924. Attorney General Harlan Stone abolished the GID, banned probes of individuals' political views, and insisted that the activities of the bureau be limited to investigations of violations of federal laws. He also fired the director and appointed assistant director Hoover, who had a reputation as a "stern taskmaster," to head the bureau. Hoover complied with Stone's orders, announcing that since there was no federal law against "radical ideas," the bureau would not collect political information. However, he continued to have agents "monitor radical activists and organizations" under the pretense that such information resulted from public informants rather than direct bureau operations. He used Roosevelt's 1936 request to secure the official resumption of the collection of political intelligence and to re-create a General Intelligence Division within the FBI.[10] In September of that year, Hoover instructed to his agents "to obtain from all possible sources information concerning subversive activities being conducted in the United States by Communists, Fascists, [and] representatives or advocates of other organizations or groups advocating the overthrow or replacement of the Government of the United States by illegal methods."[11]

Although Hoover's instructions to his agents may have appeared to exceed the president's directive, he sent the results of his findings to the White House, indicating that "Roosevelt know exactly what Hoover was doing."[12] Historian Kenneth O'Reilly points out that Roosevelt was "not insensitive to civil liberties"; he often relied on less extreme security measures that those advocated by Hoover, and the steps he did take were often characterized "by restraint and not excess."[13] However, like most presidents, Roosevelt put the nation's security, or his view of it, above any other concerns. Athan Theoharis, recognized authority on the FBI and its history, maintains that historically, Roosevelt's action and Hoover's response initiated a trend: that after 1936, presidents and their attorneys general "increasingly turned to the FBI in a quest to anticipate foreign directed threats to the nation's internal security." Hoover, already adept at monitoring the political views of suspect individuals, not only had an official sanction to continue this work, but since his targets operated by "stealth and subterfuge," he too could "rely on inherently intrusive and invariably illegal investigative techniques." The results of most of these investigations could not be used in court, but the FBI could "contain" subversives by passing the information on to the White House.[14]

Congress provided a more overt mechanism for safeguarding the country against foreign intrigue. As the continuing unrest in Europe increased the number of political exiles entering the county, the fear that their public appeals for support could divide the foreign language community or serve as the nucleus of a fifth column increased as well. To protect American citizens from being used unknowingly to advance a foreign cause, federal legislators proposed a registration and disclosure system for individuals, organizations, and media outlets working on behalf of a foreign entity.[15] The resulting Foreign Agents Registration Act (FARA) of 1938 required groups or individuals who acted on behalf of a "foreign principle" to register that connection by submitting a relatively simple three-page form and a photograph to the Department of State, which administered the law.[16] To further reduce the appeal of foreign exiles, the government stressed the importance of naturalization for immigrants intending to reside permanently in the United States. Immigration authorities, the United States Bureau of Education, and local citizens organizations and school districts formed partnerships to standardize citizenship classes and make them widely available. Yet the average immigrant took more than ten years to become a citizen, while some waited for as long as twenty.[17]

To accelerate the naturalization process, the federal government sponsored a radio series called "Americans All . . . Immigrants All," which celebrated the contributions that ethnic groups had made to American life while emphasizing the virtues of citizenship and a common culture. The Federal Radio Project of the Office of Education, Department of the Interior, developed the series of twenty-six programs in 1938, with the assistance of the Works Progress Administration and in cooperation with the Columbia Broadcasting System and a private organization, the Service Bureau for Intercultural Education. George Seldes, a playwright who was also a CBS executive, wrote the scripts, and James L. Houghteling, Commissioner of Immigration and Naturalization in the Department of Labor, who had expressed his support for the project in its earliest stages, reviewed them. To Houghteling, the name perfectly suited the program because it conveyed his belief that "we are all Americans," and that immigrants, "by changing their birthplace" through naturalization, "make better natural citizens than those who were born to it."[18]

In the promotional materials for "Americans All," the commissioner of education declared that the people of the United States "do not know racial or national boundaries . . . we're one people!" The series highlighted the "little-known triumphs of the American spirit of tolerance and hospitality to all who have pledged allegiance to the United States."[19] The programs were broadcast from late November 1938 through the spring of 1939; as more refugees entered the United States, the government hoped the series would popularize "a cosmopolitan definition of American nationality which would make nativism unpatriotic."[20]

The goals of the Service Bureau for Intercultural Education were more immigrant centered. The Bureau had originated among high school teachers looking for a way to defuse "ethnic tensions" in their classrooms. Inspired by an article Louis Adamic had written for *Harper's* in 1934, in which he called attention to the "feelings of inferiority" and alienation among second-generation ethnics, who felt little attachment to their parents' homeland or to America, the Bureau focused its attention on the "importance of building ethnic pride" among the children of immigrants.[21] However, the government agencies involved were not comfortable with a strong celebration of ethnicity, and insisted that the thrust of the programs center "on the contributions of ethnic cultures to American culture, not appreciation for ethnic culture per se."[22]

The Service Bureau complied, describing the series as one designed to achieve a "better understanding for and among all cultural and racial groups through the dramatization of the contributions made by each group in American life." CBS broadcast the programs on Sunday afternoons but schools and colleges could obtain recordings for their own use and the Office of Education provided leaflets supplementing the information in each episode without charge. In addition to programs on each ethnic group, the series covered crucial periods in American history and the contributions made during those periods by immigrants, as well as the immigrants' record in specific areas, including science and the arts.[23] Listeners were encouraged to discuss each program in "listening-in" groups, preferably with members of different cultural groups in attendance.[24]

A persistent theme throughout the series was the interaction between immigrant groups; the program on the English, for example, took special care to acknowledge their crucial role in shaping the country's institutions and history, while also stressing "that nothing here has ever been done exclusively by one group."[25] The prospectus for the first program, called "Opening Frontiers," summarized the history of immigrants who had come to America and the gifts they gave to their new home, from the "customs, foods, place-names" of the Spanish to the "aggressive democracy" and "mountain music and dances" of the Scotch-Irish. The script depicted most as seeking freedom and as contributing to the wealth and power of the United States; the "Negroes," though identified as slaves, were credited with helping to "transform southern wilderness into prosperous plantations."[26] With more of an emphasis on creating an image of a united, democratic country than on historical truth, the program described the Spanish as "accompanied by Catholic priests, Jewish scientists, an African negro sailor" in their quest for empire; the Puritans as seekers of religious freedom and William Penn of the Quakers as a man dedicated only to "liberty of conscience." The Irish came to America "to escape famine, to find political freedom," but the script made no mention of the hostility and prejudice they had encountered from American nativists.[27]

The only ethnics featured in more than one program were the Slavs, who, the Office of Education maintained, had "contributed to every phase of America's cultural and industrial expansion." Southern Slavs "did battle with the soil" to clear the plains, helped establish the metropolitan centers of the East, and through their "wit and brawn" became "the backbone of the coal, steel, and meat-packing industries." The Yugoslavs constituted part of this general history of the "thousands of robust laborers" who helped to "build an American empire of cities and railroads and skyscrapers," but they could also boast of the achievements of individuals such as the Serb inventor Michael Pupin and the Slovene scientist Nikola Tesla.[28]

The series was a great popular success, but the government did not realize its goal. Native-born Americans had not listened to the programs; only the foreign nationalities community had, and they had taken away "a self-assurance and a sense of prestige about their own nationality." The educators involved were no doubt pleased, but the policymakers, who were more interested in unity than diversity, were not, and future programming featured more of an emphasis on the American system and its values.[29]

Among the general public, the political beliefs of immigrants commanded more attention than their cultural contributions. For the average American, citizenship carried with it an aversion to radical ideas, with "radical" usually defined as a commitment to leftist or communist ideology. By the 1930s, the rise of fascism, with its skillful use of propaganda and "fifth column" tactics, added fears of right-wing radicalism to more traditional concerns about dangers emanating from the left. Roosevelt himself often spoke of fifth columns, usually in the context of avoiding the problems of the last war, but also in reference to more open attempts by exiles to influence American policy. At a news conference on September 8, 1939, in the wake of the outbreak of war in Europe, Roosevelt recalled the need to guard against "some of the things that happened over here" from 1914 through the beginning of 1917, when a number of "foreign governments" had attempted not only sabotage but also propaganda designed to influence American public opinion. He announced a number of preparedness measures, including an increase in the "personnel of certain investigating agencies" and the primary role to be played by the Justice Department and the FBI rather than the State Department in investigating "espionage, sabotage, and violations of the neutrality regulations." These measures were designed to "guard against that and the spread by any foreign nation of propaganda in this country which would tend to be subversive—I believe that is the word—of our form of government."[30]

The president's announcement made public the result but not the details of a power struggle that had been waged between the State Department and the FBI. The war emergency had given Hoover the opportunity to centralize all "domestic intelligence operations" within the FBI. However, since Hull had approved the bureau's investigations in 1936, with the authority conveyed by the statute passed in 1916, the State Department technically retained authority over the FBI's intelligence activities. When the State Department attempted to exercise that control in 1939, Hoover and the attorney general secured a secret directive from Roosevelt ending the department's supervisory role.[31] Roosevelt made that arrangement public during his September news conference.

Assistant Secretary of State Adolf A. Berle, the State Department's Coordinator of Intelligence and liaison with the FBI, did not accept this defeat gracefully. Berle, who had served as an Army Intelligence officer during World War I, viewed intelligence as "an elitist, intellectual extension of foreign policy."[32] Throughout the war, Berle would attempt to regain at least a measure of authority for the State Department in gathering intelligence from foreign nationalities groups.

The American public seemed to prefer more rather than less security. By the spring of 1940, several state legislatures had discussed measures barring aliens from certain areas of employment and a number of states (mostly in the South where few aliens resided) demanded that aliens be registered and photographed. American citizens also flooded the Justice Department with requests for investigations of specific aliens, whom loyal Americans suspected of espionage.[33] Berle understood the need for security but worried about the perils more stringent measures involved. The danger, he said, was that as we try to "get hold of people who are violating our laws, we gather in a lot of perfectly respectable citizens who are suspected of having had an idea at some stage of the game." The government had to balance the need to "prevent a 'fifth column' who are really either foreign agents or people who are trying to commit crimes" with the imperative "to prevent this machinery from being used hysterically, in violation of civil liberties and every decent idea of progress."[34]

The government attempted to counteract this anti-alien sentiment through the "I Am an American" program, which celebrated the attainment of citizenship by immigrants. The "I Am an American" concept had its roots in World War I, when Congress had proclaimed the Fourth of July "Americanization Day" and the country had sponsored ceremonies honoring new or naturalized citizens. These celebrations had continued intermittently throughout the 1920s and 1930s. In 1939, at the behest of Labor Secretary Frances Perkins, dozens of towns and cities held "New Citizens Day" celebrations, and in 1940, Congress authorized the president to designate "Citizenship Day," the third Sunday in May, as "I Am an American" Day.[35] That same year, the Immigration and Naturalization Service (INS) and the National Broadcasting Company developed a radio series entitled "I'm an American," which featured "distinguished naturalized Americans" discussing their recently acquired citizenship, "a possession which we ourselves take for granted but which is still new and thrilling to them." The program was designed not just for immigrants, but, as the title suggested, "for all Americans from Plymouth Rock to Ellis Island."[36] Librarian of Congress and poet Archibald MacLeish, who was native born, inaugurated the series by reading his poem "America Was Promises": the "promise of wealth, of well-being, of escape, of freedom, of new beginnings" made by the country to people around the world, but which the people themselves had to bring to fruition.[37]

Subsequent broadcasts featured Thomas Mann, Louis Adamic, and Albert Einstein, with the latter taking his citizenship examination just two hours before the broadcast. Eleanor Roosevelt participated as well, in a program during which young, recently nationalized citizens asked her about their role in democracy. Each episode ended with the announcer providing an address where listeners could write to obtain a free copy of the United States Constitution, provided by the Daughters of the American Revolution.[38]

Even though some of the same people appeared, the tone and content of the "I Am an American" radio series differed from the more dramatic, sentimental, and immigrant-centered accounts given in "Americans All." The programs took the form of a conversation between a government official and the guest, and featured small lectures by the latter on the meaning of democracy, the impact of science and technology on individual freedom, or the role of the intellectual in American life. The tone was often liberal and internationalist, as émigrés such as Albert Einstein spoke of the need to create a new and stronger world organization, "a federal organization of the Nations of the world" to keep the peace.[39]

Specific references to a guest's country or ethnic background usually occurred only in the introduction to each program and sometimes not at all. Louis Adamic said nothing about his homeland in Slovenia or his own experiences as an immigrant, but spoke of the shortcomings of the American system, the "weaknesses which the dictators of the totalitarian countries are counting on" and the "fresh opportunity" to correct those defects that the current need to defend democracy presented. At the end of this broadcast, listeners were invited to write for a copy of Adamic's own pamphlet, *Plymouth Rock to Ellis Island.*[40] Thomas Mann, after being prompted to discuss the loyalty of refugees and exiles toward "the land which offers them sanctuary," with a view toward "preserving that tolerance which is one of the greatest of our democratic virtues," replied that America possessed "a definite national unity, a communal spirit of loyalty peculiar to itself," and that recently arrived immigrants shared that "national characteristic." Americans, Mann said, "need not fear that foreign-born citizens will remain foreign," since history shows they "have always sought to become true Americans as quickly as possible."[41]

Attorney General Robert H. Jackson, who, like Berle, was increasingly troubled by the conflict between security and the Bill of Rights (which the public's demands represented), also exercised what power he had to urge restraint and to discourage state or private action against aliens or suspected subversives.[42] In April 1940, Jackson created a Neutrality Laws Unit within the Department of Justice to cope "with the problems of internal security created by the expanding forces of the war abroad" and to develop "remedies for the special problems created by the war." As the role the United States played in the war changed, the duties and the name of the unit changed as well, from the Special Defense Unit in March 1941 to the Special War Policies Unit (SWPU) in March 1942. By the end of that fiscal year, the SWPU had become the major component of the new War Division within the Department of Justice, serving, according to a SWPU annual report, "as a control tower in the Government's fight to eliminate subversive activity . . . by suggesting, coordinating, and assisting in all affirmative action on the internal security front." The nation's "internal security problems could not be met solely by use of the ordinary formulas of indictment and prosecution" because modern warfare included "sophisticated techniques of propaganda and psychological sabotage" that demanded the coordinated use of "all available preventatives and legal remedies."[43]

Jackson took care to emphasize that the unit did not itself investigate or prosecute but authorized "prosecutive action in cases growing out of the espionage, sabotage, foreign agent, neutrality and other national defense statutes." It would not replace the "Criminal Division, the United States Attorneys or the Federal Bureau of Investigation" but working through "research, study, consultation and recommendation" would complement their efforts by "initiating preventive and corrective action of a non-prosecutive nature." However, the unit did exercise control over national security cases by displacing the FBI as the entity that would recommend what action should be taken in such matters, much to Hoover's displeasure.[44]

Brett Gary, in his study of American liberalism, points out that in creating the SWPU, Jackson hoped to "accommodate . . . the growth of the modern administrative and regulatory state" and to "fuse" it with the conviction that the state had to act as "the primary vehicle for the protection of civil rights and civil liberties, including unpopular speech and opinion."[45] Jackson's choice to head the unit, Lawrence M. C. Smith, an attorney who had worked at the Securities and Exchange Commission (SEC), had no experience with internal security, but he shared Jackson's conviction about the need to protect both individual liberties and national security. Jackson gave Smith a great deal of freedom to set policy but, in a gesture that indirectly showed his disdain for Hoover's methods, made available all of the records of the department's anti-radical activities during World War I and the subsequent Red Scare to insure that Smith did not repeat that history.[46]

Chester Lane, who had also been at the SEC and who served under Smith as associate chief of the SWPU, later recalled that the War Division existed more or less in name only. The unit was largely autonomous, with Jackson trusting Smith and Lane "to run the shop as [they] saw best." Jackson believed that the Department "just [could not] sit on its hands" as the fascist threat increased; he expected Smith to ascertain what needed to be done to protect the United States from fascist propaganda and its effects. Lane and his chief "took the whole field of American internal security as our province" and, in Lane's words, worked "to make the protection of our internal security as smooth and unrestrictive in operation as we possibly could, consistent with internal dangers as we saw them."[47]

The SWPU took shape just as Hitler's invasion of the Low Countries in mid-May increased the American public's demand for security. Congress accelerated its discussion of anti-radical and anti-alien measures, and by June support for an omnibus bill, known as the Alien Registration Act (or the Smith Act, after its major sponsor), enjoyed wide support. The bill required not only the registration of aliens but included prohibitions concerning the overthrow of the government, the incitement of disobedience in the armed forces, and membership in organizations advocating such activities. Although much of the impetus for the bill came from anticommunist quarters, debates in the Congress linked fifth-column fears to a general concern about subversion. Liberal groups, such as the American Civil Liberties Union, which had opposed similar measures in the past, did so again, but they were in the minority.[48]

A companion measure also under discussion in the Congress, the Voorhis Act, compelled the registration of organizations engaged in "political activity" if they were controlled by a foreign entity and sought the overthrow of the United States government; "political activity" included the dissemination of propaganda.[49] Like the previously enacted Foreign Agents Registration Act, authorities viewed the Voorhis Act as "a preventive measure, being designed to disclose hostile activities of organizations and thereby to permit the taking of remedial action and the prevention of overt acts."[50]

Despite such assurances, the sentiments voiced in Congress on the above measures could only have alarmed members of the foreign nationalities community. On the day of the Smith Act's passage, Congressman Robert Reynolds of North Carolina submitted to the Congressional Record a newspaper editorial that declared that aliens in the United States should be "watched, fingerprinted and tabulated so that their every move will be known to the powers that be." There were already enough "unknown, unregistered, and unwatched aliens in the United States to pose a serious 'fifth column'" menace, the paper claimed, and only residents of "malicious intent" could object to measures taken to guard American security.[51]

The Common Council for American Unity (CCAU), known as the Foreign Language Information Service (FLIS) until the middle of 1940, did not agree and mounted one of the most visible campaigns opposed to the general registration of aliens. The FLIS had originated during World War I as the CPI's Division of Work with the Foreign Born and had become a private, nonprofit agency by the early 1920s. Representative of the pluralist approach to Americanization, the FLIS relied on education to promote unity and tolerance among the native born. Read Lewis served as the agency's director, assisted by a board and an advisory council consisting of government officials, activists and news people, ranging from Louis Adamic and James Houghteling to Ida Tarbell and William Allen White.[52]

Money was often scarce, but various New Deal relief agencies occasionally provided funding. The FLIS sent "weekly educational releases" to foreign-language papers in their own languages and also "interested itself actively in legislative problems concerning the alien." By the late 1930s, under Adamic's influence, the organization broadened its focus to furthering "an appreciation of what minority groups have contributed to America," encouraging "the growth of an American culture" representative of both the immigrants and the native born, and overcoming "intolerance and discrimination." The reorganization and name change in 1940 and the publication of a magazine called *Common Ground* reflected this new emphasis. Adamic edited the magazine and designed it to promote "the public's understanding of the nation's multiethnic character." A legislative newsletter on state and federal laws affecting aliens, edited by Alan Cranston, who served as the Council's Washington representative, strove "to keep informed those who wish to facilitate American citizenship, defeat unjust discrimination with regard to the alien and maintain our democratic tradition." Grants from a variety of institutions such as the Carnegie Foundation and B'nai B'rith supplied operating funds not covered by dues and subscriptions.[53]

Writing in the *Contemporary Jewish Record* in the spring of 1940, Cranston summarized his agency's opposition to registration. He feared that Congress would use the alien as "an official scapegoat for the nation's ills." Many members of the public, including "patriotic American groups" who did not realize that their attempts to restrict alien rights "strikes at the very principles of democracy that they would defend," and the country's "would-be dictators and their storm troopers and dupes," who see that "an attack upon any minority group can be turned into an assault upon an entire nation," had contributed to this "mild and fanatic anti-alien sentiment." States had barred aliens from working as "junk dealers . . . pool room operators" and from "the profession of garbage collecting," while the federal government had excluded them from the Works Progress Administration. So many bills dealing with the deportation of aliens on so many grounds were pending in the Congress that the chair of the House Immigration Committee declared the intent to be nothing short of "alien-baiting." Cranston predicted that alien registration measures would lead to a "domestic passport system," with citizens having "to produce evidence of citizenship or face arrest as suspected unregistered aliens." If even a few of these measures became law, he said, Congress "may one day be held in part responsible for the decline of American democracy."[54]

On a more practical level, Read Lewis advised Houghteling that "only the good aliens will register" and the government will have to use procedures already in place "to get hold of the bad aliens." The result would be a great waste of time and money better utilized elsewhere.[55] But as Cranston told Lewis in late May, the press in Washington was "full of items about 'fifth columns,'" and even Houghteling, though against registration, "is beginning to feel it may be necessary . . . and can't openly oppose it."[56]

The FLIS continued its campaign of opposition in its legislative newsletter, where Cranston reflected the same tension between security and civil liberty that Berle and other liberals had confronted. Alien registration would not enhance national security, since people with something to hide would avoid complying with the law. If aliens were operating clandestinely, "under cover of legal entry and a legitimate occupation," they would abide by the law to avoid suspicion. Even if all three and a half million aliens registered, all of "their daily doings" could not be monitored. The administration officials who would administer the law agreed with these objections, but Cranston said they hesitated to "express themselves in face of the semi-hysteria that now exists," and supported the pending measures only to "protect the alien from something worse." The laws under consideration were divisive because enforcement "would result in putting millions of citizens who have 'foreign' names, or who look or speak differently from the majority under suspicion." Until the administration declared registration "a necessary defense measure," the FLIS would remain in opposition and urged its readers to protest the passage of such a measure to their representatives.[57]

As Congress debated the registration act, the State Department began to consider reforming the passport and immigration service in order to maintain better control of aliens already here. Such matters were under the jurisdiction of the Department of Labor, but Secretary Frances Perkins had become the target of a Dies Committee investigation because of her refusal to deport Harry Bridges, a resident alien and left-wing union leader. Perkins based her position on the legal ambiguities surrounding the case, and the Supreme Court eventually ruled in Bridges' favor. Solicitor General Biddle believed Perkins had acted with "her usual courage and independence," but the Dies Committee had attempted to impeach her; when that failed, they continued to charge her with communist sympathies. Under Secretary of State Sumner Welles was anxious to take more precautions after receiving disturbing accounts "about the 'fifth column' activities in Norway," and Berle believed he was right. In Berle's view "the blunt fact is that the Labor Department is so honeycombed with Left Wing and Communist intrigue that you can never quite trust what they are doing. This does not mean," he said, "that there is any great amount of disloyalty, though I suspect there is some. It means that there is a lot of inefficiency and sheer soft-headed foolishness."[58]

The bureaucratic rivalry inherent in Berle's comments represented one of the few constants in the administration's approach to foreign nationalities issues. When Welles outlined the "defects" in the country's practices regarding aliens and immigrants to the president in May, he made much of the shortcomings of the Labor Department, citing a lack of adequate controls on the entry of aliens and a general inability to keep abreast of alien activities. He suggested that alien and immigration issues could be more effectively dealt with by a department that did not also have "labor matters as its major function," a situation he thought created "a duality of interest" for the Labor Department. Since many problems related to immigration (such as deportation and investigations associated with naturalization cases) already fell within the purview of the Justice Department, Welles proposed that "administrative practices would be simplified" by a transfer of the INS to the Justice Department. The "coordination of the activities and interests of the various governmental agencies" dealing with immigration should, Welles emphasized, be housed in the Department of State, where "it was exercised during the years 1917 and 1918."[59]

Welles acted despite the objections of Attorney General Jackson, who was not as quick to equate aliens with sabotage and subversive activities. To Jackson, mixing "the pursuit of criminals with the control of aliens" conveyed "unfortunate implications." The Justice Department would have to act as "a litigant in the courts over these matters," which would put the department in the position of defending its own acts. He also did not share in the general criticism of Frances Perkins but held "a very high opinion [of her] motives [and] complete confidence in her loyalty."[60] Jackson agreed that the State Department could serve as a coordinating agency in immigration matters, but he was reluctant to accept the Bureau of Immigration and Naturalization and informed Welles he would do so only as "a matter of duty."[61]

At a luncheon meeting with the president, where he was abruptly presented with a copy of the executive order announcing the INS transfer, Jackson again demurred, remarking that "there was somewhat the same tendency in America to make goats of all aliens that in Germany had made goats of all Jews." Jackson agreed that aliens should be more strictly supervised, but he was "utterly opposed to a new policy of persecuting or prosecuting aliens just because of alienage." He suggested they create an entirely separate agency "as part of the national defense to handle the whole matter of alien control, sabotage, espionage and subversive activities." While the president concurred with Jackson's statement that aliens should not be persecuted, he was not, however, persuaded to grant Jackson's request. Jackson then acquiesced to the proposed change.[62] Frances Perkins also opposed the transfer of INS to the Justice Department; she disliked linking immigration issues with criminal behavior and believed the Department of Interior to be a more suitable home for the immigration service. However, Roosevelt, in his conversation with her on the eve of the announced change, tied immigration to security and simply informed her of the new arrangement.[63]

When Roosevelt announced the transfer of the INS to the Justice Department from the Labor Department, he couched the move as part of an ongoing government reorganization plan but said also that "obvious national defense reasons" made the change an important one. When a reporter asked him if this "fit in with the general measures to prevent espionage and sabotage," the president answered "Yes."[64] Biddle, to whom Jackson gave the task of integrating the INS into the Department of Justice, viewed the president's decision on the transfer as consistent with his policy of "toughness" on such issues, an indication of Roosevelt's belief "that it was all very well to be liberal . . . but you must not be soft."[65] Perkins had not wanted the INS in her department and had neglected its administration, but Biddle considered the underlying cause for the transfer to be the president's resolve that "immigration control should be tightened."[66]

Jackson held a news conference as well, trying to "break the news . . . as gently as possible." To alleviate immigrants' fears about being associated with the FBI and its criminal investigations, Jackson stressed that immigration services would be separate from the rest of the department. However, he also declared his support for alien registration and "for fingerprinting all aliens before their entrance to this country," along with his conviction that most of the three and a half million aliens in the United States were "loyal to our principles" and "have the makings of good Americans."[67] Jackson had lost none of his resolve to resist the kind of anti-alien hysteria that he had opposed as a young attorney during the Red Scare, but as attorney general, he understood that the "American people need to be reassured" and that he had to appear to be as "tough" as the president.[68]

Read Lewis saw a more positive side to the Justice Department's role, believing that Congress, as it finished its deliberations on the alien registration bill, would be more willing to provide "adequate discretion" for enforcement of some of the bill's provisions "because Congress would probably be more willing to vest in the Attorney General an authority they would not give to the present Secretary of Labor."[69]

Read Lewis was correct. The Alien Registration Act passed the Congress by overwhelming margins in late June, and Roosevelt signed it into law on June 28, 1940. In addition to its anti-radical provisions, the law required that resident aliens (those in the country for more than thirty days) register with the federal government, submit to fingerprinting, and carry an identity card. The president, in response to critics who considered the law a violation of the Bill of Rights, insisted that the legislation protected the country and safeguarded the rights of loyal aliens.[70] Those "loyal aliens" who were the "guests" of the United States, Roosevelt said, should not view the registration process as bearing "any stigma or implications of hostility" by the country to their presence. Americans understood that aliens had come here because they "believed and had faith in the principles of American democracy," and they must be protected from "harassment." Since the federal government had acted, any additional action by individual states would result only "in undesirable confusion and duplication."[71] The Justice Department also released a statement, prepared by Jackson and Biddle, assuring the public that registration carried no stigma, and discouraging individual states from enacting similar legislation.[72]

However, the anti-radical provisions in the bill, which, in the words of Maurice Isserman, "established the first peacetime federal sedition law since the Alien and Sedition Acts of 1798," strengthened any connection that existed in the public's mind between ethnicity and disloyalty.[73] In his memoirs, Biddle recalled that the term "fifth column was on everyone's lips," and in the public's mind fifth columnists "came from the alien population—the very word alien suggested those who had been estranged and excluded." Making the same analogy as Jackson, Biddle observed that European aliens "who had seen Hitler register the Jews as a preliminary to stripping them of their rights" could not help but be alarmed by the law, but "the beginning of a witch hunt was on."[74] For Biddle, the law simply elevated the canard of "guilt by association" to the status of a federal statute.[75]

Once the bill passed, the Common Council conceded that the precautions implicit in the law seemed wise, given fears about fifth columnists, and hoped that it could serve as a means of "channeling off anti-alien sentiment." The cooperation of "educators and liberal groups" would enable the process to become "a step toward citizenship and a constructive rather than a divisive influence."[76] The Justice Department did what it could to soften the law's impact. Because of Biddle's "known sympathies for the foreign born," Jackson assigned him the task of alien registration, even though it did not fall within Biddle's purview as solicitor general.[77] Biddle, in turn, appointed Earl G. Harrison, a young attorney with a "social outlook unusual among most successful lawyers" to administer the program. The two arranged to have registration of the people Biddle referred to as "American aliens" take place at the Post Office, rather than the FBI, and secured the ready support of the foreign-language press in publicizing the process.[78]

Harrison delivered a nationwide radio address in August, a few weeks before registration was to begin, to explain the provisions of the law. He called the act "an important phase of our National Defense Program," but he assured aliens that registration "means merely that you are recording your presence with your host, the United States Government." Aliens had nothing to fear; the postal authorities, not the police, would conduct the registration and all of the information given by the registrant would remain confidential. Aliens must remember that the act was a necessary measure "intended to safeguard the land that has given many of them a sanctuary from oppression; the land that has given many of them physical security and a chance to earn a living." Harrison cautioned American citizens to be circumspect in their treatment of and attitude toward aliens, observing that "in the matter of real loyalty and devotion to America and to the American way of life, there is no inevitable magic in naturalization."[79]

The Department of Justice also produced a radio program, "Good Guests of America," which featured a conversation between an immigration official, an average alien and an alien of distinction, with the latter advising his fellow countryman about the merits of the registration program. In the first broadcast (September 1940), Thomas Mann eased the fears of a "Mr. Kirsch," who claimed the registration program signaled that he was not welcome and that American authorities "are angry with me." Mann responded that America asked little of its guests other than registration, and in return provided "security and peace." When Kirsch persisted, saying in German that the law indicated a suspicion "that I belonged to the Fifth Column—that I was a spy, an enemy who should be deported," Mann explained the derivation of the term "fifth column" and its misuse in this context. The "fifth column" of civilians who had brought victory to the fascists in Spain and later to other parts of Europe had been natives of the countries in question, not aliens. In any case, Mann speculated that aliens such as himself, who had fled tyranny in their native lands, might be more conscious of American freedoms and "anxious to defend them" than native-born citizens who accept these rights "as a matter of course." Kirsch at last agreed with "Herr Docktor" and declared himself happy, as a member of the American community and an aspiring citizen, to register so "that democracy may be saved!"[80]

Most of the mail Biddle received from registrants concerning the process was positive.[81] Press accounts agreed. In a *New Yorker* article published in early November 1940, the author described the registration procedure as simple and brief. Registrants filled out a short form with fifteen questions, one of which asked whether they were engaged in any activity on behalf of a foreign government, and submitted it along with their fingerprints. Officials estimated that the entire procedure took about twenty minutes. While a few people were embarrassed to have their fingerprints taken, most dressed in their best clothes for the event and were quiet, cheerful, and cooperative.[82] The *Survey Graphic* considered the program a success as well, noting that it "was carried out with surprising lack of friction, confusion and resentment." The author attributed this to two factors: that registration had taken place in the post office rather than in the more threatening environment of a police station, and that Harrison, who was active in liberal and social causes, had resolved to make the process as efficient and friendly as possible. The registration law had been enacted in a time of "hysterical fear and suspicion which easily might have boiled over in anti-alien demonstrations," but this had not occurred because of Harrison's skill.[83] Cranston and the Common Council also praised Harrison—"an American born son of an immigrant from England and a man of deep tact and decency"—and his superiors, Biddle and Jackson, for developing a program that was educational at its core and represented "Americanization at its best, aiming to draw the alien to America."[84]

A positive outcome served a political end for Roosevelt, as he sought re-election to an unprecedented third term. Roosevelt and the Democratic Party took care in 1940, just as they had in previous years, to include foreign nationalities groups in the campaign. In 1938, the Foreign Language Citizens Committee of the Democratic National Committee established twenty-six "nationality divisions" to secure the ethnic vote; the Yugoslavs were among those represented. Bernard G. Richards, who directed these efforts for the party, assured the president in October 1940 that after "active and continuous contacts with the representative groups of naturalized citizens hailing from different lands, their people are in largest numbers, as devoted as ever to your policies and programs." Louis Adamic, who was traveling throughout the country on a lecture tour, agreed, writing to Richards that "it looks like a Roosevelt landslide to me." The irony of the political parties "dividing and splitting the American electorate into numerous nationality blocs" as the government was equating ethnicity with dangers to the nation's security did not appear to register to anyone concerned.[85]

By February 1941, when the attorney general released a report covering the administration of the Alien Registration Act over a six-month period, more than four million aliens had registered in the United States, and another one hundred thousand had done so in America's territories. The release quoted Jackson praising the efforts of everyone involved and declaring that the department's initial conviction that the "overwhelming majority of non-citizens . . . were peaceful and law-abiding residents, in sympathy with the tenants of Democracy" had been affirmed.[86]

*　*　*

Registration alone did not remove the dangers believed to exist in the foreign-language community. In October 1940, R. Keith Kane, an attorney working in the Justice Department's Neutrality Unit as a special assistant to the attorney general, proposed the trial formation of a "Nationalities Section" to serve as the foundation for "an educational program for the alien and foreign language population, especially in relation to alien registration." The section also would analyze the foreign language press and prepare periodic reports on the attitudes of the foreign-language population and on the extent of foreign influences exerted upon them. Such analyses would aid in ascertaining which foreign influences or individuals operated as "foreign principles" within the meaning of the foreign agents registration act and could also be of assistance to other agencies with interests in foreign population groups.[87]

After the trial section's initial reports illustrated that the attitudes of the foreign-language press were "certainly much more extreme than in the English language press," Smith asked that the section's activities be maintained. The influence of extreme views on the foreign-nationalities population could not yet be measured, but since foreign-language publications were often the only reading material available to aliens and immigrants, Smith reasoned that such papers "may be assumed to have on the whole more influence" than the English-language press had in the native-born community. Combining regulation with the protection of basic rights, just as Jackson wished, Smith argued that continued study was warranted not only for the reasons Kane had originally proposed but also to uncover "infringements on civil liberties of alien and foreign language populations or of disaffection." Such work could serve as the basis for a "peacetime propaganda analysis and propaganda section which could be readily expanded in case we went to war." Liberalism, however, had its limits. In a final recommendation reflective of the manner in which policymakers devised separate categories for the foreign born, Smith advised against any similar program for the English-language press because he saw no evidence of need and because of "the opposition which would be stirred up and the danger to freedom of speech" it would entail.[88]

By the end of 1940, the prospect of disaffection had not diminished. Kane warned of the use of the foreign-language community as "a vehicle of foreign propaganda" and of the danger that they might spread "contagion . . . as the standard of living is forced down by the sacrifices required in total defense."[89] To combat this danger, the Neutrality Unit proposed a number of amendments to strengthen the Foreign Agents Registration Act, principally by suggesting that those subject to it should disclose more information regarding their activities and that the enforcement of the act be transferred from the State Department to the Justice Department. Chester Lane believed the recommendations were justified; the original law "had been drafted without any substantial teeth and had a great many loopholes." The State Department, which still maintained "ancestral concepts of being a group of diplomats who were bound by the precedents" of the eighteenth and nineteenth centuries, had "no conception of how to administer the registration statute" and had done so in a "thoroughly ineffective" manner.[90]

All of the agencies involved agreed to the proposed changes in FARA by the summer of 1941, but not without more bureaucratic infighting. Berle recorded "rows between Justice and State—chiefly as to who should administer the proposed new act covering registration of alien agents—Justice ought to do it; and the control of persons going in and out of the United States—State ought to do it."[91] He offered to mediate, and the dispute was finally settled by the end of the month, with Berle crediting Biddle who "acted very fairly and very decently about it." He concluded, "I don't know which side is at fault; I suspect both."[92]

The proposed amendments left most of the original legislation intact. The intent of the law remained the regulation of "propaganda in terms of disclosure as opposed to censorship," with the terms "foreign principle" and "agents of a foreign principle" broadly defined. Propaganda was subject to regulation only when it was intended to be distributed "to more than one person" or by someone "who is an agent of a foreign principle." The term "foreign principle" included any organizations, ranging from the German-American Bund to the Communist Party, that "constitute a ramification of a foreign political party." All propaganda material disseminated within the United States by a foreign principle, even one operating abroad, "must be labeled, copies sent to the Librarian of Congress, and copies filed with the

Department of Justice, together with a list of the addresses to whom it is being sent." The Post Office had the power to "declare propaganda material non-mailable" when it had been sent to the United States by an agent of a foreign principle who had failed to register.[93] The attorney general could grant and terminate exemptions to the act's provisions. Biddle, in recommending the bill to the Congress, argued that the transfer from the State Department to the Justice Department seemed sensible since the Justice Department already administered the Alien Registration Act and the Voorhis Act, and the activities covered by the legislation "impinge on the functions of the Department of Justice rather than on those of the Department of State."[94]

Biddle made his case for the bill as attorney general. Roosevelt, after elevating Jackson to the Supreme Court in the summer of 1941, had allowed Biddle to serve as acting head of the Justice Department but had been reluctant to appoint him to the position permanently. The president, who often found Jackson too hesitant to support security measures, feared Biddle was not "tough enough" for the job and that his commitment to civil liberties might be at odds with the demands of a war emergency. Roosevelt also expressed concern about Biddle's ability to work with Hoover. Finally reassured by Biddle's performance as acting attorney general, Roosevelt announced the appointment in late August and Biddle took up the post in early September.[95] Liberals applauded the president's action, with the Common Council expressing its gratitude that "a man who has demonstrated his sympathetic understanding" of issues relating to the foreign born "should be Attorney General at this difficult time." While he had been steadfast in enforcing the law, Biddle had "courageously defended civil liberties and the rights of aliens and other minorities."[96]

Hoover and Biddle also worked well together, largely due to Biddle's efforts and the fact that Biddle heeded the advice given him by Harlan Stone, that Hoover could be a formidable enemy but that he appreciated and reciprocated loyalty. Biddle, who had promised Hoover more direct access to the attorney general, included Hoover in his policy planning meetings and came to enjoy "within limits" the gossip Hoover shared at their regular luncheons. Biddle harbored no illusions about the FBI director; he found his collection of personal files "disturbing" and also objected to Hoover's "obsession" with Communists, which usually netted him "fish . . . hardly worth catching." Yet he valued Hoover's administrative abilities and lack of corruption.[97]

By the time Congress passed the amended FARA in January 1942, the United States had entered the war. Roosevelt returned the bill to the Congress in February, without his signature and with the request that members of the United Nations be exempt from its provisions. The original law had been "drafted in peacetime to protect a nation at peace," with the intent of forcing the "disclosure of the activities of foreign agents who . . . weaken our national unity by fostering discord and distrust." However, now that the United States was part of a coalition, the president believed that there must be "a minimum of interference with the strengthening and perfecting of joint action," and "the fullest and most constant exchange of representatives" between the United States and its Allies.[98]

Most of the objections to the bill had originated with the British and centered on intelligence gathering. The Justice Department crafted provisions to meet these objections by exempting from the law those agents of foreign governments deemed "vital to the defense of the United States" when engaged "in activities which are in furtherance of the policies, public interest or national defense both of such government and the Government of the United States, and are not intended to conflict with any of the domestic or foreign policies of the Government of the United States."[99] As Biddle told the Judiciary Committee, the activities of Allied representatives had to be kept from the enemy, and the positions of U.S. representatives abroad safeguarded as well. He suggested a "less onerous type of registration and labelling" for these individuals, including personnel in military and economic missions, "and persons engaged in supplying information to the extent that their activities are in furtherance of the joint interests and defense of both their country and ours and not intended to conflict with the policies of our government." Each Allied government would furnish the attorney general with information on the identity and activities of the persons in question; if such individuals abused their position or engaged in activities prohibited by FARA, or if the defense of their country was no longer vital to the United States, the exemption could be terminated.[100]

In late March 1942, James R. Sharp, who had been recruited by Smith to run the section within the SWPU that would administer FARA, suggested that the president issue an executive order, under the First War Powers Act of 1941, transferring the administration of the old act to the Justice Department to enable his unit to make the necessary preparations for administering the new amended legislation. Biddle expected "a vigorous program of enforcement and administration" to secure more information to use as a basis for prosecutions and to obtain a larger number of registrations, particularly from those who had failed to register under the old legislation. The State Department had administered the act as "a two man position," but if the Justice Department were to act as Biddle wished, Sharp would need "the necessary authority and personnel." The time frame included in the law also called for haste: the act became effective sixty days after its approval, and those required to register under it had only ten days to do so. Sharp also raised a number of jurisdictional issues: he requested freedom of action in all but major policy decisions (such as whether to insist that the German-American Bund or the Communist Party of the United States register under the Act); a full exchange of information by the Criminal Division of the Justice Department of any prosecutions undertaken; the ability for the section to ask the FBI to conduct investigations, while engaging in its own limited and preliminary inquiries; and the full exchange of information by the FBI.[101]

President Roosevelt signed the amended Foreign Agents Registration Act on April 28 and transferred its administration to Justice on June 1. The law became operative on June 29, 1942, and those subject to its provisions had just ten days—until July 9—to register. The act required public disclosure, in the form of registration with the Department of Justice, by persons engaging in propaganda or other activities as "agents" of "foreign principles," with the latter defined as a government, political party or individual affiliated or associated with a foreign government or political party, or a group of individuals organized or doing business in or subsidized by a foreign country. An "agent" consisted of a person acting for, collecting funds or information for, or from a foreign principle, or any person who assumed or purported to act within the United States as an agent of a foreign principle in any of the respects described in the law.[102] Every six months, registered agents had to file reports on their activities and provide copies "of all political propaganda they disseminate" to the Justice Department and to the Library of Congress. The material itself had to be "labeled in a manner designed to acquaint recipients with the fact that the material they received is being distributed by a registered agent of a foreign principle."[103]

The Justice Department carefully spelled out who was exempt from the law (individuals connected to a foreign government or principle but who did not engage in "propaganda or public relations activities," for example), as well as the definitions of "foreign principle" and "political activity." Although the department made clear the meaning of "political activity," it did not explain the exact meaning of "propaganda." Penalties for violating the act consisted of not more than five years imprisonment and/or a fine of not more than ten thousand dollars.[104]

In practice, the FARA section strove to minimize prosecution and instead attempted to "negotiate registration." Nonetheless, entities from friendly countries resented the law, which they saw as designed to safeguard the

United States against enemies, not against friends. This often made the task of the section a "delicate diplomatic job." It was also a daunting one. As the law took effect, Lane and his colleagues estimated that there were one hundred thousand foreign agents in the United States. Although many would be exempted from registration, approximately three thousand individuals and organizations were likely to file registration statements, with another hundred "foreign propaganda agencies" requiring surveillance. The latter "would require familiarity with the languages, allegiances, and competing political ideologies of virtually all of the foreign language groups in the United States."[105]

This connection between a law governing "foreign principles" and the foreign-language community in the United States provoked controversy. The FARA section investigated ties between American ethnic organizations and "foreign principles" with the aid of the FBI and initiated proceedings against any organization the department deemed liable under the law, but which refused to register. The intent of the act was disclosure: the public to whom the agents appealed would know what interests or ideologies they represented and could better judge whether to offer or withhold their support. The government perceived these procedures as preferable to censorship, but the law "represented a step in the direction of enforcing consensus by employing a label that demoted foreignness and un-Americanness."[106] Immigrants, such as those in the Yugoslav-American community, who believed they were supporting the American war effort by assisting their former homelands, deeply resented these designations.

*   *   *

Measures such as the Smith Act and FARA may have been necessary to protect national security, but they provoked fear and feelings of alienation within the immigrant community. The government also had done little, beyond radio programs and naturalization ceremonies, to promote the patriotic fervor and feelings of inclusion that would more effectively negate the allure of foreign influences. In November 1940, Secretary of the Interior Harold Ickes, with the support of other members of the Cabinet, proposed that the president set "up some machinery for propaganda." He argued that "pro-Nazi sentiment in such places as the German communities of Nebraska could not be combated by someone's getting up on a platform and haranguing. We ought to send into those communities citizens of German birth or descent who can talk to their fellow Germans in their own language and against their own background."[107] Roosevelt expressed some interest, and Ickes formed a group of relevant cabinet and executive officers "to consider the advisability and possibility of setting up some machinery to combat subversive activities."[108]

The committee quickly focused its attention on a plan for an information service that presidential advisor Louis Brownlow had presented to Roosevelt some months before. Brownlow made it clear that Roosevelt had not accepted the proposal and had cited the excesses of the propaganda effort of World War I as the reason. Nonetheless, the committee favored the agency's proposed rationale, which included charges "to analyze and combat propaganda menacing the national security and defense, to fortify national morale . . . and to acquaint the people with the nature and source of the present threats to their liberties, civil, economic and political."[109]

This produced a lengthy dissent from Attorney General Jackson, centering on the foreign nationalities issues that had prompted Ickes' initial concern. In speaking of the foreign born, Jackson said: "We try to convince them that the Government means well toward them. We want them to register. We don't want to treat them hatefully. We don't want to make Fifth Columnists of them. And then somebody introduces the bill that no alien should be given relief and no alien should be given a job, whereupon all your good will is shattered." If aliens continued to be made to feel unwelcome, then "the alien and the alien's naturalized friends become antagonistic and very fertile ground for the work of discontented elements."[110]

Jackson acknowledged that the foreign-language press published "constantly, very subtle propaganda in support of, particularly, Fascism" as well as anti-Semitic material. The Justice Department had acted against articles that were "subversive within the definitions of the law" but the question of how to deal with the propaganda published in the foreign-language press was "a very, very difficult one because this propaganda takes a form that is hard to answer. It is imbedded in general articles." While Jackson did not object to a unit that gathered information on the press, much as his "own squad" at the Justice Department did, it should not have any prosecutorial function. He cautioned that if the public believed "we are trying to prosecute them for their views," they would resent it. If the proposed organization were composed of representatives of the government, he did not want the Justice Department to be included, and in general he believed the undertaking should be part of a "separate defense effort." He had a little more success that he had had when making a similar proposal to the president; the group agreed to omit the Justice Department, and a subcommittee of three began to draft a memo for the president outlining their plan.[111]

The subcommittee's report proposed the creation of an agency "to analyze and combat propaganda menacing the national security and defense" with a committee of cabinet members setting its policies and developing its programs. The director, who would be appointed by the president, "should be a man of great executive ability, trained in one of the major fields of public information and relations, with a wide knowledge of foreign affairs" and without "active partisan affiliations."[112]

Despite Ickes' hope that the president would "act without undue delay,"[113] Roosevelt did not implement the suggestions contained in the report. As his conversation with Brownlow indicated, Roosevelt had not forgotten that the World War I–era CPI had too often aroused hatred and rancor, serving in the end as a source of discord rather than unity. The lofty rhetoric that Woodrow Wilson had used to generate support for the war had ended in a postwar disillusionment and a resurgence of isolationism that had hindered Roosevelt's own foreign policy. He had no desire to repeat any of these mistakes.[114] Ickes, more concerned about the present, despaired that his committee's suggestions would remain only that "until we pay the cost that France and other countries have paid for stupidity and inertia," and he asked the president that he "be relieved of any further responsibilities in this whole matter."[115]

Others were less reluctant to attempt to shape the public mind. In the summer of 1940, Col. William J. Donovan, one of the personal emissaries Roosevelt used for a variety of diplomatic and intelligence missions, had been sent by Navy Secretary Frank Knox, with the president's approval, to Great Britain to report on that country's defense capabilities. Donovan's mission was designed in part to rally support in the United States for increased assistance to the British. Edgar Mowrer, a newspaper correspondent who had covered the fall of France, accompanied Donovan; the British, anxious to secure as much aid as possible, "helped Mowrer gather appropriately horrendous tales of German fifth column activities." Donovan and Mowrer then wrote a series of newspaper articles, published as a pamphlet in 1941 under the title *Fifth Column Lessons for America,* to warn Americans of the dangers of totalitarian propaganda.[116]

In the introduction to the pamphlet, Secretary Knox discussed the objectives of such propaganda, which included the creation of "suspicion and dissension among the masses" and the promotion of neutrality as a means of protection. A country such as the United States, a democracy that valued civil liberties and that "springs from many nationalities," was "particularly vulnerable to this new kind of warfare." Because of this danger, Knox regarded "defense against enemy propaganda as second only to defense against enemy armaments." In the articles themselves, Donovan and Mowrer continued to sound the alarm. The fifth-column tactic, which operated "most freely and effectively in democratic states," was Hitler's "decisive weapon." Among Hitler's primary agents were Germans living abroad, many of whom were residing in the United States, "naturalized, but still essentially hyphenate . . . ready to annex the United States as a returning prodigal son."[117]

Donovan also apprised Roosevelt of Britain's will and ability to fight on; the president, in turn, supported increased aid to the British. As the volume of American aid grew throughout 1940 and 1941, the two countries also co-operated in collecting and sharing foreign and military intelligence. In the United States, more than a dozen agencies collected intelligence, but "bureaucratic infighting" prevented any genuine coordination of these activities.[118] Donovan, who had made a second trip abroad to report on the war in general and on British intelligence operations in particular, returned in the spring of 1941 to urge Roosevelt to create a centralized intelligence organization in the United States.[119] Roosevelt, who "enjoyed muddling authority" and who had even created his own spy network, usually relied on the State Department for oversight of intelligence activities. However, the war rendered these arrangements inadequate, and Roosevelt and his advisors agreed on the need for an intelligence agency.[120]

In July 1941, the president established the Office of Coordinator of Information (COI), with Donovan at its head, to collect, analyze, and distribute information to various government departments and perform "such supplementary activities as may facilitate the securing of information important for national security and not now available to the government."[121] Still reluctant to establish clear lines of authority, Roosevelt stressed that Donovan's work was "not intended to supersede or to duplicate, or to involve any direction of or interference with" the activities of any existing intelligence service or any departments or agencies.[122]

The creation of the COI did not address the needs of those who believed it essential for the United States to engage in an overt campaign to defeat enemy propaganda. The COI's connection to the wider public in general and to America's foreign-language community in particular was minimal. Although the COI contained a foreign-language section within its radio bureau,[123] and its staffers interviewed members of foreign-language groups, the agency's executive order did not include a specific mandate concerning foreign nationalities. As a result, the pressure on Roosevelt to act in this area did not abate. Harold Ickes, writing to the president in September 1941 in violation of his previous resolve to "never again mention to you the question of national morale," confided how "frightened" he was about the public's state of mind. Despite the approaching danger of war, the people of the country had "no conception of the issues involved that are vital, not only to their security but to the future well-being and happiness of themselves and their children." Because of this, they had no "wish to fight" and no "will to victory."[124]

Finally, the president, in another half-measure that did little to dilute his own ability to control information, created the Office of Facts and Figures (OFF) under the leadership of the Librarian of Congress, Archibald MacLeish, in October 1941. The OFF would "formulate programs designed to facilitate a widespread and accurate understanding of the status and progress of the national defense effort and of the defense policies and activities of the Government" and work with other agencies to disseminate that information.[125] The agency would not be a "super-press bureau" but existed "to correlate the unwieldy mass of disconnected and sometimes contradictory information emanating from various departments." With the goal of presenting a full picture of government policy, the OFF would be able to prevent "one department, which does not have all the facts about the defense program at its command, from issuing information which distorts the over-all picture." MacLeish already chaired an Interdepartmental Advisory Committee that was designed to "minimize the differences of opinion between departments before they get in print," and he would expand these efforts as head of the OFF. Office of Civilian Defense head Fiorella LaGuardia, to whom MacLeish would report, insisted that the OFF was not "a propaganda agency," because the United States did not believe "in artificially stimulated, high-pressure, 'doctored' nonsense."[126]

The bland language of the executive order may have been designed to reassure those who remembered the excesses of World War I, but it did not suit MacLeish. A veteran of that war, which also claimed the life of his brother, MacLeish had trained as an attorney before turning to a literary career in the early 1920s. Most known for his poetry, he also wrote prose pieces for several years for *Fortune* magazine. MacLeish, believing that writers had a "social role" to play, used his writing to promote "the need for brotherhood and a common cultural tradition." Initially a pacifist, he began to write speeches for Roosevelt and gradually embraced an interventionist stance. A foe of both communism and fascism, his association with the president led to attacks by right-wing congressmen when the president nominated him to serve as Librarian of Congress, but he secured confirmation for the post.[127] MacLeish viewed the war as a moral crusade and was not content simply to route information from the government to the people. Like the members of the Ickes committee, he wanted to acquaint the public with the main issues of the war through "a strategy of truth," and to stimulate discussions about its goals and aims.[128] MacLeish and other members of the pro-war liberal intellectual community described the war in "intensely moral and idealistic terms," as "a democratic revolution and an international civil war between democracy and fascism." The "future of democracy and progressive reform were at stake" and the conflict had meaning only as "a united struggle for the liberation of the common man and for a new world order."[129]

The man MacLeish chose to head the Foreign Language Division of the OFF shared his activist approach. Alan Cranston, who came to the OFF from the Common Council for American Unity, was eager to demonstrate that immigrants were united in their support of the American war effort.[130] He was convinced that the threats America faced from foreign sympathizers in the technologically advanced and sophisticated 1940s were far more dangerous than those experienced during the previous world war. As he wrote in a 1942 Foreign Language Division memo: "No Josef Goebbels was trying to turn American against American in 1918, no shortwave was piercing America from Europe and the Orient in 1918. Today there are many more countries involved in the war, many more occupied lands, many more governments in exile, several million more enemy aliens in our midst."[131]

Cranston's background shaped his attitude. In 1934, as a student journalist, he had traveled in Germany to report on the rise of the Nazis. After graduating in 1936, he had worked for the International News Service in London and Rome; in Rome, he had developed a sympathy for the Italian people and an understanding of the fear so many seemed to have of Mussolini's regime. These experiences, coupled with a stint in Ethiopia, left him with "an abiding concern for the rights of a free press." He also had an abhorrence of fascism. After returning from Europe in 1938, he became concerned that the sanitized version of *Mein Kampf* published in the United States did not convey the real dangers of Hitler's philosophy. He and a friend published their own edition, only to have Hitler successfully sue for copyright infringement and stop distribution.[132]

In the years immediately preceding American belligerency, Cranston continued to work as a reporter, covering stories of refugee ships arriving in New York and working on occasion to gain asylum for people fleeing fascist persecution. These activities brought him to the attention of Read Lewis, who hired Cranston to lobby Congress on laws relating to immigration and aliens for the Common Council. Cranston also wrote for the council's publication, *Common Ground*.[133] It was Lewis who recommended Cranston to MacLeish, and at age 27, Cranston became head of the Foreign Language Division (FLD) of the OFF.[134] Cranston brought to his work the conviction that the government had to disseminate war information to the millions of Americans who "can only be reached effectively in their mother tongue," and to "prepare and adapt . . . war information and material intended to assist" the foreign nationalities community in order to "meet their special problems and to participate in the American war effort." If existing facilities proved inadequate for these tasks, new avenues would have to be created.[135] Cranston was not reluctant to make attempts to influence the editorial policies of the foreign language press and the broadcast practices of foreign language radio stations, or to direct the ways in which ethnic groups joined together to support the war.

Cranston enlisted two friends to assist him: Lee Falk, the creator of *Mandrake the Magician* and *The Phantom* served as associate chief of the FLD and handled radio issues; and David Karr, a fellow reporter, headed the press section.[136] In his letter inducing Falk to take the job, Cranston explained that Falk would compose radio scripts for use in foreign-language broadcasts designed to provide information about the war, to boost morale, and to "sell the war to the German, Italian, and other groups in this country." For this, Cranston said, Falk would have to relocate to "a Washington slum," work constantly, and "take thyroid pills."[137]

Assistant Secretary of State Berle was equally concerned about the foreign nationalities community, but his focus was a more negative one. Too many refugees and exiled diplomats were active in America's ethnic communities, soliciting support for their governments or creating "free movements" to replace discredited regimes. Even if democratic in nature, this agitation threatened the government's ability to craft a foreign policy based on American interests, which to Berle did not include a hyphenated component. Berle had some experience with the foreign nationalities community; his parents had been active in the Progressive movement, and as a young attorney, he had lived in and provided legal services for the famous Henry Street settlement in New York. He held the typical Progressive's view toward minorities: he favored their assimilation into American society and had no sympathy for those who resisted, and "militance or even a strong self-consciousness among racial, religious or ethnic groups defied his vision of Americanism."[138]

In his liaison work with Hoover and military intelligence, Berle repeatedly expressed the need for a positive program (in addition to the "usual espionage, arrest, etc. mechanism") that would be designed to identify and alleviate the grievances upon which foreign agents fed. He had begun devising such a program in the summer of 1940, because it was "about time that some of the attempts to organize American groups in the interest of foreign governments—paid for by secret caches of money (usually held in bills)—should stop," but he despaired by the fall that nothing had been formalized.[139] He planned to "try to get hold of Francis Biddle [U.S. Solicitor General] and two or three others and see what we can rig up." He said, "It seems to me that there is a legitimate line between propaganda and control (totalitarian style) and the reasonable handling of groups in this country, aliens and others, who might be made really dynamic democratic forces."[140]

In the fall of 1941, Secretary of State Cordell Hull addressed some of this concern by assigning Harold B. Hoskins, Berle's executive assistant, the task of using the Division of Foreign Activity Correlation to maintain contact with all unofficial foreign groups and "free movements" in the United States. Hoskins, a former vice president of Cannon Mills, had previously served as the State Department's liaison with the OCD.[141] Hoskins and the division would interview "all foreign political leaders promoting movements in the interests of their peoples and committees of foreign born groups visiting the Department" to ascertain their "activities, purpose, organization and membership."[142] The intent was to prevent individuals or groups from "drifting in to see various officials in the State Department and then utilizing such contacts to create the impression of State Department approval." Hoskins would also work with the foreign language components of the OFF and the COI to apprise the State Department of "any changes in orientation which may take place" within the foreign-language groups he was monitoring.[143]

As Hull's charge to Hoskins indicated, the approach of the department would be one designed to discourage and control ethnic activity. Berle made this clear in mid-October 1941, when Archduke Otto von Hapsburg approached him to ascertain the American government's views on "the formation of committees representing national aspirations, which committees might eventually be recognized as governments." The archduke understood that the United States did not welcome such groups, but he did ask about "what activities were permitted to informal groups representing national aspirations." Berle confirmed that his government had "not been in the habit, ordinarily, of establishing relations with national committees claiming to be governments" but that "any group of people who were willing to abide by our laws could quite legally unite to further the interests of their people." The United States viewed "with sympathy" the desire of aliens to see their homelands freed from German control, but this did not imply "any recognition of such groups as present or future governments." When the archduke asked if the same sentiments applied to "American citizens of foreign descent," Berle, neatly disposing of the idea of divided loyalties, replied that while the United States was "a composite country ... we [do] not like endeavors to divide American citizens into blocs or categories based on race or descent from previous nationality." The government understood "the natural interest which Americans of foreign ancestry had in the fate of the countries from which they had sprung," and acknowledged that these sentiments "formed a part of American public opinion." But when asked to support "political ends overseas," Berle insisted that immigrants must remember they are Americans, that "it [is] contrary to our interest to try to involve them in disputes based on overseas nationalist quarrels, or to make the territory of the United States and United States citizens an area of political battles based on overseas ambitions." The government would accept "legitimate appeals for the sympathy of American citizens for nationalities overseas which desired to regain their freedom," but nothing more.[144]

Knowledge of the content of the foreign-language press was crucial to the work of Cranston and Berle and the other agencies concerned with foreign nationalities issues. The OFF used the services of the Common Council to translate foreign language material; all of the agencies also relied on the scanning done in Smith's unit at the Justice Department. However, the State Department and the COI considered the product produced by the Department of Justice to be inadequate since it centered on uncovering subversive activities in the United States but did not secure political intelligence abroad.[145] Donovan, after discussing this with Berle and Welles, proposed the establishment of a separate foreign nationalities division within the COI, claiming that it would be a better source of intelligence for his agency and would also fill the gap identified by the State Department. For his task, Donovan enlisted the assistance of John C. Wiley, a seasoned diplomat with experience in central and eastern Europe who had moved over from the State Department to the COI in August. Wiley in turn called on DeWitt Clinton Poole, who had served in the American embassy in Russia during the Bolshevik Revolution, headed the Division of Russian Affairs in the State Department, and had been affiliated with the School of Public and International Affairs at Princeton University after leaving the foreign service in 1930. Poole and Wiley held discussions with Smith, Hoover, and R. Keith Kane, who had joined the OFF's Bureau of Intelligence, and by November 1941, the two had devised a plan outlining the creation of a "foreign nationalities" branch within the

COI, and Poole had completed a draft of the proposed branch's rationale and functions.[146]

As Poole envisioned it, the Foreign Nationalities Branch would cast a wider net than the Hoskins group. The FNB would maintain contacts with foreign nationals who had recently arrived from abroad and who hoped to influence American public opinion and foreign policy. However, the new branch would also prepare reports for the State Department, by whose "particular request" the FNB was being created, and for other agencies on the "sentiment, activities and cross currents within foreign nationality groups," particularly as they pertained to foreign affairs. There would also be reports pertaining to foreign nationals' leaders and the contents of their press reports and radio programs. Such services would enable the United States to secure intelligence about conditions abroad and to use this information for the benefit of American policy.[147]

This description occasioned immediate controversy. First, the mention of press reports caused concern at the OFF. Both Poole and Wiley had previously explained to MacLeish that the kind of analysis they intended to do of the foreign-language press, which involved the acquisition of "political intelligence," involved a different expertise than the OFF had available. The work Kane had done for Justice had involved "the detection of subversion," and now that he had moved to the OFF, they presumed his work in their office would follow the same pattern. However, MacLeish wanted it made clear that monitoring the foreign language press was to be performed by R. Keith Kane's group in the OFF. He saw no reason for duplication, since Kane's material would be available to other agencies. The OFF had responsibility for "programs for government information on the war effort," and since foreign nationalities groups "make up part of the population of the United States, any governmental communications to them directly or indirectly should be handled by OFF." In order to avoid charges from the Bureau of the Budget that the FNB's work would duplicate that of the OFF and to secure a good relationship with the OFF, Poole amended his outline to illustrate the expertise his press section would require. He also used his contacts in the academic community to organize a network of volunteer readers to perform the task.[148]

The second opponent was not as easily placated. Donovan sent Poole's draft to Welles, who, despite Poole's reference to the State Department's "peculiar request," allowed the draft to sit for three weeks. At last, on December 20, Donovan appealed to Roosevelt to intervene, on the grounds that

"Sumner Welles, on behalf of the State Department, requested me to set up a branch in my office which would study and report upon foreign politics as they unfold in the United States in connection with our foreign nationality groups." The president approved the creation of the FNB two days later.[149] However, friction persisted, with Berle in particular continuing to see the FNB as a potential source of interference with the State Department's policy and with his own approach to foreign nationalities issues. Berle also harbored a "dislike or distrust" of Wiley. To surmount this last obstacle, Donovan appealed to Hull, assuring him that the proposed branch would collect information but not "interfere in questions of policy, . . . the province exclusively of the Department of State." Hull agreed, since Welles "on behalf of the State Department" and with the president's approval had asked that the FNB be created.[150]

Although Wiley served as the FNB's head during its first year, it was Poole—Wiley's second in command—who had the most influence on the branch's direction. Poole's approach to foreign nationalities issues occupied a middle ground between that of the OFF and the State Department, reflecting his diplomatic experience and his stint at Princeton, where he had edited the *Public Opinion Quarterly.* To Poole, the war provided both opportunities and obligations; his proposed branch would take advantage of the first while discharging the second. As a result of Axis conquests, most of the world was "closed to political activity of any free and democratic kind." The United States, center of world economic and military power with a "multi-national population which shares with all the other nations their thoughts and fears and aspirations," was now, because of those events abroad, "an ever busier arena of foreign political activity and intrigue." During World War I, America had not had sufficient information about foreign political activity taking place on its soil and had found itself at significant disadvantage. Now that another conflict was in the offing, the national interest of the country demanded "an organization which can function in this environment but only with the most skilled and reliable of personnel."[151]

The far-reaching task of the FNB would be "to study and report upon foreign politics—but upon foreign politics as they unfold in the United States." This work had three components: to be aware of and in contact with the "foreign political personalities" in the United States; to know the views of "all the foreign nationality groups . . . their leaders and factions, and the movements of political sentiment within these groups"; and to evaluate the information gathered and "submit timely and well considered reports . . . to the policy-making branches of government." All of this would require "an unusual degree of discretion, tact, and knowledge of world politics" from the men and women employed in the FNB's service.[152]

Since "direct observation" of much of Europe was not possible, the FNB's primary resource for political intelligence would be the country's foreign nationalities population, thus enabling the agency to use an "indirect method of looking in a mirror in order to catch the lineaments of a foreign situation."[153] Poole's definition of "political intelligence" was broad and included "reflection in the United States of situations abroad" and any "foreshadowing here of possible developments abroad"; information concerning "unrecognized movements and dissident agitations"; and examples of the "American democratic process—pressures at Washington touching points in international relations."[154] Poole considered his agency's work as comparable "to the political reporting of an American diplomatic mission abroad . . . or that of the foreign correspondent of a first-class American newspaper." The means used were "not secret or inquisitorial, but open and free, though always discreet," and the operation as a whole represented "an interesting addition to the American democratic process."[155]

Poole, while mindful of the audience to whom his information was sent, did not lose sight of the sensibilities of the people from whom the information was gathered. He frequently reminded his colleagues in the foreign nationalities field of the need to develop policies that did not question the loyalties of America's foreign-born citizens. The government should not urge "anyone to be loyal to the United States of America" but to "the ideals of freedom and democracy" for which the war was being fought.[156] He cautioned FNB personnel not to think of their task as limited to the preparation of reports. Their duty was rather to possess "at every moment a complete familiarity with the foreign political situation" assigned to them; reports and memoranda would then be "by-products of a more fundamental operation."[157] The most important of the FNB's services consisted of "direct personal contact (what might be called diplomatic contact) with important foreign political refugees in the United States and also with the politically important members" of foreign nationality groups. Poole did much of this work himself because of the "high level of professional competence, and in some cases not a little diplomatic experience" the task required.[158]

The branch produced a variety of materials whose circulation and readership depended on the subject matter and security classification of the document. *Reports* consisted of comprehensive analyses of particular foreign nationalities issues, such as the Serb-Croat dispute within the Yugoslav-American community, or the political views of the foreign-language press.

Bulletins were more timely newspaper-like accounts of current developments, such as ethnic conferences and the activities of foreign nationalities organizations. *News Notes* featured announcements of "spot news" items gathered mostly from volunteer readers. Poole also composed his own *Specials* which were accounts of interviews he had had with various leading foreign nationalities figures. The *Specials* had a limited distribution, since they usually dealt with Poole's candid assessment of sensitive subjects or controversial personalities.[159]

* * *

By the time the United States entered World War II, a number of agencies existed to deal with foreign nationalities issues, but the administration had not developed a common approach to guide them. Berle and the State Department quickly moved to fill that vacuum by issuing a policy statement on "free movements" and the European exiles who led them. The statement, released a few days after Pearl Harbor, echoed Berle's comments to Otto von Hapsburg by acknowledging that the United States contained citizens of varied European backgrounds but insisting that these people "owe, and have, an individual allegiance to the United States." Ethnic Americans could take pride in their countries of origin, but the American government would not favor "any activities designed to divide the allegiance of any group of American residents between the United States and any foreign government, in existence or prospect." Washington also would not approve of attempts by aliens or "free movements" to recruit Americans "of like racial background on the theory that they are 'fellow nationals.'" Aliens from countries occupied by the Axis naturally desired to liberate their countries; loyal Americans, concerned about their former homelands might "organize in sympathetic and friendly support of such aspirations." The United States welcomed information about such activities, but it did not favor "free movements" that advocated policies at variance with those of the American government. The State Department, which at the time of the statement's issuance still administered the original FARA, also preferred that the governing committees of such movements be comprised "of citizens of the foreign country, rather than American sympathizers."[160]

Yet free movements continued to proliferate, much to Berle's annoyance. His frustration peaked on January 9, 1942, when he made the following entry in his diary:

> I am likewise having a lot of trouble with the foreign language groups in the United States. The leaders from overseas want to do a lot of proselytizing and

general politics in the United States; and in many cases we sympathize. On the other hand, the first and central interest of any proper United States authority must be to see to it that the United States is not fragmented or Balkanized by disputes between groups. I am trying to draw a clear line between groups of Americans or intending Americans of European background who want to express sympathy; and frank exiles who are here because they have to be and propose to go back as soon as they can. But it is sometimes a tough line to draw. Some of the governments-in-exile want to give us lists of all of the immigrants in the United States so that we can start in recruiting them for army service, etc.—which would be fatal.[161]

Berle, whose Division of Foreign Activity Correlation had the most contact with free movements, proposed a solution to his troubles in a late January memorandum sent to all of the agencies working on foreign nationalities issues. Berle acknowledged that several people within the government had suggested that the foreign nationality groups in America be used "as a bridge" to communicate the ideals of the war to their former homelands and thus encourage resistance to the fascists. Nothing had been done, however, because the task involved working with certain free movements in the United States as well as political groups in Europe. This would not only involve the United States in European quarrels, but it would also allow exile groups to utilize an official American sanction. Because no solution to these impediments had been found, Berle argued, "a powerful weapon had remained unused." As a remedy, he suggested the formation of an American committee representing the chief foreign-language groups in the United States, whose members would be American citizens, not associated with any factions or free movements. The activities of this committee would be steered by a government panel composed of officials from the State Department, the OFF, and the COI, with each agency having its own definite responsibilities. The State Department would determine the "political orientation" and the "line" the committee would take; the COI would ensure the best use of the "propaganda and publicity developed on the continent of Europe;" and the OFF would direct the propaganda and publicity disseminated in the United States. The committee's propaganda line would emphasize the desire to see the countries of Europe free and independent, but it would not concern itself with the political complexion of postwar governments, a subject Berle considered inappropriate and unacceptable. Before the undertaking commenced, Berle deemed it essential for the agencies involved to arrive "at a perfectly clear definition of function among them. If there is a struggle between the three offices to try to determine the policy, or to make policy, independent of the other," he said, "the results will of course be disastrous."[162]

Berle's comment concerning a "clear definition of function" addressed one of the major deficiencies of the administration's foreign nationalities policy. Yet in making his suggestion, which ignored the work being done by both the COI and OFF, Berle was attempting to limit the scope of the FNB and reassert a dominant role for the State Department. As he was composing his memo, Berle, making certain that he was on firm ground, asked the president to clarify "Bill's functions." The COI had an overseas mandate, but the FNB operated domestically, and Berle observed that Donovan wanted "to get into the United States via the alien or foreign-language groups here." Roosevelt replied that he thought "Bill was doing a pretty good job on propaganda and something of a job in terms of intelligence" but confirmed that he did not want him "in Canada . . . South America . . . or inside the country." He saw Donovan as the head of "a war operations agency operating by propaganda and intelligence, etc.," but under no circumstances did Roosevelt want him to operate in the United States. Berle, having secured the statement he wanted, rather disingenuously replied that this understanding would help "because Bill had got crossways of the Attorney General and Secretary Hull and so forth."[163]

Berle next warned Hull that the efforts of "various governments in exile and race groups" to extend their influence over the foreign nationalities population with which "they have affinity" had reached dangerous proportions. Attempts by various foreign intelligence agencies to develop contacts within the foreign nationalities communities would prevent the assimilation of ethnics into American life, in violation of America's historic "melting pot" tradition. As a variety of social and political movements in occupied Europe struggled for postwar power and position, the seriousness of the issue, Berle said, "cannot be overestimated." The State Department had only three choices. It could give foreign governments "considerable latitude" and accept the results; it could close down all "foreign operations" in the United States and "discourage" American immigrants or race groups from becoming involved in European quarrels; or it could be selective in what it allowed each group or government to do and "attempt to guide the forces unleashed."[164]

In addition to issues of power, Berle's statement also reflected the philosophical differences that had surfaced as newer organizations like the OFF and the COI had taken shape. While some of these disputes pitted conservatives against liberals, a few involved New Dealers themselves. Liberals such as Cranston and MacLeish trusted the common people of Europe, once liberated, to govern themselves and resist tyranny, while liberals like Berle believed that traditional elites were better suited to re-establish order and combat the Left. Each set of bureaucrats thoroughly distrusted the other, and this was especially true of Cranston and Berle. According to the biography written by Cranston's sister during his unsuccessful bid for the presidency in 1980, Cranston engaged in "constant combat" with Berle because of their contrasting approaches to foreign issues. Cranston believed that Berle wanted the war to restore "the old order" of monarchies and hierarchal governments; that he appeared to "flirt with Otto of Austria and . . . King Zog of Albania" and preferred "Laval and Petain to deGaulle and the Free French."[165] Jordan Schwarz, in his equally sympathetic biography of Berle, acknowledged that Berle, a man variously described as "arrogant," "brilliant," and "didactic," with easy access to the president, "had more than his share of enemies," but that in wartime Washington, "ideology was in the eye of the contemporary beholder." The Nazi attack on the Soviet Union "had swung Washington's liberal politics sharply leftward, leaving a liberal anti-Nazi and anti-Communist such as Berle looking conservative and isolationist." He seemed "out of sympathy with the war's Grand Alliance with the Soviets." To Schwarz, Cranston's "misguided" hatred of Berle was based on the latter's refusal "to accept the Communists Cranston favored" to lead European refugee groups.[166]

Although the views of both biographers are extreme, it was Cranston who quickly enlisted MacLeish in opposing the plan Berle had outlined in his memo. The proposal, which he believed was designed "to launch a brand of appeasement within this country, and to slap down the 'Free' movements," was "the most dangerous" the State Department could make. Hoskins, although "a fine human" was "inept politically" as well as "appeasement minded;" to give the State Department the kind of control Berle envisioned would lead to the "rise of the questionable groups the State Department would inevitably choose to support." Cranston urged MacLeish to "kill this project" unless the other agencies involved would join in opposition to Berle. If the latter occurred, then "the project might well be of extreme value as a way to modify out-dated policy."[167]

Nonetheless, Berle forged ahead. Along with Hoskins and James Dunn, the State Department's political advisor on European affairs, Berle met with Wiley and Poole of the COI, MacLeish and Ulric Bell of the OFF, and Nelson Rockefeller of Coordinator of Inter-American Affairs to announce his intention to create a committee "on which would be represented the several agencies concerned with foreign-language groups in the United States." All present agreed that such a "steering committee" should be formed,[168] but before that committee met, each agency continued to sort out its tasks and responsibilities and to burnish its prerogatives.

MacLeish again queried Donovan about the relationship between the FNB and the OFF. To MacLeish, the task of the FNB was to conduct intelligence work among "alien groups" in the United States and to furnish whatever strategic or military information it gained to the State Department, but not to supply information to any group or attempt "to direct or influence their behavior." This insured, for MacLeish, that there would be no conflict with the OFF and that the FNB would work to keep the OFF informed of any actions which might influence the OFF or its duties.[169] Wiley, for his part, conferred with Dunn, who expressed the view that Berle's actions "were about as provocative as they could be" but that the idea of a working committee where the views of FNB could be represented was probably sound. Such a group also might eventually "work itself out of Mr. Berle's orbit, which would be very desirable." When Dunn commented on MacLeish's "personal antagonism to Berle," Wiley responded that he had sensed "an atmosphere of battle" but that "a collaboration with the State Department had to be successful no matter what the obstacles might be."[170]

Little collaboration occurred during the initial meetings of the Berle group, tentatively named the Interdepartmental Committee for Political Warfare. Hoskins, who served as chair, recorded that all present had agreed that an interdepartmental committee could be of use "to insure coordination and maximum governmental effort" in the area of psychological warfare. However, his proposal that they discuss "the proper policy regarding the use of aliens" in United States military forces met with immediate opposition, as the others insisted the issue was outside of the group's purview.[171] Ultimately, the representatives of the FNB and the OFF asked not to be held to an official position on the question, and Poole requested that each representative obtain specific instructions from his agency before agreeing to any general policy statement concerning foreign nationalities. Hoskins expressed his regret at this lack of progress and at the uncertainty those present seemed to harbor about the committee's "mandate," but he agreed to suspend the meeting.[172]

The uncertainty to which Hoskins referred stemmed in part from what Poole and Wiley rightly saw as Berle's attempt to subordinate the FNB's functions to State Department control; nevertheless, Wiley advised Donovan that Poole should remain in the group and "play along with it on the assumption that it will lead nowhere and probably talk itself to death en route." As the official history of the FNB put it, both officials "were tactfully trying to hold

Berle at arm's length and tacitly discourage on his part too enterprising an initiative." In the meantime, the FNB could use the meetings to work out a closer collaboration on foreign nationalities issues with the OFF and the Justice Department.[173]

Wiley was more or less correct in his assessment of the Berle committee's future. By its third meeting on February 11, 1942, the committee had changed its name to the less ambitious "Interdepartmental Committee for Foreign Nationality Problems"[174] and evolved into more of a forum for the discussion of specific issues than a grand policy-making body. Poole later surmised that Berle's initial wariness concerning the FNB ranged from fears that Donovan's ambitions would "eclipse the State Department" to concerns that the branch "was actually a cover for some kind of internal Gestapo." By the spring of 1942, Berle seemed resolved to work with the FNB, and Poole, conscious of Donovan's advice "that we must avoid fighting with anyone except the enemy," met Berle more than halfway. Yet he told Donovan, "[I]t would have been easier and pleasanter to have joined issue on several counts and had a good fight."[175]

*   *   *

By the time the United States entered World War II, the American public had become used to equating immigrants and exiles with concerns about national security. In part, this identification was traditional, as the nativist outbreaks in America's past had shown. However, this fear also arose from conditions, such as fifth-column hysteria, peculiar to the 1930s and 1940s. Roosevelt, more sensitive to civil liberties than Wilson had been (but also reluctant to share power), was unwilling to create any one agency to deal with the public's concerns. He supported legislation and issued executive orders to guard the nation's security and relied on the people who executed them to deal with any repercussions that occurred. However, this strategy did not allow for the kind of coordination, or agreement on a single purpose, that many of the people dealing with foreign nationalities issues wanted. When a contentious ethnic group, such as Yugoslav-Americans, interacted with equally contentious bureaucrats, the results did little to enhance either domestic unity or national security.

2

A Feud Entirely European in Origin

No single group served as a better illustration of America's conflict between ethnicity and national security than the Yugoslav-American community. Although a relatively small percentage of the general population, the concentration of Yugoslav-Americans in defense plants and the publicity afforded to the Chetnik resistance group within Yugoslavia earned them the attention of policymakers and the public. Yet it was the depth of ethnic and political conflict within the ranks of Yugoslav-Americans that most troubled the agencies involved with foreign nationalities issues. The community suffered from a severe and apparently irreparable split as Serb monarchists loyal to the exiled king battled the liberal Croat and Slovene supporters of Tito and the Partisans. This tension not only demonstrated the problems that ethnic conflicts caused within the United States, but it showcased the different approaches taken by each agency involved, the concerns about communist sympathies in immigrant communities that influenced some policymakers' views, and the diplomatic complications inherent in many ethnic quarrels. Although American officials eventually developed a common approach with regard to the Serbs, that did not translate into a single, coherent policy toward Yugoslav-Americans or ethnics in general. The administration's divided views on the value of ethnic ties in a nation at war proved as difficult to alleviate as the divisions between Serbs, Croats, and Slovenes.

*   *   *

The conflicts between Yugoslav-Americans arose from their homeland's troubled past. Yugoslavia, originally called the Kingdom of Serbs, Croats, and

Slovenes, came into existence in the wake of World War I. Though multi-ethnic in name, the new state "had a Serb majority, a Serb dynasty, a Serb capital, and a predominately Serb government."[1] The Serbs, in short, dominated the country to the extent that, according to Jozo Tomasevich, leading expert on the economic and political history of Yugoslavia, the "majority of non-Serb South Slavs probably soon came to feel that they had merely exchanged one form of foreign rule for another."[2] Throughout the 1920s, political parties were organized along ethnic lines as Slovenes and Croats chafed under this Serb hegemony and demanded more autonomy. The Communist Party, though prohibited, remained active underground. In 1929, King Alexander, with the full support of the Serb-controlled military, attempted to end ethnic strife by abolishing the constitution, banning all political parties, and assuming dictatorial powers. Croats who opposed Alexander's regime, such as Croatian Peasant Party (CPP) leader Vladko Maček, were jailed; others, such as Ante Pavelić, fled to Italy to create resistance groups. With the support of Mussolini, Pavelić formed the Ustasha, a violent revolutionary movement dedicated to Croatian independence. In 1934, the Ustasha participated in the conspiracy that led to Alexander's assassination; a regency, led by Prince Paul, then ruled Yugoslavia in the name of Alexander's eleven year old son, Peter. Prince Paul governed with a lighter hand than Alexander and released Maček and other dissenters from jail, but his actions only made Croat opposition to the regime more effective.[3]

By the late 1930s, as the threat of war became tangible, Paul reached an accommodation with Maček and the CPP, lest the country's ethnic tensions make it vulnerable to Axis aggression. The accord, made final just as the European war began in 1939, increased Croatian representation in the government: Maček became vice-premier and four other Croatians served as ministers of state; Ivan Šubašić was named Ban, or governor, of "Banovina Croatia," which received a large measure of autonomy on local issues.[4]

Throughout the winter and spring of 1941, as the Axis increased their hold on southeastern Europe, the Germans pressured Prince Paul to adhere to the Tripartite Pact in return for a promise of neutrality. The United States, not yet in the war but anxious to limit Axis gains, encouraged the Yugoslav government to resist. The American minister in Yugoslavia, Arthur Bliss Lane, appealed to Prince Paul, still acting as regent for the underage Peter, to stand firm. Cordell Hull and Sumner Welles met with Yugoslav minister Konstantin Fotić to convey the same message and to enlist his support in convincing his government to withstand Germany's demands. After a few of these meetings had occurred, Lane advised Welles, whom he knew to be "on close terms" with Fotić, that Fotić was "one of the most highly regarded Yugoslav diplomatic representatives" and that his talks with the Americans had strengthened the will of those in the government who wanted to defy the Axis.[5]

The efforts of the Americans failed. Prince Paul signed the Tripartite Pact at the end of March but was immediately overthrown by a military coup. Its leaders proclaimed Peter king under a new government headed by a Serbian general named Dušan Simović. In reporting to President Roosevelt, Welles characterized Simović "as an officer of great ability and of strong Serb tendencies," but he conveyed Fotić's assurance that the Cabinet was reflective of the country as a whole, "with full representation given to the Croats." Welles also recommended that Roosevelt approve a personal message from Roosevelt to the king since it "would be of great value at this moment."[6] Roosevelt complied and Lane later told the president that the king valued Roosevelt's support "more than that of anybody next to his mother." Lane had also conveyed Roosevelt's wish, originally expressed two years before, that Peter and his mother visit the White House, only to learn that Prince Paul had never relayed this information to Peter, who "would have gone like a shot" at the invitation. Lane was impressed by the young king's "moral courage . . . and . . . his evident desire to rely on the United States," a country for which he had "genuine admiration."[7]

The young king's government, fearing a German attack, remained divided over whether or not to formally repudiate the Tripartite Pact. However, popular demonstrations in opposition to the accord prompted the Axis to invade Yugoslavia. Exploiting the ethnic divisions between Serbs and Croats, the invaders partitioned the country in order to forestall resistance and to provide their Balkan allies with spoils. Most of Croatia and all of Bosnia-Herzegovina became the "Independent State of Croatia" ruled by the "fanatically anti-Serb" Ustasha leader Ante Pavelić and an absentee Italian king. Italy, Bulgaria, and Hungary received portions of Serbia, with the remainder placed under a German-Bulgarian occupation force commanded by General Milan Nedić. Germany directly annexed the eastern part of Slovenia; Italy took western Slovenia, most of the Adriatic coast and all of the Adriatic islands and Montenegro. Albania and Bulgaria annexed land in Slovenia and Croatia.[8]

Peter and his ministers fled their now-divided country, and, after weeks of temporary abodes in the Middle East, established a government-in-exile in London in late June. The cabinet remained dominated by Serb nationalists who seized on their country's quick collapse as proof of the instability of a multiethnic state and justification for the creation of a "Greater Serbia" after the war. In Yugoslavia, where most of the army had been captured and deported to Germany, one of the officers who had escaped, Draža Mihailović, mounted a guerrilla resistance in Western Serbia. Mihailović was a Serb colonel with a relatively undistinguished but pan-Serb career, and by June, when he made his first contact with the Yugoslav-Government-In-Exile (YGIE), he had approximately ten thousand "Chetniks" under arms. His movement, which was primarily Serbian, was "anti-Croat and anti-Communist" as well. A second resistance group, led by Josip Broz Tito and known as the Partisans, engaged in acts of sabotage in the spring but did not launch their movement fully until after the German invasion of the Soviet Union. The Partisans, who supported the re-creation of a united but federated Yugoslavia, attracted all three ethnic groups to their banner and, though communist led, were "Yugoslav" in character.[9]

In the *Handbook* of America's foreign nationalities groups published by the Foreign Nationalities Branch (FNB) during the war, DeWitt Clinton Poole observed that one-sixth of the American population with origins in central and eastern Europe "tend predominately to represent minorities and dissidents." However, numerical "distortions" often occurred as these groups moved to America; in the case of the South Slavs, while "Serbs outnumber Croats and Croats outnumber Slovenes" in Yugoslavia, in the United States the reverse was true. The vast majority of all three groups had emigrated to the United States before the formation of the Yugoslav state and had no personal knowledge of the state's history, or any experience of living as "Yugoslavs." Their overall numbers were not large: in the 1940 census, 383,000 Americans listed Yugoslavia as their country of origin; 178,000 were Slovene, 115,000 were Croat, and 37,000 were Serb. Of the 160,000 Yugoslav-Americans born in Yugoslavia, 61 percent were naturalized American citizens. As a group, they were centered in the industrial states of Ohio, Pennsylvania, Illinois, and Michigan.[10]

This population's concentration in factories and plants essential to the war effort would have caused the government's attention to fall on the Yugoslav-American community, but another factor was at work as well. By the spring of 1940, in the midst of public fears about fifth columnists, the State Department had singled out the "benevolent, social, and burial societies among our alien population" as having "already, in a measure, become the instruments of foreign agitators."[11] Although the context in this instance involved the work of fascist propagandists, ethnics from non-enemy areas also raised concerns, as the passage of laws such as the Smith Act and the relocation of the Immigration and Naturalization Service (INS) to the Justice department showed. Like most immigrant groups, Serbs, Croats, and Slovenes had their own fraternal or benefit societies and newspapers, but all of them were divided along ethnic lines. The newspaper editors, like the general Yugoslav population, had arrived in the United States before 1914, and having little expertise or knowledge, had, as Poole observed, "readily accepted the cooperation and guidance of better educated and more recently informed political spokesmen" who had entered the United States as refugees after the beginning of World War II. Because Yugoslavia itself was occupied and divided, to a greater extent than even Poland, "the political life of Yugoslavia since the outbreak of the present war has been lived in the United States."[12] Ethnic divisions within the community—and the potential use that exiles and "foreign agitators" could make of those divisions—made Yugoslav-Americans a prime example of the dangers that America feared existed in its ethnic enclaves.

The largest Croatian group in the United States was the Croatian Fraternal Union of America (CFU), formed in the 1920s through the merger of several smaller organizations. Headquartered in Pittsburgh and described by the FNB as too faction-ridden to have a clear stance on political or foreign issues, its members published a number of small circulation foreign-language papers. The National Council of Americans of Croatian Descent, also based in Pittsburgh and established by an American Croatian Congress held during the war, was perceived by the Roosevelt administration as leftist. The Serb National Federation (SNF), the largest Serb group in the country, published *Amerikanski Srbobran* and established the Serbian National Defense Council in 1941 to collect relief funds for the Serbs and to publicize the Chetnik cause. The SNF, located in Pittsburgh, had close ties to Fotić and the YGIE. The "liberal" Slovene National Benefit Society of Chicago was the largest of the Slovene organizations and supported a reunited Yugoslavia. Its president, "an old-time Socialist" named Vincent Cainkar, published the group's daily paper, *Prosveta,* which was "leftist-liberal" on political issues. The Slovene American National Council, created by a Slovene Congress held during the war, had a pro-Partisan leadership but a clerical rank and file. The leftist and pro-Partisan United Committee of South-Slavic Americans (UCSSA) did not organize until 1943, but it was, along with the SNF, a major concern of the agencies involved in foreign nationalities issues. Louis Adamic, the most prominent "American of Yugoslav origin" in the United States, served as the UCSSA's first president and the editor of its *Bulletin;* the United Committee's strength came primarily from the Slovene and Croatian communities. The

American Slav Congress (ASC), though more generally Slavic than Yugoslav, also aroused interest in government circles because of its connection to the Soviet Union. The International Workers Order (IWO), a pro-Soviet association tied to various labor groups, worked closely with the American Slav Congress. It had more than a dozen foreign-language sections, including the Serbian American Federation and the Croatian Benefit Fraternity of America; each was relatively small but each had its own press.[13]

Ethnic tensions in the Yugoslav-American community initially surfaced after the Axis invasion of Yugoslavia. In April, John Butkovich, head of the Croatian Fraternal Union and the Croatian representative on one of the Democratic National Committee's nationality committees, sent a telegram to President Roosevelt on behalf of the Croatian National Council, an umbrella organization that had been formed in the 1930s to protest Alexander's dictatorship. In his message, Butkovich pledged his group's loyalty to the United States at a time when "the country of our birth and Croatian people are subjected to an unprovoked aggression."[14] A few weeks later, Dr. Vladimir Rybar, the counselor of the Yugoslav Legation, met with officials at the State Department to assure them that the Slovene population in the United States remained "100 per cent pro-Yugoslav and anti-Pavelić" and that the fall of Belgrade had caused the factions within the community to bury their differences and "to proclaim their solidarity behind the idea of a united Yugoslavia."[15] Within a few days, however, Rybar reported that he had just returned from Cleveland where he had learned "to his distress" that Catholic priests there supported the creation of a separate Croatian State and "in effect are supporting Pavelić." He attributed this to the Catholic Archbishop of Cleveland, "who is of German descent."[16]

This pattern of division was fully set by Fotić, who had continued to represent Yugoslavia in the United States. In late April, in accordance with a request from his government, Fotić asked that the United States issue a statement supporting the re-establishment of an independent and united Yugoslavia at war's end. Welles agreed but advised Hull "that such a statement, if made by us, should be made in a rather formal and not in too casual a way."[17] According to Fotić's memoirs, Welles ultimately suggested that the president deliver his statement in the presence of representatives of the various loyal Yugoslav-American groups within the country, only to have Fotić claim that the Croatian Fraternal Union attached so many conditions, including a request that a member of the Croatian Peasant Party be present, that General Simović ultimately asked that the whole endeavor be abandoned.[18] Fotić then branded CFU president Butkovich as "sympathetic with the Croat separatists" and unwilling to join an all Yugoslav relief effort. Welles passed the memo on to Adolf A. Berle and his division with the suggestion that "it might be desirable to have some investigation made of Mr. Butkovich's present activities and connections."[19] Fotić also gave Welles a newspaper article which threatened "Yugoslav residents of the United States that if they do not support the new Croatian Government of Dr. Pavelić, their relatives in Yugoslavia will suffer for it." Welles sent this on to Berle, asking that it too be included in "our present investigation."[20]

Within a few weeks, Berle met with two officers of the CFU, one of whom was Ohio State Senator William Boyd-Boich. They were cooperative and eager to offer assistance, and they "confirmed the feeling" that Butkovich was "an undercover Nazi." They also supported Fotić's claim that a newspaper sympathetic to Pavelić was being distributed in a large number of cities and speculated that it "must be getting money from somewhere." The two men described the majority of Croatians as being anti-Pavelić and proposed "to try to get a firmer control on newspapers published by the Croatian Fraternal Union and thereby counter some of the Pavelic propaganda." Berle asked "them to keep in general touch with us so we could know what went on."[21]

The policies of the government-in-exile also exacerbated Yugoslav-American tensions. Mihailović, far outnumbered by Axis and Ustasha forces, quickly decided to conserve his resources until the Allies landed; the London government approved this strategy, as did the British, who cautioned Mihailović against "premature actions." In September 1941, the Germans issued a decree that called for the execution of one hundred civilians for every German killed by the resistance, and for fifty lives in exchange for every wounded German solider. As a result, the Chetniks, who believed that the Serbs had suffered and lost too much in the last war, became even more determined to husband their forces and avoid "national suicide." Tito's Partisans, despite almost continual German attacks, remained in the field and pursued a more offensive strategy, but the government-in-exile celebrated only the Chetniks, who gained a popular following as the first and most effective resistance force in occupied Europe.[22] Although the Partisans and Chetniks attempted to coordinate their activities, neither could accept the tactics or postwar visions of the other, and by the end of 1941, they battled each other as Yugoslavia slipped into what Simon Trew, expert in battlefield studies, has termed a "war of almost unparalleled savagery."[23]

The royal government's eagerness to circulate atrocity stories concerning the alleged massacres of thousands of Serbs by Croats in Croatia, and the willingness of Serb newspapers in the United States to publish the accounts, created additional tension. While Serbs and Croats wantonly murdered one another throughout the war, the numbers cited in the atrocity accounts and their general authenticity were suspect. This was particularly true of the so-called "Danckelmann Memorandum," which emanated from the Serbian Orthodox Church but was transmitted to the German occupying authorities in Yugoslavia and eventually sent to London. *Amerikanski Srbobran* began to publish this material in early November 1941.[24] Prior to publication, Fotić gave Welles a series of telegrams, whose "general accuracy" he vouched for, which detailed the torture and massacre of Serbian priests and other civilians by Croatians, with the collusion of the Catholic Church. Serbian churches had been demolished, monasteries robbed, and "the people forced to accept Catholicism." The death toll, Fotić claimed, stood at more than three hundred thousand.[25]

In January 1942, the League of Majors, the young Serb army officers who had supported the March coup and fled with the king into exile, engineered a change in the royal government in London. After claiming that Simović exercised too little leadership, the Serbs elevated an elderly but well-respected historian Slobodan Jovanović to the post of prime minister. More important, they promoted Mihailović to the rank of general and awarded him the cabinet post of Minister of the Army, Navy, and Air Force. Mihailović was the government-in-exile's "chief asset," and the Jovanović regime resolved to do all in its power to enhance his position with the Allies.[26] To publicize the Chetniks' activities and to illustrate the regime's commitment to all of the country's ethnic groups, the YGIE also established a Yugoslav Information Center in New York, staffed by ministers representing each ethnic group: Franc Snoj for the Slovenes; Ivan Šubašić, the last governor of Croatia, for the Croats; and Sava Kosanović, who also headed the Office of Economic Reconstruction, for the Serbs. Little unity resulted since the ministers, though loyal to the government-in-exile, were federalists who opposed the Greater Serbia tendencies of the cabinet in London and of Minister Fotić in the Washington legation.[27]

The Serb-Croat dispute, which Poole characterized as "a perfect example of the reproduction on American soil of a feud which is entirely European in origin,"[28] served as the subject for two of the FNB's earliest reports. The branch judged that before the fall of 1941, most of the strife within the Yugoslav-American community had stemmed from the Croatian National Council of Pittsburgh, which supported the Nazi puppet state ruled by Pavelić. Butkovich, president of the Croatian Fraternal Union, served as "nominal head" of the council, but Dr. Dinko Tomashich, a visiting professor of sociology at Washington University in St. Louis, actually wielded power. The majority of American Croats, however, sympathized with Croatian Peasant Party leader Maček, who had been confined by the Germans for refusing to cooperate with the puppet Croatian state. Beginning in early November, 1941, the Serbs had emerged as the prime instigators of conflict, with the Serb National Federation, the largest Serb fraternal and mutual aid society in the United States, championing the Chetnik and Royalist cause. In the past, the federation and its newspaper had "invariably supported every Yugoslav Government currently in power and had upheld the unity of the Serb, Croat, and Slovene peoples in the Kingdom of Yugoslavia." This had changed late in 1941, when the federation, under the prompting of Jovan Dučić, an exiled Yugoslav diplomat living in the United States but still on the Yugoslav government's payroll, created the Serbian National Defense Council (SNDC), ostensibly to collect relief funds for war-torn Yugoslavia. Michael Dučić, Jovan's brother and a wealthy dairy owner in the Midwest, served as the SNDC's president. After the creation of the council, *Amerikanski Srbobran* called for the creation of a Greater Serbia under the slogan "One People, One State, One King." The paper justified this "pan-Serb" campaign by charging that all American Croats supported the Croatian National Council, and that the Croats in Yugoslavia had all collaborated with the Axis, thus negating the ideal of the multinational South Slav state established in 1919.[29]

The FNB believed that "Serb nationalism seems plainly the main source of all this turmoil"; Fotić and the YGIE, if not behind the *Amerikanski Srbobran* campaign, showed their silent approval by not countering the paper's charges. While Fotić's public actions had thus far been "discreet," he had "ceased to refer to Yugoslavia by name." How much support the anti-Croat campaign had outside of the SNDC remained in doubt, since several hundred Yugoslav-Americans had attended a pro-Yugoslav rally in New York in March, organized by the Union of Yugoslav Americans, which was affiliated with the International Workers Order. At that rally, Šubašić, who was a frequent target of *Amerikanski Srbobran,* and his fellow ministers at the Yugoslav Information Center, Sava Kosanović and Franc Snoj, had condemned the paper and called for the support of the king and Mihailović.[30]

The FNB also analyzed the religious differences between Serbs and Croats and the clergy's role in perpetuating division, concluding that the "thousand-year quarrel" between the two "is thus in part a religious quarrel." The Croats were predominately Roman Catholic, while the Serbs were Orthodox. Bishop Dionisije Milivojević, the head of the Serbian Church in Canada and the United States, and a member of the official state church of Yugoslavia, had accepted the position of honorary president of the Serbian National Defense Council and had blessed the group's activities. In sum, the "divisionist tendencies among the Yugoslavs in the United States" came from three sources: the "ethnocentric tendencies" of Croats and Serbs; "the conflicting interests of the clergy in each group"; and "perhaps from the Yugoslav legation in Washington." The FNB recommended that if pan-Serb sentiment was not that widespread, several men, such as Šubašić and Louis Adamic, who had "enormous prestige among all branches of Yugoslav-Americans," could be used by the United States government to reconcile the Serb and Croat factions.[31] Poole, although careful to note that his agency was limited only to "the gathering of information," also suggested to Berle that someone from the State Department speak to Fotić about the material in *Amerikanski Srbobran*.[32] He did not deem it necessary to ascertain whether Fotić was "in some degree back of the Serb agitation." If Fotić "is asked to use his influence with his Serbian compatriots . . . to induce them to avoid controversies . . . this will serve as a warning to him in case he has been guilty of an indiscretion." If he were blameless, he could "only receive in a friendly spirit a request from the State Department for his assistance."[33]

Some of Poole's information on the Serbs came from an informant in Pittsburgh identified only as "S. Karan" or "S. K.," who involved himself in the ethnic controversy, much to Poole's distress. S. K. worked under Allen Dulles in the Coordinator of Information's New York office, and his employment "was known to FBI pursuant to the general arrangement existing between Mr. Dulles' office and FBI."[34] In one of his communications, S. K. related that Branko Pekich, an officer in the SNF, had complained to him of a visit from two FBI agents who had inquired about the federation's anti-Croat campaign, which Pekich had defended as a simple exposition of Croat atrocities. S. K. confided that the local Yugoslav consul had asked the FBI to do this as a warning to the SNF and that for years the consul had "been combating all anti-Yugoslav propaganda and has closely cooperated with U.S. authorities." S. K. also reported that Pekich "honestly believes" all of the atrocity stories published by the paper and was convinced that the Serbs must respond "in kind and totally divorce themselves from the Croats." Pekich could not conceive that Dučić and others might selfishly be using the SNF "to promote their plan of action against the realm of Yugoslavia."[35]

Nicholas Mirkovich, who worked with Kosanović at the Office for Reconstruction, also confirmed to Adamic that "the FBI had raided the offices of the Pittsburgh *Srbobran* and taken editor Mladen Trbuhovich." The results seemed immediate; subsequent issues of the paper did not contain any attacks on Croats, and Mirkovich advised that "the next step would be to break the ring of the actual backers of the anti-Croat drive (the notorious Jugoslav diplomats)."[36]

S. K. took credit for these developments, telling the Coordinator of Information (COI) that "as a result of strong representations on his part respecting the displeasure of the American Government as a result of the recent activities of the *Srbobran*," Trbuhovich had been dismissed as editor and the paper had adopted "a general line . . . looking to pacification between the Serbs and Croats." However, Trbuhovich planned to visit Washington with Michael Dučić, and Poole speculated that they would call at the State Department and the FBI to inquire what authority S. K. had to speak for the government. Poole asked the same question, only to have S. K. reply that he had acted on his own because "the circumstances demanded such action." Poole countered, as forcefully as he could, that S. K.'s "conduct had been quite unauthorized" and ordered him to return to New York "at once and report to the office there."[37]

When Trbuhovich and Dučić came to Washington, they visited the Office of Facts and Figures (OFF) to submit their own account of recent Yugoslav events. Their first paragraph gave credence to the FNB's analysis of the Serb-Croat dispute, by proclaiming that throughout its brief history, Yugoslavia's ethnic groups have lived "under a queer strain of mutual distrust—even hatred." The Serbs, a people with a history of empire and a superior culture, agreed to merge with the "small suburban state" of Croatia and the "suburban province" of Slovenia but quickly discovered that the "Kingdom of Serbia had made a poor bargain." The Croats waged a "systematic campaign of sabotage" against the new state and Alexander's dictatorship had been "a last desperate measure" to preserve the country. This pattern continued during the spring crisis of 1941, when the "noble" Serbs defended Yugoslavia's honor and the Croats "betrayed" it. An "unusually reliable source" had confirmed to Trbuhovich and Dučić that the "subsequent blood-brother murder toll" caused by the Croats' slaughter of Serbs stood at five hundred thousand; this rendered impossible any "mutual life between the two peoples in the future." Given this history, attempts by the "so-called leaders" in London to create an information service in the United States to promote ethnic unity was "beyond comprehension." The ministers in New York were nothing but liars who denounced the "authentic facts" about Croatian treachery published in *Amerikanski Srbobran*.[38]

The Serbs also complained that S. K., who "appeared planted" and who they believed was acting in the service of the ministers in New York and the Serbs affiliated with the IWO, had visited federation offices on several occasions. He claimed to be a member of British intelligence and then an FBI agent, and he told the Serbs that the government considered them to be fifth columnists and planned to shut down both the SNF and the paper. The SNF viewed this as an attempt by their enemies to "create a defeatist fright" among them.[39] By the time this story appeared in *Amerikanski Srbobran* in August, Karan was described as impersonating "an American detective," and the paper claimed his services had been paid for by funds sent to the Information Center in New York for "pro-Yugoslav propaganda," funds routinely used for "corruption and bribery."[40]

The continuing ability of a paper such as *Amerikanski Srbobran* to engage in ethnic quarrels stemmed in part from the Roosevelt administration's decision, early in the war, to rely on a system of voluntary censorship for press and radio. In January 1942, the Office of Censorship issued printed guides explaining what kind of print and broadcast material was acceptable and what practices should be avoided. By the spring, the refusal of some publications to conform led Roosevelt to begin pressuring Francis Biddle to move against "subversive" newspapers. The attorney general resisted any blanket action and instead endorsed prosecution of only a few offenders, under the provisions of the Espionage Act. However, the issue remained alive, as the president insisted that something more aggressive be done.[41]

Although Roosevelt's concern centered on domestic fascists such as Charles Coughlin and his publication *Social Justice,* the foreign press as a whole did not escape scrutiny. In early April, at the weekly meeting of the Berle committee, Lawrence M. C. Smith asked Alan Cranston for the OFF's opinion on the issue of "control of the foreign language press in wartime." Smith confided that such a step was under consideration by the Justice Department and the Post Office, and that Congress was expected to act as well. Cranston suggested a practice used during World War I, when the Post Office had "exercised a licensing power whereby it could require any foreign-language newspaper to submit complete English translations of all material before it could use the mails." Papers considered "pro-American" received a license exempting them from this requirement. This policy—which would "put out of business . . . the violently anti-American newspapers which should be put out of business" while assisting "loyally American papers" which should be "free from harassment"—should be re-adopted, provided "the Post Office will lean upon the judgment" of the OFF and the Justice Department. Cranston warned that the "disastrous" alternative would be a shutdown of "the entire foreign-language press."[42]

These deliberations became public when the *New York Times* reported that the departments of Justice and War were debating whether to restrict the foreign-language press, with the Justice Department favoring no more than a licensing policy, "to be used to weed out undesirable periodicals."[43] In an accompanying editorial, the *New York Times* indicated its opposition to any repressive action. The Common Council for American Unity praised this stance, since "language is no test of loyalty." Foreign-language papers served a crucial function in communities where even naturalized Americans remained more comfortable with their native tongue than with English. The government itself has recognized this and utilized the foreign-language press to "explain and spread the American way of life." Now that the country was at war, it was even more important for the foreign-language press to assist in communicating America's war aims to the ethnic community.[44]

Biddle's more lenient policy continued to prevail, and the Justice Department finally concluded that "they would not ask for any radical repressive legislation to apply generally to the foreign-language press" and believed it would be "more satisfactory" if an interdepartmental committee reviewed evidence submitted to it on individual papers.[45] By the end of April, Charles Coughlin's mailing privileges had been suspended and his paper, *Social Justice,* ceased publication; a few other papers of most concern to the administration were dealt with in similar fashion.[46] The Justice Department also issued a press release that included a letter that Biddle had written to Congressman Samuel A. Weiss. Weiss had told Biddle of his concern about the loss of advertisers suffered by foreign-language publications because of the assumption that Justice was about to suppress them. Biddle assured Weiss that the "policy of the Department of Justice is not to suppress foreign-language newspapers." Papers that are seditious, regardless of the language in which they are printed, would be subject to "appropriate action" but "those loyal to the United States [would] have nothing to fear from the government."[47] In a late-May press conference, War Secretary Henry Stimson agreed with the attorney general that "indiscriminate suppression" of the foreign-language press "would do an injustice and serve no useful purpose."[48] While this policy struck the right balance between civil liberties and security, it left the government with few options, other than informal pressure, to deal with troublesome but not seditious publications such as *Srbrobran.*

*   *   *

Poole's endorsement of Šubašić as a conciliator was one informal option, but given the Serb attitude toward the Information Center, it carried little hope of success. Poole's other candidate, Louis Adamic, also eventually proved to be a divisive force within the Yugoslav-American community. Adamic had been born an Austro-Hungarian subject in Slovenia and had emigrated to the United States as a teenager after being expelled from school for participating in the Yugoslav National Movement. By the late 1930s, he had published a number of successful novels and was widely known for his use of immigrant and ethnic themes. Adamic was active in organizations designed to promote tolerance and helped shape the pluralist approach of the intercultural education movement. As the country moved toward war, he feared that the public's security concerns would lead to an anti-alien campaign that would undermine these efforts, and he used his work with the Common Council and his writings in *Common Ground* to bridge ethnic and class differences. He was, ironically, a more controversial figure within Yugoslav-American circles because of his writings in opposition to King Alexander's dictatorship and his support for closer ties between Yugoslavia and the Soviet Union.[49]

Carey McWilliams published a sketch of Adamic in 1935, and (previewing Poole) referred to Adamic as "an interpreter of American life." An "apostle of the excluded," Adamic was moved by and gave a voice to "those who stood beyond the portals of the established order" because of class or ethnicity. McWilliams also observed traits that would render Adamic less suitable for the role Poole would assign him: although charming, Adamic was "a highly strung, nervous, amazingly vehement individual who experienced ideas so intensely that it seemed difficult for him to taper his sentiments down to a conversational pitch." His thought and his writing were "dramatic"; this quality made him "an excellent propagandist" but also caused him to commit "certain errors" to the extent that a reader could not accept "the actual facts or elements in a given situation without verification."[50]

Adamic's skills as a "propagandist" for immigrants became obvious during the war. Speaking to the Common Council in April 1941, Adamic linked the congressional passage of the Lend-Lease Act in early March to the coup that occurred later that same month in Yugoslavia, claiming that the first had helped insure the second and that both had demonstrated the devotion of each country's people to democracy. His native country and his adopted one "have in this moment of crisis begun to achieve the most dynamic and effective unity." Describing himself as "an American who was born in Yugoslavia," he said that he and others like him, who had sent "hundreds of cables" urging the Yugoslavs to resist the Axis, "had played a role in the Yugoslav drama." He believed that in all of their actions "our American and our old country motives met and worked together, and in this we are typical of new Americans of other strains." He was certain that the "loyalty to the United States of most of the foreign-born, including the aliens, is almost beyond adequate statement" and that the United States was beginning to understand that "this diversity of its population" was one of the country's "greatest advantages."[51]

One of Adamic's most famous works, *Two-Way Passage*, combined his interest in ethnicity with his concerns about the outcome of the war. In the book, published before the United States became a belligerent, Adamic emphasized the need to avoid the mistakes of World War I and to make specific postwar plans while the war was still in progress. The United States, as "the one great country which was not interested in grabbing anything," could serve "as the source of sanity, moral strength and material supplies" for the postwar world.[52] America had a unique resource to use in this endeavor: its immigrant population. Adamic suggested that Americans descended from more recent immigrants ("Plymouth Rock" vs. "Ellis Island") be organized, according to their country of origin, into advisory groups that would go to Europe temporarily at war's end to administer the liberated countries' governments. The object of this "passage back" would be to re-create the American Revolution in Europe, to establish democracies in place of the discredited regimes of the prewar period. The result would be a democratic European Federation, with a single currency and a just economic order, but with the sovereignty of each state preserved.[53] Adamic warned that the British, though long a power in European affairs, could not, with their history of imperialism, serve as a model. Only America could "open the passage to the future for all the world" because the Europeans "will trust only us."[54]

Adamic presented an inscribed copy of his book to Eleanor Roosevelt, accompanied by a letter in which he wrote eloquently of the fear in America that chaos would follow the war. Such a development was certain, he claimed, unless the United States helped "to create a universal democracy." Hitler had conquered Europe with an idea, and America must undo this with an idea of its own. As he told Mrs. Roosevelt, "V for Victory is all right but *we need also V for Vision.*" *Two-Way Passage* offered such a vision, and he urged the president's wife to read it soon.[55] Mrs. Roosevelt apparently agreed, telling Adamic that she found the ideas in the last chapters of the book (which contained the "passage back" concept) "quite exciting" and "should like to see them tried."[56] A short time later, Mrs. Roosevelt invited Adamic and his wife, Stella, to dinner at the White House to discuss his work.[57]

After the war, Adamic published an account of the dinner party, which took place on January 13, 1942, in *Dinner at the White House*.[58] The Adamics thought they would be dining alone with Mrs. Roosevelt; to their surprise, President Roosevelt and British Prime Minister Winston Churchill joined them. Churchill, upon whom President Roosevelt had pressed Adamic's book, found it "int'r-resting," while the president candidly admitted to Mrs. Adamic that the "passage back" section had generated a great deal of controversy. However, he said: "I like the last part. It has something. It has something. It opens vistas. It appeals to the imagination. Will you tell that to your husband? Tell him that *I* like the *last* part of the book."[59] Yet the president's agenda for the evening did not center on an endorsement or even a discussion of the passage back. Although he and Churchill had an excellent working relationship, Roosevelt knew that the prime minister did not share his commitment to anticolonialism or grasp the range of attitudes present in America toward European affairs; nor did he understand "what a mixture of races, religions and nationality backgrounds we are, and that our backgrounds persist." As Roosevelt told Mrs. Adamic, he wanted the prime minister to realize that part of the American mixture harbored anti-British sentiments and that "as a people, as a country, we're opposed to imperialism—we can't stomach it."[60] Adamic and his wife were present merely to demonstrate that anti-imperial ethnic mix.

Disappointed that he had not been able to discuss his ideas at the dinner party, Adamic later dispatched a "longish memorandum" to the First Lady that discussed the points he had made in *Two-Way Passage* in the light of America's entry into the war.[61] In the twenty-three page explication, he referred to his idea as "a scheme tossed out for discussion" rather than as a fixed plan. The United States had to take the lead in filling the vacuum that would exist in Europe once the "totalitarian power collapses," lest "the leeches and scoundrels, the intellectually and spiritually bankrupt, the hating and defensively-minded" re-establish their control. Only a "breathless moment" will exist between "the cessation of hostilities and the outburst of vindictiveness" and only America can "take intelligent advantage of it." Government and private relief agencies were already developing plans to feed Europe after the war, and he hoped that "we will have the sense to use food and other services not only to relieve immediate distress but also for immediate and long range political purposes—to enhance the influence and power of the genuine democratic leaders who will appear and to thwart their opponents."[62]

If American followed his proposals, Adamic, using the same reasoning as liberal intellectuals like MacLeish, argued that the country would be taking the "American Revolution, the American Experience" with its commitment to federalism, diversity, and individualism, to Europe—and this "will preclude another crisis like the present." He knew that those in power would oppose these actions, but he was certain that "the plain people of Europe," the multitudes that cheered Wilson in 1918, would approve. The European war was not just a military conflict; it was a "political, ideological conflict," and Hitler could best be defeated "by a military effort in conjunction with a revolutionary idea which is sound and more powerful in its appeal than his." That idea was "a democratic revolution" that could "originate only in the United States," and, if used as a tool in "psychological warfare . . . would pry open the passage to the future" for both Europe and America. If President Roosevelt implemented the plan now, it would preclude a postwar American return to "escapist isolationism."[63]

Adamic knew the task would not be an easy one; the Soviets might offer stronger objections to the American role that he outlined than the British would. The Soviet Union, because of "her war showing and her widespread, resourceful (but intellectually and morally corrupt) Communist Party apparatus," had strength in many of the occupied countries. The attitude of the governments-in-exile would vary, just as the competency of their people ranged, Adamic said, from the few "excellent men" in the "Yugoslav outfit" to "personal symbols of spiritual and political failure, incapable of developing any kinship with a future which is bound to be revolutionary." The various free movements in the United States were not all led "by people conditioned or equipped to further democracy." This did not help morale, nor did the propaganda emanating from some of the legations and governments-in-exile in Washington. However, such tendencies could be offset by the "Passage Back movement and action."[64]

Adamic believed the effect of his ideas on immigrant groups would be particularly beneficial, as many feared that the war would end with a return to power by the old regimes, "a new Danubian empire under the Hapsburgs." The country's immigrant population was "full of rumors and worries and fears of this sort. The foreign-language press is concerned with them; . . . this is not conducive to the morale and energy of millions of new Americans as they work in war industries and serve in our armed forces." The German people, he was certain, would more quickly rid themselves of Hitler if they were "inspired by our German Americans and by German refugees, the overwhelming majority of whom are now loyal to the United States, but confused and fearful on the subject of their 'old country's' future—a fact which I know makes their participation in our common task less effective than it might be."[65]

Mrs. Roosevelt found the memo "very interesting" and assured Adamic that it was "now in the president's hands."[66] Adamic later learned that the document circulated within the administration, but that the departments of State and War "had no use for the essence of the Passage Back suggestion."[67]

Hollywood expressed more of an interest in Adamic's immigrant themes, but the final result was no more satisfying than Adamic's dinner with the president. In February 1942, while Adamic was on a lecture tour for *Two-Way Passage,* Attorney General Biddle asked Adamic's agent to release him to director King Vidor and Metro-Goldwyn-Mayer for a motion picture "dealing with American industry and immigrants." In its press release, Adamic's publisher boasted that this was the first time a writer had been "drafted" and announced that Adamic and Vidor were touring war plants prior to writing the screenplay. The release also noted that Adamic had recently dined at the White House and that "both the President and Mr. Churchill had read *TWP.*" Vidor's proposed film, which centered on three generations of an immigrant family, was to be set in the steel mills of Gary, Indiana, with Spencer Tracy as a possible leading man.[68] The final product, released as "An American Romance" late in 1943, actually bore little resemblance to Adamic's work and did not list him among the twelve writers who had worked on the film. The OWI, which had also supported the project as one that would celebrate wartime productivity, objected to the anti-union stance in the original version Vidor produced and negotiated with him to secure a film more in line with the pro-labor stance of the New Deal. The final story merged the life of an immigrant-turned-mogul with an account of industrial productivity, but there was no passage back by the hero to the land of his birth.[69]

Adamic had more success with radio when the Treasury Department used his book as the basis for a program in the "Treasury Star Parade" series. "Two Way Passage" first aired in 1942 and featured Paul Henried and Fay Bainter as the immigrant Johann Schmidt and his American-born wife Jenny. Johann had emigrated from Germany, "looking for the right to work, the right to worship, and the right to say what he believed." He settled in Minnesota, educated himself by reading books in the town library, married the librarian, and changed his name from "Johann" to "John." He and his wife prospered, buying "a little bungalow on a little street in a little suburb" and paying scant attention to the world outside. Letters from John's family in Germany about Hitler and the Nazis disturbed him, but Jenny insisted he was "an American now" and should let "*them* fight it out between themselves." This indifference ended when local Nazi sympathizers threatened harm to John's family in Germany if he did not cease doing business with "Jewish firms" in his town. He suddenly saw the danger in the Nazi boast that "it will be easy to make a bloody revolution" in America because of the "many social and racial tensions" present there. Jenny assured him the Nazis were wrong; America had a tradition of "harmony and equality," and, as a nation, the American people were "a union united in a common cause."

When America became a belligerent, the Schmidts sent their son to war and John vowed that he too would be going "and using my other ticket . . . my ticket back." Now that he and others like him had helped build a democratic America, "it's time for us to use our passage back—time to take what we have learned here back to all of the places that we and our forefathers came from." Stressing Adamic's theme that the war presented "an opportunity . . . for us, the ordinary people everywhere" to build a better world, the program ended with "God Bless America" playing in the background and John warning the evildoers of Europe, "you liars, you gangsters, you traitors and murders! We're coming back!" The announcer pledged that America's goal was "to take liberty and freedom again to all the oppressed, the downtrodden peoples of the earth" and that the purchase of war bonds would accomplish that goal and provide for "the future security of America."[70]

The messages of this program were that totalitarianism in Europe threatened democracy in America; that all citizens had a role to play in defeating that menace and that *Americanized* immigrants could make a unique contribution in the fight; and that America, though multi-ethnic, was a unified democracy. These were the same messages the government as a whole directed to the foreign nationalities community. By the middle of the script, as Johann married Jenny and changed his name to John, the Schmidts were referred to as "Americans." Only the Nazi who threatened them spoke German when he reminded John of his "good German blood," and brought the dark hatreds of Europe into the Schmidt's grocery store. When John returned to Europe, he would return as an American, who, to paraphrase Adamic, happened to be born in Germany.

In his contacts with Poole, Cranston, and other government officials, Adamic usually acted as an advocate rather than a peacemaker. He was initially concerned with Slovene issues, but after he embraced the Partisan cause, he became a spokesman for this faction within the Yugoslav-American community. Šubašić played a more substantive role in Yugoslav politics, and Poole interviewed him many times, usually in the FNB's New York office and often in the presence of his fellow minister Sava Kosanović. At one such meeting in May 1942, Šubašić assured Poole that the "masses of Croats and Serbians in the United States" were not involved in the Serb-Croat controversy, which was limited to "the intelligentsia and a few political leaders," including the clergy of both groups. The clergy were especially influential "for the Serbs" since "their religion and their country were one and the same." Although both ethnic groups were at fault for the unrest, Šubašić placed more blame on the Serbs, most notably Bishop Dionisije and Minister Fotić. Because of the latter's involvement, "the idea has now become widespread among the Serbs and also among the Croats that the movement against a confederated Yugoslavia and for a Greater Serbia had at least the tacit approval of the United States Government." This agitation would end only "if the American Government made it plain to Minister Fotich that his undiplomatic activity must cease" and issued "an equally strong warning" to the bishop.[71]

Sava Kosanović was even more "frank and bitter" in his criticism of the Yugoslav Legation, which "had closed all doors in Washington" to him and his New York colleagues. The material that Fotić had furnished to *Amerikanski Srbobran* "of alleged Croatian atrocities upon Serbians" was nothing but "German propaganda designed to divert attention from the atrocities committed by the German troops in Serbia." Kosanović promised to provide this material to Poole as proof of the complaints against the minister.[72]

Poole subsequently discovered, in private conversations, that the "State Department may be preparing to take rather severe action" against the Serbs. Cavendish Cannon, who commended FNB for their excellent memoranda on the Serb-Croat dispute, had gone to Welles personally to acquaint him with Fotić's "excessive activity." Like the FNB, Cannon thought it probable, though not "susceptible of proof," that the Yugoslav legation supported *Amerikanski Srbobran.* He surmised that Welles "was likely to be especially outraged by evidence of undiplomatic activity" by Fotić because Welles had supported him in the autumn of 1941 when Fotić had claimed that other members of the YGIE were attempting to have him dismissed. Fotić had "presumed excessively" upon this support by telling "the Croatian members of the Yugoslav Government that they dare not interfere with him since he has the backing of the United States Government."[73]

The Berle committee looked for a solution as well after Poole told his colleagues that "in some instances feeling has run so high between American citizens of Serb and Croat descent that workmen of these two races cannot be placed next to each other in workshops. That is especially serious in view of the great numbers of them at present engaged in heavy industry." The FNB and OFF agreed to pressure the Serbian editors "active in the present agitation," and the committee as a whole discussed "the possibility of an investigation of the *Amerikanski Srbobran* on the grounds that it was being subsidized by the Yugoslav Government." In aid of this, Poole sent copies of "the more polemic articles" in *Amerikanski Srbobran* to Smith at the Justice Department at his request.[74]

*　*　*

Attempts to limit ethnic activity would prove to be the norm for Berle's committee, but one member of the group argued for a more aggressive strategy. For Alan Cranston, supporting organizations that united ethnic groups across national borders was a more positive way to alleviate the sort of strife rampant among Serbs and Croats. One such group, the American Slav Congress, had ties to the Yugoslav-American community, but Cranston's support of it generated controversy on two grounds: the reluctance of Berle and like-minded others to promote "race movements," and the usual concerns about manipulation, in this instance by communists rather than by foreign exiles.

The origins and nature of the American Slav Congress were matters of controversy. Critics claimed that the organization was nothing but a Communist front formed in response to orders from Moscow; defenders insisted that government officials urged American Slavs to join together after Pearl Harbor to support the war effort.[75] An official of the Congress identified the attorney general as the group's founder, since Biddle had been addressing a Slav meeting when news of Pearl Harbor broke and immediately asked those present to help organize all Slavs behind the war effort.[76] The FBI, hostile to both the ASC and OWI, asserted in 1944 that the Slav Congress had been formed "at the suggestion of the Office of War Information."[77] Initial invitations to government officials from labor organizations and Slavic groups to support a Slav Congress actually dated from the fall of 1941, but the meeting was cancelled because of the refusal of "leading Polish, Czechoslovak and Slovenian organizations to participate." Rather than contribute to disunity in the country, the organizers decided to postpone until a "genuinely representative Congress" could be held.[78] The COI later learned that the groups declining to attend the Congress had done so because of a concern that the meeting was being "conducted under influence of the pro-Soviet and communistic elements." The postponement thus constituted a "diplomatic withdrawal."[79]

By the spring of 1942, the ASC's organizers, which included prominent labor leaders such as Leo Krzycki, vice president of the Amalgamated Clothing Workers, and Blair Gunther, a Republican judge who "energetically practiced ethnic and fraternal politics," had rescheduled their meeting for late April.[80] Cranston, true to his activist approach, saw an opportunity for the government to support a group that could unite thousands of diverse Slavs, representing millions in the general American population, behind the war effort. The sole point of the meeting, Cranston advised MacLeish, was support for the war effort; the group had agreed to "avoid completely the subject of future boundaries in Europe." Communists had joined the ASC, but Cranston insisted that they were not a dominant force and that many priests, representing a variety of Catholic groups, would also be in attendance. The leaders of the Congress "want us to help them put this over," and Cranston urged that they "take the thing in hand, land a really prominent government speaker for the meeting and make it a success." Support by the government "will vastly increase the will to produce and win among American Slavs and it will hearten the Slavs in Europe." MacLeish thought this important enough to send on to Berle, with the request that he persuade Welles to address the group either in person or by radio. Welles, however, declined.[81]

Poole was willing to try Cranston's approach and offered all possible assistance, but he also cautioned Cranston "that he must look out for the Communists, who are smart fellows and would naturally endeavor to obtain control of the meeting." He assured John C. Wiley that the "resolutions to be adopted have already been drafted with the informal assistance of the OFF and under the chairmanship of Mr. Krzycki of the Amalgamated Clothing Workers, who is well and personally known to us."[82] Berle, whom Hoover had told that Communists intended to dominate the proceedings, was more cautious and emphasized the importance of keeping the meeting focused on the United States and its war effort. Berle also asked Poole to look into alleged "plans for a continuing Slav organization" and to ascertain "who was backing such a plan."[83]

That left Cranston and the OFF as the ASC's major and most enthusiastic supporters. The radio bureau within the Foreign Language Division (FLD) mailed news releases to foreign-language radio stations asking that they promote the gathering, which was "of vital importance" since "over 50 percent of our war plant workers are of Slavic origin." The announcements called on Slavs, including the ethnic groups in Yugoslavia, to express their support for "a mighty crush-Hitler movement to help our country win the war."[84] Cranston requested permission from his superiors to travel to Detroit for the Congress, which the OFF supported "to the hilt," in order to "see that all goes well and also to meet the leaders of the various Slavic groups in America, who are considerably indebted to us at this moment."[85]

MacLeish also suggested that President Roosevelt send a message of greeting and support to the ASC, again citing "the tremendous proportion of the workers in war industry" who were Slavs. The Slavic community had been split politically, and the OFF had hopes that the meeting would succeed in healing those divisions. MacLeish provided an appropriate text for the president's use, but the White House passed the package on to the State Department, where it eventually fell to the Division of Foreign Activity Correlation. Harold B. Hoskins, echoing Hoover, advised Berle that there was "a communist tinge to this Congress," and that it would divide, not unite, the Slavic community. He recommended that the president send no greeting and that Berle supply the scheduled administration representative, Federal Security Administrator Paul McNutt, who also chaired the War Manpower Commission, with points to emphasize in his speech. Berle, who was more flexible than Cranston gave him credit for, adopted a middle course, explaining to the White House that it was possible that Communist groups were in the ASC and that Communists may attempt to control the meeting—but he was not sure "that this is particularly important at this time." He advised that Roosevelt send a message emphasizing the "common struggle" of the United Nations, the contribution of Slavs to the war effort, and the American intent "to unify all racial groups in a common effort" for victory and freedom. It was Berle's version that went out over the president's signature.[86]

The American Slav Congress met in Detroit at the end of April, with approximately twenty-five hundred delegates, representing twenty-two organizations, in attendance.[87] The resolutions adopted included a message of greeting to President Roosevelt; a "manifesto" to all Slav Americans, proclaiming the ASC's loyalty to the United States, its devotion to unity, and the intent of all Slav Americans to "double and treble" their commitment to war production and to victory; and a report from the "Panel on Fifth Column Activities" calling on the Congress to combat "pro-fascist elements."[88]

After the meeting, Cranston assured Berle's committee "that the Slav Congress had not fallen into the hands of the Communists and that their discussions and resolutions confirmed this fact."[89] The FNB's report on the Slav Congress sustained Cranston's judgment, with a few caveats. The new committee sponsoring the event rested on "avowed non-Communist sentiments," but the Communist press had heavily publicized the meeting and the All-Slav Congress in Moscow had sent a message of greeting. The congress thus took on "the coloring of a pan-Slav movement directed from Moscow" and a number of Slavic organizations, particularly among the Poles, ultimately declined to attend. Yet the proceedings themselves "justified neither the worst fears of the Poles nor the most hopeful predictions of the democratic leadership which successfully controlled the meeting." Attendance had exceeded expectations, with estimates of Communist participation at less than ten percent of the total, and with "all important Slav organizations" represented. Blair Gunther, an American-Polish lawyer who served as chairman of the congress, and Leo Krzycki, the union leader who was elected president of the permanent American Slav Congress, kept the meeting focused on "the home front." The group elected a number of vice presidents representing each of the nationality groups, including Vincent Cainkar (Slovenes), Samuel Werlinich (Serbs), and John D. Butkovich (Croatians). The congress also created an executive committee to direct future activities, and three members of this group were "reported to be communists."[90]

The FNB also used the congress to highlight a general danger that existed within the Slavic communities. The "rank and file" of Slavs in the United States "do not follow any definite political ideology" and their loyalties to Europe were "cultural rather than political." The Church has lost its old position of leadership, "with the result that small groups of the more recent political refugees, harboring their own passionate resolves and seeking compensation for their loss of status and prestige in Europe, try to work through the leaderless Slavs and win them over to a 'cause.'" The Communists were "taking advantage of our present alliance with Soviet Russia" and using "propaganda and intrigue . . . to make inroads wherever they can," but FNB doubted they could gain "actual control of, and a large following among, the American Slavs." Slavs remained committed to the war effort and to their part in maintaining war production. Despite the "Old World squabbles which in some instances divided the delegates into rival banqueting parties," they all agreed at the ASC on the need to completely defeat the Axis powers. Because of the meeting, American Slavs enjoyed the recognition of highly placed U.S. government representatives and saw themselves as an integral part of American life.[91]

The FNB's optimistic but cautious appraisal validated the OFF's support for the All-Slav Congress and the importance of making ethnics feel included in the war effort. However, Cranston criticized the report for placing "a bit too much emphasis upon the negative victory achieved in Detroit." While it was true that "the Communists were kept well in hand," Nazis, not Communists, were the enemy, and the congress represented "a distinct victory over the Nazis." He quoted extensively from a *Christian Science Monitor* article on the ASC, which stressed "the unity of will" that had dominated the meeting. Many Slavs who stayed away because of their "strictly nationalistic" views or because of a fear of Communist influence "suffered by abstaining." To Cranston, "the fact that the resolutions were sound, American, and concerned solely with the job of winning the war should not be emphasized as a defeat of the Communists, who wanted violent resolutions on certain subjects," but should be understood as expressing the will of the majority of those present.[92]

Despite Berle's dislike of race movements, his actions toward the ASC showed that the Slavs' importance to the war effort gained them a measure of official support. This support continued when the ASC proclaimed June 21 as National Slav Sunday "to bring home to each Slav community the program of the Congress." Most of the celebrations occurred in cities where war industries were centered, and mayors in each city issued proclamations recognizing the day. Interior Secretary Harold Ickes addressed the meeting in Pittsburgh; Eleanor Roosevelt sent greetings to the one in New York. The rallies in turn sent messages of support to the president for his war policies and raised money for war relief. Although some Slavic groups still viewed the ASC as Communist directed or inspired, the FNB, continuing to see both advantages and dangers, concluded that the ASC had "worked to unify" Americans of Slavic descent behind the war effort and had done so "by appealing to their patriotism as Americans." The result might have been a "better understanding between the Slav groups in America . . . and eventual assimilation of the American Slavs." The congress had, as promised, minimized disputes over "post-war territorial settlements" and acted "as a cordon thrown around about 15,000,000 Americans who otherwise might be open to Axis-inspired defeatism as well as unopposed Communist infiltration." However, since the congress organized Slavs to support the war program, it also implied that a lack of loyalty existed in the Slav community, and many Americans of Slavic descent believed this emphasized "racial differences at a moment when American national unity is most essential." Another danger existed as well: while the present leadership had staved off Communist influences, "in the end the Congress might well serve the interests of the pro-Communist rather than of the pro-democratic elements in the United States."[93]

* * *

In contrast to the different approaches taken toward the ASC, the visit of King Peter to the United States in June 1942 occasioned a high level of cooperation between the agencies engaged in foreign nationalities issues. Despite its concern about Yugoslav-American factionalism, the U.S. government maintained cordial relations with Yugoslav representatives in America and had relatively little direct involvement in the war in Yugoslavia. It fell to the British, who hosted the government in exile but who were constantly at odds with the Pan-Slavs who surrounded the king, to play a greater role in Yugoslav military affairs. The royal government, as a way out of its dependence on the British, hoped to obtain direct American assistance for the Chetniks, and with that in mind suggested that the king visit the United States.[94] The presence of Peter seemed certain to increase ethnic tension, but Fotić, beginning in the summer of 1941, repeatedly spoke to American officials of the king's wish to come to America.[95] Roosevelt, who had extended an invitation in the past, demurred, telling Welles he believed "it is a mistake for the young king to come here this summer. He would be a target for the Croats and would be hard to guard. How can you get that thought across?"[96] The president prevailed temporarily, but continued requests by the YGIE made further postponements impossible, and Welles informed Fotić in April 1942 that Roosevelt "would be very glad" to receive the king in June.[97]

Before the king's arrival, Oscar Brown of the FNB conferred with British diplomats Sir Ronald Campbell and Donald Hall, who were sympathetic toward the young king but found him "stubborn." Hall was obviously upset about the visit and complained that the governments-in-exile in London, especially Yugoslavia, "were engaged in frequent disputes with the British Government and were inclined to take their complaints to Washington." The British were "none too pleased about these routine voyages 'to papa'" and hoped that Churchill's trip to Washington, occurring at the same time as King Peter's, would "crowd the King's visit out of the newspapers."[98]

The potential for the kind of disturbance Roosevelt feared quickly surfaced, but it was the Serbs who were the provocateurs. Every year on June 28, the Serbs observed a national holiday commemorating their fourteenth-century defeat at the Battle of Kosovo and honoring the memory of those Serbs who had "fought for liberty and independence." In the United States, Serb-Americans, combining the old and the new, traditionally held this Vidovdan celebration on the Fourth of July. The Serbian National Defense Council moved the celebration back to the traditional June date, supposedly to correspond to the SNDC annual meeting being held in Chicago. The event, dubbed an "All-Serb Congress" was to be held near Libertyville, Illinois, at St. Sava Monastery, which was the seat of the Serbian Orthodox Church.[99]

This change, which accommodated the king's scheduled visit to the United States and was no doubt designed to insure his appearance, produced a flurry of activity within the U.S. government. Cannon met with Fotić to question the necessity of a visit by the king to the monastery, only to have Fotić assure him the visit would be informal and "no one would know about it." The fact of the congress meeting seemed to put the lie to that, and Cannon saw this as "another proof that the King's visit is part of the Serb campaign, and will be a further provocation to the Croatians." As he told Hoskins and Berle, "I am not liking that at all!"[100]

Cannon also received information from Cranston about "a new and disturbing development" in the Serbian-Croatian conflict: the SNDC had invited the attorney general to attend the Libertyville meeting and had asked the president to declare the day "an official holiday" in honor of Serbia. Cranston, after briefing the attorney general's office, had been assured that Biddle would decline the invitation. He asked Cannon to apprise the White House that to proclaim this holiday would please the Serbs but "infuriate" the Croatians. Cannon did so, agreeing that the congress "would be a direct provocation on the part of the Greater Serbia faction to those elements representing the real Yugoslav idea."[101] Roosevelt declined to designate the day as "Chetnik Day in America" on the grounds that all of the allies were already commemorated on June 14, which had been designated United Nations Flag Day.[102] The FNB planned to send an observer to the meeting, "because it seems very important to have a first-hand impression." Poole was certain the information gleaned would be valuable for all of the agencies involved.[103]

Poole also took note of a "new editorial direction" in *Amerikanski Srbobran*, which featured an end to attacks on Yugoslavia but a continued promotion of the "idea of Serbian dominance." The paper claimed that all Serbs, regardless of residence, should be "united in a single territorial unit," which Poole took to indicate "a move to remove the greater part of Croatia from the future Yugoslavia." The paper also featured the Serbian flag rather than the Yugoslav flag, and a banner on the front page read "All Serbian Lands Under a Serbian Banner."[104] More splits and provocations followed. After another group of Yugoslavs announced plans to celebrate an alternative Vidovdan in Detroit in early July, *Amerikanski Srbobran* charged that the meeting had been called by "a group of intriguers and renegades" who "were only yesterday enemies of democracy." This "destructive element . . . crammed into one basket, university professors, disillusioned clerics, unsuccessful businessmen, corrupted workers and every kind of 'specialist' without permanent occupation." Only "ignorant Serbs" who believed that they were "Yugoslavs" or "Internationalists" and thus enemies of "Serbianism" would go to Detroit. The Serbs in Libertyville loved both America and Serbia and were loyal to their Orthodox faith, while those in Detroit were led by the Communists "who gather around the '*Slobodna Reč.*'" The choice of which meeting to attend should be clear to all "honest Serb men and women."[105]

This sniping prompted Berle to meet with Fotić to complain that his government was "a little disturbed by the recrudescence of the Great Serbian Movement in the United States." Most Yugoslavs in America were Croats, and "any controversy between Serbs and Croats in the United States could only lead to sterile disputes here." The United States did not wish "to take sides in the controversy itself, since that was of interest only to Yugoslavia but . . . did not feel that the controversy ought to be permitted to divide groups of people" in this country. Fotić assured Berle he had already taken effective steps to reduce tensions, but he immediately belied that and played into Berle's concerns about the ASC when he argued that the real intention of the SNDC propaganda was "to establish its position as against the Serbian Communists." This put them in opposition to the Pan-Slav Congress, which "was really dominated by the Communists, through its Executive Secretary, who was an agent of the Third International, and nothing else." The Serbs stressed their ties with the State Department. Fotic said, in order "to make headway against the Communists, who were trying to convey the impression that the United States specifically sanctioned the Communist movement."[106]

A few days before King Peter's arrival, Poole attended a meeting in Cranston's office with Cranston, Donald R. Perry of the INS, Adamic, Stoyan Pribichevich of *Fortune Magazine,* and Nicholas Mirkovich of the Yugoslav Office of Reconstruction in New York to talk about a strategy for addressing the "agitation now in progress between the Serbs and Croats in the United States." Pribichevich, a member of a prominent Serb family who had been forced to leave Yugoslavia in the 1930s because of his opposition to King Alexander, had recently returned from London where he had gathered material for an article on the YGIE. He told the group that British authorities were concerned about "the weakness of the Yugoslav Government in the face of the Serb-Croat agitation," but Pribichevich's attempts to convey this to his Serb friends in the Yugoslav government had failed. He attributed this to the prime minister, Slobodan Jovanović, "who is an historian by profession and will never take sides;" to the "machinations of Fotich;" and to the army officers advising the "young King." Fotić had convinced the YGIE that the Americans and the British planned to create "a Catholic federation in Central Europe or the Danube Valley" and that the "Serbs had better grab all they could get, including as much as possible of Croatia." The Nazi propaganda concerning Croatian atrocities that was finding its way into *Amerikanski Srbobran* was being brought out of Yugoslavia by military men who claimed to be Chetniks but who were actually connected to the Nedić regime. Pribichevich promised Poole he would furnish this information to him.[107]

In this written account, which the FNB issued as a report, Pribichevich cited the YGIE in London as the "storm center of the anti-Yugoslav and Greater Serbia movement in the United States." Both Jovan Dučić and Bishop Dionisije were on the payroll of the YGIE, and the "separatist political line of propaganda" in *Amerikanski Srbobran* was "directed from London" and in the United States by Fotić. Atrocity stories, either invented or exaggerated by the Nazis, made their way to the pages of *Amerikanski Srbobran* because "pictures of massacred people are photographed by the Germans, who take great pains to see to it that Serbians who leave the country take them with them." Since London was the source of this, he did not believe that action against *Amerikanski Srbobran* or Fotić alone would be effective and suggested that Biddle speak to Jovanović and the entire Yugoslav cabinet because "a complete cure can be effected only in London." A small group was open to drafting a new Yugoslav national policy, but Jovanović, who was Pribichevich's former professor and one of the foremost scholars on the Balkans, was too old and inexperienced to stand against the "Serbian extremists" and was "terrorized by them." Pribichevich asserted that the "bureaucratic apparatus in exile . . . is nearly one hundred percent the remnant of the former pro-Axis Serbian apparatus." They needed a legitimate explanation for their prewar Axis sympathies and for their country's quick collapse in 1941, and so "the blame is now put on the Croats who, it is alleged, betrayed the Serbs." The eighteen-year-old king was "very immature mentally," and his mother, whose husband had been assassinated, "constantly has before her eyes the fate of her husband and fears that a similar fate might befall her son." Peter was fascinated by America but Pribichevich feared his visit "would create a great deal of harm unless it is handled very carefully." He warned that extremists like Fotić would use the event and the king's reception by important American officials to solidify their positions.[108]

King Peter, for whom Roosevelt's invitation was welcome news, since the king had been asking to "make the trip for some time," arrived in the United States with his entourage on June 21. Roosevelt held a dinner in his honor and he remained overnight at the White House. Winston Churchill was visiting the president as well, and he, Roosevelt, Yugoslav Foreign Minister Momčilo Ninčić, and King Peter discussed the situation in Yugoslavia at length. In his memoirs, the king claimed that Roosevelt expressed his support for the Chetniks, and though his resources were limited, he "promised to do all possible to send long-range bombers to drop food and supplies" over Yugoslavia.[109] Berle, who had feared the king's visit might "be taken for a signal for eruption by the Pan Serbs," was not impressed. He found Peter to be a "nice boy who would like to be out playing somewhere, and is completely in the hands of Nincic and a group of Serbian officers. He is entirely sincere. We can expect nothing better of a boy of eighteen."[110]

The king's account of his trip made only subtle mention of the tensions in the Yugoslav-American community. In discussing John Butkovich's remarks in support of Yugoslav unity and the Chetniks, made at the Information Center reception held for the king, Peter recorded that "a few weeks later, alas, the same Butkovich . . . attacked me for my continued support of Mihailović."[111] Yet the king himself did not remain above the fray. Before leaving Washington for his tour of the country, Peter delivered a national radio address during which he "first publicly proclaimed that the rank of full general would be conferred upon Major General Mihailovich on the following Sunday, the national holiday of Yugoslavia."[112] In Detroit, he met with Yugoslav-American workers at the Ford Motor Company's Willow Run plant and made another radio presentation, which was beamed back to Yugoslavia via shortwave.[113] Officials from the War Production Board (WPB) had prepared the script of the king's speech and made sure that the workers who appeared with him represented all of divided Yugoslavia. The FNB's Oscar Brown, who had assisted the WPB with the speech, found the Yugoslav diplomats at the legation willing "to eliminate all semblance of disunity from the King's public utterances." During the broadcast, for example, the king had announced the promotion of Mihailović, "my dearest friend and sterling solider," but he also had spoken repeatedly of "the Serbs, Croats and Slovenes" of Yugoslavia and the fight they waged against the Axis. Brown found the king "a pleasant and intelligent young man" and Ninčić something of a non-entity, "an old school diplomat well-versed in the intricacies of Geneva but somewhat lost in the directness and tempo of Washington." He believed Fotić to be "the most influential person and the 'power behind the throne,' at least during the Washington visit."[114]

Events seemed to confirm this assessment. The members of the Yugoslav Ministerial Mission in New York, who had opposed "Mr. Fotich's 'private diplomacy'" did not attend the king on his tour of the country. The legation in Washington later claimed that an "error" had occurred in issuing the proper instructions. Fotić hosted a reception for King Peter, during which representatives of the Serb National Federation presented him with a bound copy of all of the back issues of *Amerikanski Srbobran*. Dučić and Bishop Dionisije attended this event, but no representative of any American Croat or Slovene organization was present. The Yugoslav Ministerial Mission later charged that Fotić again "found it expedient to misinform" the other ethnic groups about the date of the reception. Members of American-Croat organizations subsequently sent a message to the king, saying essentially that they would meet him "anywhere but in the presence of Minister Fotich," and Boyd-Boich, Butkovich, and several communist leaders, such as Mirko Markovich, the editor of *Slobodna Reč*, attended a reception for the king at the Yugoslav Information Center in New York.[115]

This gathering had long-term consequences. During the reception, in addition to the comments made by Butkovich that the king later found duplicitous, Croatian-Americans discussed the need for a new organization that would unite all Yugoslavs in opposition to the SNF and their divisive tactics. Cranston soon endorsed the move, which put him in greater conflict with Berle and other officials who sought to discourage any additional fragmentation in the Yugoslav-American community. By September, the FNB reported that a Croatian-American Congress Committee, chaired by Butkovich, had held a meeting attended by Šubašić and "dominated by a group closely identified with the Communist movement in Yugoslav-American circles" and had decided to proceed with plans to form a permanent organization. Opposition to the decision had come from Boyd-Boich and another officer of Butkovich's Croatian Fraternal Union, who believed that Šubašić and members of the YGIE were too involved in the affairs of Yugoslav-Americans.[116]

Amerikanski Srbobran made no mention of the disunity among Yugoslavs during the initial days of King Peter's visit but launched a "particularly vicious attack" on Šubašić after the New York reception for the king. The FNB viewed this as an attempt "to impair what was evidently a friendly relationship between the King, Kosanovic, Subasic, and Snoj." Foreign Minister Ninčić told a journalist in the United States—the correspondent, Andre Visson, who was friends with Fotić—that the Yugoslav ministers in New York were conspiring to have Fotić removed, and if that occurred, he, Ninčić, would resign.[117] He confided that the YGIE had put Croats into influential positions only to "satisfy our British friends, whose help we now need" and thought it something of a joke that the addresses delivered by the king in Washington and New York, which the Croats in America "liked very much" and whose sentiments they wished Fotić would adopt, "[were] written by Fotich."[118]

Ethnic issues surfaced again at the end of the king's stay. Upon his return to Washington to take his leave of President Roosevelt, Peter presented a document detailing atrocities committed against the Serbs by the Axis and the Ustasha. When Roosevelt remarked that Croats complained about the American media's emphasizing only the resistance of the Chetniks, Fotić reminded the president that the puppet state of Croatia was at war with the United States. Roosevelt replied that he had instructed the OWI to refer to "guerilla activities in Yugoslavia as 'Yugoslav'—a label which would cover all those who were resisting."[119] Yet the joint statement ending the visit referred only to "General Mihailović and his daring men" by name.[120]

The agencies concerned with foreign nationalities continued to follow a common course throughout the king's visit. As most officials had predicted, the SNDC dominated the Vidovdan ceremony held at St. Sava Monastery, with speeches by Louis Christopher, Michael Dučić, and the bishop all conveying Greater Serbia sentiments.[121] To Cranston, the SNF was "definitely following a Fascist pattern" and the meeting "closely resembled the early gatherings of the Brown shirts."[122] The Foreign Language Division followed a "hands-off" policy to demonstrate "that the Government does not approve of the Libertyville meeting" but did completely support the 4th of July Vidovdan meeting in Detroit, which was attended by all three of the major ethnic groups, as well as Poles and Czechs.[123] Featured speakers at that meeting, all of whom pursued the theme of unity, included the three Yugoslav Ministers from the Information Center in New York, Boyd-Boich of the CFU, Krzycki of the ASC, Cranston, and a variety of communist and non-Communist editors, labor leaders, and clergy.[124] Both Biddle and Berle sent messages, with Biddle stating that those gathered could best serve the war effort "by abandoning any conflict which threatens to engulf your ranks—by barring any elements which seek to divide your ranks." Berle echoed this same theme, but also followed the State Department's position by heralding "the courageous example which General Mihailovitch and his heroic men are displaying in Yugoslavia today" and urging the "need for complete abandonment of any conflicts of a petty nature."[125] Yet, as the FNB concluded, it could not be said "that the King's visit has helped to unite the dissident Yugoslav groups in the United States."[126]

The general public's view of the king's visit was probably more positive, since Yugoslavia's status as one of the few occupied areas with an active resistance earned it continuing and favorable press attention. As Fotić later wrote in his memoirs, in reference to the publicity surrounding Mihailović during the early years of the war: "In the gloomy days which followed the Blitzkrieg against France and England, Pearl Harbor, the lightening Japanese attack in Indonesia, and the swift advance of Nazi armies in Russia, the news that a small people had had the courage to start an armed resistance to the totally superior German Wermacht brought great moral encouragement. It inspired other conquered nations to resist the Nazis, and it was also evidence that the Nazi conquest of Europe was not final."[127]

A *New York Times* article that appeared before the king's visit in June typified this sentiment. Carrying the headline "Yugoslavs Claim 1,500 Axis Troops," the story called Mihailović's Chetniks "the leading force in the revolt in occupied Europe." Quoting information supplied by the government in London, the paper reported the capture of fifteen hundred enemy soldiers, despite "heavy casualties" suffered by "the patriots" in their battles with Italian, Bulgarian, and "traitor" Croat forces.[128] The same paper revealed that the YGIE would soon announce the young king's engagement to Princess Alexandra of Greece. The two had met at Cambridge, where Peter was an undergraduate and Alexandra a Red Cross nurse. The *Times* speculated that the marriage "would be welcomed" by both governments and "by their peoples whose relations have always been friendly and who have suffered at the hands of the Axis."[129]

However, as the British had hoped, King Peter's visit, along with the presence in Washington of a host of other foreign leaders, was, in the words of *Newsweek,* "overshadowed by that of the British Prime Minister" who had come to consult with FDR on crucial war and postwar issues. The various dignitaries, including royals from Greece, the Netherlands, and Norway, as well as political leaders from China, were "drawn to Washington by the same magnet, the Anglo-American negotiations." King Peter planned to "seek Lend-Lease aid for the guerrilla fighters" in Yugoslavia, while Queen Wilhelmina planned a formal visit to the White House "to outline Dutch needs."[130]

What little coverage focused on King Peter was sympathetic and light-hearted, emphasizing the king's youth and affability. The *New York Times* featured pictures of a smiling young man, laughing with the president and throwing out a baseball at a major league game. An account of the king's trip to Detroit centered on his test drive of an army jeep "at high speed over the rugged terrain of a factory proving ground," accompanied by a photograph of an exuberant Peter behind the wheel and an anxious looking Edsel Ford in the passenger seat.[131] In an editorial, the *New York Times* detailed the tragic history of the king and declared that his "youth, his misfortunes, and those of his people make his coming welcome."[132] *Newsweek's* final story reported that the young king "really won the heart of Washington on his visit last week"—in contrast to the "cold and standoffish" king of Greece.

Peter's "shy and democratic manner" made him "more popular on Capital Hill than anyone else in the recent procession of foreign notables."[133]

Public and government outlets kept the story of Yugoslavia's resistance alive long after the king's departure, and did so in ways that usually suited the aims of the YGIE. The OWI, in a pamphlet entitled *The Unconquered People* published in late summer 1942, celebrated the resistance being mounted all over Europe to the Nazi occupation, and those who made their stories known to the outside world. The latter included not only people who had themselves escaped from Europe, but the "agents of the governments-in-exile" who obtained news from Europe "which they release to an anxiously waiting world." One such story involved the "brave Yugoslavs" who were "in open armed revolt against Hitler." The only leader named was Mihailović, "a fiery Serb" whose Chetnik guerrillas, representing all of the country's ethnic groups, conducted sabotage against the enemy and controlled "three-fourths of old Serbia and parts of Herzegovina, Bosnia, and Montenegro." The Germans had at first disparaged these fighters as "communists and criminals," but now "Axis troops are unsafe outside their barracks."[134]

Radio did its part as well. CBS aired a series called "The Twenty-Second Letter," which was dedicated to "those anonymous underground workers in every part of occupied Europe, who continue to fight against the invader." A program in mid-August featured Yugoslavia and quoted the Serbian church's account of Nazi atrocities as well as a German correspondent's report that the "entire country was infested with Chetniks and armed peasants." To a soundtrack of "the Song of the Chetniks" and repeated Chetnik battle cries, the narrator and actors spoke of the "plain everyday folks" who had become "the most expert bomb throwers in all of Europe." The script followed a young engaged couple, Ferenc and Ilya, who killed several German soldiers terrorizing the people in their town and who then fled to "join the Chetniks." Although most of their actions took the form of sabotage, "two-thirds of Yugoslavia [has] been recaptured by these mountain troops" representing a people who "will not accept defeat."[135]

*   *   *

Divisions within the Yugoslav-American community surfaced before the United States entered World War II; American belligerency caused those divisions to become a focus for the agencies involved in foreign nationalities issues. However, the problems the Yugoslavs posed were not only internal. Yugoslavia, though occupied and partitioned, was a member of the United Nations; its resistance against the Axis gained it early and consistent media and public attention. The YGIE, unhappy with their British hosts, tried to curry the favor of the United States, but Roosevelt was prepared to play only a superficial role in an area of more interest to his British and Soviet allies. The agencies working with foreign nationalities did not have the luxury of that detachment; each of the Yugoslav-American factions had ready access to one or more of the officials working at the State Department, the OFF, and the FNB. American officials could not decide, collectively, whether those contacts were an asset or a nuisance and whether the political activity of ethnics represented a danger to American interests. The OFF favored support for an inclusive Slavic group, such as the ASC, as a way to reduce ethnic tension, but the State Department was particularly wary of ethnics with left wing attachments. Although all of the officials involved in foreign nationalities issues worked together to limit the harmful effects of King Peter's visit, that did not erase their fundamental differences in approach and philosophy.

3

A Question of Public Order

Official concern about Communist influence within the Yugoslav-American community became more acute in the summer and fall of 1942 as the Communist press attacked Draža Mihailović for collaboration, and the ethnics' quarrel moved into the public spotlight. The effects of the divisions within Yugoslavia on the Grand Alliance and on the shape of the postwar world began to preoccupy the State Department and the Foreign Nationalities Branch (FNB), while the foreign policy questions involved limited everyone's options. The Coordinator of Information (COI) and the Office of Facts and Figures (OFF) were renamed and reorganized, but the members of Adolf Berle's committee continued to quarrel over strategy. The "good fight" between bureaucrats that DeWitt Clinton Poole had wished for finally occurred, but it pitted the Office of War Information (OWI) against the State Department. By the spring of 1943, the State Department and its strategy of control had gained ground, but how effective that would be in dealing with the apparently unbridgeable conflict between Croats and Serbs remained to be seen.

* * *

King Peter's visit to the United States took place against a backdrop of change for many of the agencies involved in foreign nationalities issues. Over the spring and summer of 1942, the COI became the Office of Strategic Services, under the administration of the Joint Chiefs of Staff. The reorganization made the fate of the FNB again an object of contention, with officials in the State Department, anxious to protect their power, questioning the reason for the branch's existence. As Berle told Cordell Hull after attending a Joint Intelligence Committee meeting where the fate of the FNB had been discussed, a "question came about this strange unit Colonel William J. Donovan organized to follow foreign nationality groups in the United States, nominally to 'assist the State Department.'" The "present recommendation that it shall stay with the espionage work of course violates the President's order that this group shall not do espionage in the United States." The State Department "had an interest in this unit by its creation" but Berle was not sure whether it "belonged to [the State Department] or to Military Intelligence."[1]

COI officials expected the FNB to remain within its parent organization, but the Joint Chiefs, apparently as unsure as Berle, proved reluctant to have the branch under their jurisdiction. To make their case to the military and establish their incompatibility with the State Department, John C. Wiley and DeWitt Clinton Poole detailed the work of the FNB and its connection to the subversive and psychological operations the Office of Strategic Services (OSS) would perform. Their field division, they explained, gathered information from foreign nationalities sources; the chancery division compiled reports and memoranda from that information; and a corps of volunteer readers, located in various universities and ethnic communities, scanned the foreign language press and were "indispensable to the best use of our resources in the prosecution of the war and the consolidation of victory." The individuals with whom the FNB maintained contact with regard to foreign political studies and investigations were the same people who were most likely to assist in intelligence operations. The FNB, then, in addition to its regular responsibilities, would be a "helpful auxiliary" to "strategic operations, and has already made considerable contributions in the field of intelligence and counter-espionage."[2]

As an illustration of the latter, Poole and Wiley detailed the success the FNB had enjoyed in "cultivating an important refugee Czechoslovak official" in order to learn the provisions of a secret treaty signed by the Czech government and the Soviet Union. That sort of work could not be done with "propriety" by the Department of State. By contrast, the FNB, "exercising no statutory authority, free from tradition or recognized position, was able to extend its contacts unobtrusively and develop relationships of an informal and . . . highly useful sort."[3]

Donovan went even further to convince the Joint Chiefs of Staff of the branch's military and overseas dimension, listing the "gathering of information of conditions, enemy dispositions and enemy policy in enemy occupied countries" as the FNB's first task. Donovan also highlighted Wiley's experience in psychological warfare and the role the branch could play "as an adjunct to the direct military effort, more particularly in connection with— Psychological Warfare, Intelligence, Special Operations."[4] In December 1942, the Joint Chiefs finally agreed to accept the FNB, but its "Golden Directive" narrowed the branch's role by specifying that the duties assigned to the OSS included "contact with foreign nationality groups in the United States to aid in the collection of essential information for the execution of psychological warfare operations in consultation with the State Department."[5]

This clarification of FNB's function, which reflected Poole's approach more than it did Wiley's, led to a change in the branch's leadership. Since its inception, Wiley had served as the FNB's supervisor, while Poole, with the title of director, acted as second in command. However, Wiley had a "temperamental fondness" for covert rather than open information gathering and the Foreign Nationalities and Secret Intelligence branches of OSS clashed repeatedly. The FNB complained that Secret Intelligence approached and upset its own carefully cultivated contacts, while Secret Intelligence bemoaned the FNB's use of undercover methods to gather information. Donovan, concerned about the effects of these quarrels, warned Wiley in September 1942 to cease his undercover activities, only to have Wiley quibble about the distinction between overt and covert methods. In truth, Donovan's views often mirrored Wiley's. Donovan had endorsed the idea of using ethnic workers in defense facilities as informants, despite the objections of the FBI, while Wiley had considered using African students studying in the United States as spies both at home and within the African-American community.[6] Nonetheless, Donovan, no longer a free agent, ruled in late October 1942 that the FNB should refrain from secret intelligence activities because the other branches of the organization had to yield to the Secret Intelligence and Special Operations functions, which were primary to the OSS. That in turn led to Wiley's departure in late 1942 and Poole's elevation to command of the FNB early in 1943.[7]

The OFF also evolved into another, supposedly more potent, entity. Since its inception, the OFF, to Archibald MacLeish's distress, had proved to be little more than a clearinghouse for other government agencies, a place where a news reporter could find out "anything you wanted to know about the government . . . a feed trough where you'd get prepared information."[8] MacLeish had no real power and very little funding, because, as he soon discovered, the president had little interest in the OFF or its work, other than to make sure it did not become another Committee on Public Information. The breezy assurance that President Roosevelt had given MacLeish at the time of his appointment— that he could run both the Library of Congress and the OFF because the latter "isn't going to amount to anything"—proved all too true.[9]

After the United States entered the war, MacLeish and others who had supported the OFF's creation urged the president to establish "a powerful and effective information service."[10] MacLeish submitted a reorganization plan for the new agency in February 1942 and suggested a name change to the Office of War Information, to conform to the interdepartmental advisory group already in existence, but he vacillated over whether to remain as director of this new organization or to step down. Eventually, concerned about the apparently retaliatory budget cuts inflicted on him at the Library of Congress by Republican congressmen who considered the OFF to be too pro-Roosevelt, MacLeish accepted Elmer Davis, a well known CBS radio commentator, as the best choice to head the new agency.[11] When Roosevelt established the Office of War Information (OWI) in June 1942 with Davis as its director, his executive order conferred more explicit powers on the agency, its director, and the renamed Committee on War Information Policy to "formulate basic policies and plans on war information" and to carry them out through the use of media and other facilities.[12] Although the agency was frequently reorganized during its brief life, the OWI's basic structure consisted of a domestic and an overseas branch and a variety of bureaus concerned with publications, radio programming, motion picture production, news, and intelligence. Many of the OFF personnel remained, at least initially. R. Keith Kane retained his post as head of the Bureau of Intelligence, and Alan Cranston continued to head the Foreign Language Division (FLD), now housed within the Special Operations Bureau.[13]

As OWI's director, Elmer Davis tried to balance the need for legitimate censorship with the resolve he shared with MacLeish "to tell nothing but the truth." Davis, a renowned journalist and former Rhodes scholar, had worked for years as a reporter for the *New York Times* and as a freelance writer before becoming a commentator for CBS. He had been slower than MacLeish to support American entry into the war because of his concern that America should protect its own interests and its domestic system. But like MacLeish and other liberals, Davis believed this war to be "the war of the people." The enemy, Davis said, used "news as a weapon, sought to divide America and destroy the unity necessary for victory." He saw his task as one of "psychological or political warfare," with his agency acting as an "auxiliary" to the armed forces.[14]

A short time after his appointment, Davis received a letter of condolence and advice from George Creel, who had run the Committee on Public Information (CPI) during World War I and whose example President Roosevelt was loath to follow. Creel warned Davis that it would be difficult to "make over an existing organization that has been running wild," particularly under a president "who does not like to see anyone get the blue slip." He also cautioned Davis, a genial man who had a "tendency to make the best of things," that when matters went awry, "nothing is more fatal than an amiable effort to make the best of them." Davis's handwritten notation on the letter reads: "He was about right on all points."[15]

Most of the material distributed by OWI to the general public stressed the need for unity and presented often-stereotypical ethnic images. OWI's *American Handbook*, after reviewing immigration patterns, stated that the "diverse origins of the American people have not prevented the development of an American character; of a certain homogeneity of traits." The "American people are not mixed but blended," and their nation was one of "unified traditions and a unified people."[16] One of the segments of the "Uncle Sam Speaks" series, called "Lady of the Harbor," featured a talking Statue of Liberty reassuring two frightened children recently arrived on Ellis Island. In discussing the contributions that immigrants had made to America, Lady Liberty referred to the smiling "Irish cop;" the "gleaming muscles of the Negro;" and the "quick grace" of the Frenchman.[17]

The reorganization of the OFF did not change Cranston's approach to foreign nationalities issues. He continued to be aggressive, supporting organizations such as the American Slav Congress (ASC) and exhorting foreign-language editors to police themselves. The foreign-language press remained crucial to the war effort; of the thirty-five million people in the foreign nationalities category, ten million had English as their native language but twenty-five million did not.[18] As Cranston told the New England Foreign Language Newspapers Association in May 1942, because of the substantial influence they had on the minds of the foreign-language population of America, they had the responsibility to explain the war to their readers, "to eliminate their doubts, . . . to win their full cooperation in the war," and to help "lay the foundation for a peace of justice and freedom for all." Some Americans, he said, "fear the foreign language press. They fear that it is a dividing force . . . that it keeps alive the hatreds of Europe and that it is now a source and a medium of enemy propaganda in this country." While only a handful of the foreign language press fell into this category, those few "doing the enemy's work" determined the reputation and effectiveness of the whole. If the press itself purged such elements, their editors could demonstrate that the foreign-language press was capable of making a "great and telling contribution to America and to victory."[19]

Cranston's internal reports conveyed the same resolve. In a profile of his division composed for its new home agency, Cranston described the task of the FLD as one designed "to stimulate and direct" the contribution of the foreign born "to our national unity, our war economy, and our morale;" to "educate the foreign born as to the personal stake each has in the outcome of the war;" and to counteract Axis propaganda that attempted "to revive in this country the old and new hates of Europe." The FLD used newspapers, magazines, and radio stations to reach its target audience, distributed material in twenty-eight languages to the one thousand most important foreign-language papers, and worked with a variety of foreign-language organizations and "important personalities within all foreign language groups." Through "direct contact" with editors and publishers, the division had caused "several sharp changes in editorial policy" and was "on the verge of replacing Nazi and Fascist editors" in the largest chains of German and Italian papers "with experienced anti-Nazi and anti-Fascist editors." The FLD also had contacts with the two hundred stations that broadcast in foreign languages; its efforts resulted in "a marked increase in the volume of pro-democratic and pro-war material" being carried by those stations. Cranston praised the FLD for supporting the American Slav Congress, "a powerful force for American unity" that had "been put on the map with our backing." He also credited the agency for its cooperation "with a Serbian group in a meeting designed to bring American Serbians, Croatians and Slovenes together," a task necessitated by Serbian nationalists whose activities had worried the State Department.[20]

The last initiatives Cranston described ran contrary to Berle's approach to foreign nationalities policy, as their continuing squabble over the ASC demonstrated. The catalyst was a story in the bulletin issued by the Soviet embassy concerning the All-Slav Movement and their new publication "Slavs," which would feature a section on the Pan-Slavic Conference in the United States. Berle told Cranston, in a meeting arranged at Berle's request, that the Communist nature of the organization did not disturb him as much as "the fact that it was a foreign government undertaking to play with the movements of American race groups here—we had pretty steadily set our face against this." He also objected to the representation that the U.S. government wanted all Slavs to join the Pan-Slav Conference, since "this excited resentment in other Slav groups." Cranston countered that he did not think Communists controlled the American Slav Congress and that "we had played with it in the beginning and he thought we had better keep on"—only to have Berle insist, "We ought to be prepared to drop it at once if it [becomes] in fact part of a foreign inspired movement." When the committee, in a reference to discussions held by Yugoslav dissidents during King Peter's visit, turned to "the proposed organization of various groups of Yugoslavs—Serbs, Croats, Slovenes" that "Mr. Cranston was rather thinking of getting behind," Berle suggested that it would be better for the OWI to invite the leaders of existing organizations (e.g., fraternal organizations, etc.) to a meeting chaired by the Office of War Information. That would be a way to avoid jealousies and claims by any one group to "have the special favor of the United States Government." Cranston agreed, and Berle "gathered that from now on the policy will be to try to keep in contact with the heads of the existing organizations of Americans of European ancestry; and when there was a desire to hold meetings or encourage them to join in the war effort, the Office of War Information would directly undertake the responsibility."[21]

Yet it was clear that Berle intended that the State Department be the entity that decided what was desirable and what was not. When Harold B. Hoskins left the State Department to join the military, Berle suggested that the interdepartmental committee, which to him had served as an important forum "for frank and informal discussion of questions of common interest," continue to meet in light of the mounting problems with regard to foreign nationalities groups and their connection to foreign policy issues. His description to MacLeish of the kind of information the State Department needed to derive from the committee indicated the control he intended to exercise. His list included: the support given by government agencies to the activities of foreign language groups, particularly if those activities "are related to political movements abroad" and the attitudes expressed toward the foreign-language press by those same agencies; "any support or encouragement" government agencies would give to "meetings or conventions" of foreign-born citizen groups; and "problems arising out of racial agitations which have a definite bearing on political controversies in other countries."[22] Cranston later joked that the main purpose of the Interdepartmental Committee was to provide a job for Berle, "the most intelligent jack-ass in Washington."[23]

As Berle and Cranston continued to fence, the FNB also worried about Communist influence in the ASC, with Poole reporting to Berle and Donovan that "the Communist elements . . . are a constant source of concern."[24] To minimize the danger, the FNB kept in touch with Leo Krzycki, who assured the agency that Communists were being removed from the ASC and that he was confident the "sore spots" had been eliminated.[25] Inconsistencies in policy, though, surfaced here as well. Late in July 1942, the FNB's cultivation of Krzycki suffered a setback when Berle, using his department's authority, denied Krzycki permission to attend the First Slav Congress meeting in Argentina, at which he was to be the keynote speaker. Berle insisted that the Slav Congress was dominated by Communists and no prominent American should attend. The FNB field agent closest to the organization, Richard Rohman, protested to Wiley that this decision "plays right into the hands of the Communists" who will capture the Congress "by default." That same objection had been raised concerning the ASC meetings in the United States, and had that view prevailed, millions of American Slavs would have, according to Rohman, "been left to the mercies of either Axis or Communist agents." Fortunately, that view had not influenced policy, and as a result, Communists had remained "a small minority and their minority is growing even smaller as more and more democratic elements are joining the [ASC] every day." To Rohman, the United States had only two choices: lose foreign-nationality groups to the Communists because "they are the only ones to offer them leadership," or "encourage democratic elements to work among these nationalities and win them for the democratic way of life." He urged Wiley to have the State Department reverse its decision.[26]

Berle stood firm. When Cranston continued to promote the ASC and "a meeting of Americans of Yugoslav descent, which will present a united front of Serbs, Croats and Slovenes,"[27] Berle complained to Davis regarding "the policy of encouraging hyphenated American groups." The State Department opposed such attempts "to unmelt the melting pot" and was especially concerned about organizations that "reflect the propaganda and organization machinery of certain overseas governments."[28] At a subsequent committee meeting, Berle made it clear that he wanted a coordinated policy with regard to foreign nationality problems, and he used the Pan-Slav movement as an example of how "all agencies are not moving in the same direction."[29]

He also wrote again to Davis, using FBI reports as evidence, to prove that the pan-Slav movement was "not a spontaneous movement in and for the United States" but one that had been "simultaneously organized and executed" in a number of countries; Berle emphasized that it would "be merely naive to assume that this was accidental only." More important, groups such as the ASC tended "to build up a separatist race bloc in the United States," which Berle saw as "directly contrary to the historical policy of the United States." He said, "We have tolerated separatist race groups and hoped they would disappear. Never in history has the United States government assisted in organizing such groups." Far from acting as a soothing force in the Slav community, the ASC, Berle contended, made the problem worse and divided groups "even within themselves, setting one against the other." The movement claimed to operate under the aegis of the OWI, but the Soviet government, Berle pointed out, took "a far greater interest in this group than is normally consistent with usual international relations." Even if the "Communist movement" were not so bent on control, Berle wrote, he would oppose such "a transmission belt for foreign influence" and "object to an attempt to Balkanize the United States by creating and setting up political blocs based on race affiliation."[30]

Davis, far from agreeing with Berle, had Cranston draft a response attacking the credibility of Berle's informants and the secretary's own biases. Berle's analysis had described men such as Blair Gunther and Leo Krzycki as reportedly "non-Communist" when, in fact, Cranston said, both men had strong anti-Communist credentials. The FLD worked closely with the ASC and always made it clear that the objective must be "to speed early victory for the United Nations." Cranston scoffed at Berle's alarm over mention of the ASC in Soviet publications, since it would be strange for an allied government, particularly a Slavic one, to not "cheer" at the support the ASC provided to the war effort.[31]

Davis told Berle that he did not see any compelling reason for OWI to "withhold such assistance as it has given and is giving to this body." The OWI believed "support given to the present leadership of the Slav Congress is the most effective means of counteracting Communist influence." The ASC did not represent all Slavs in the United States, but Davis reminded Berle that "such exaggerations are no novelty." Each of them had met Americans who claimed to speak for this or that multitude; the claim of the Slav Congress in this regard "if it proves anything, would seem only to prove the genuine Americanism of its leaders." It was OWI's experience that "citizens of foreign birth or parentage may sometimes put a little more effort into it if they are convinced that the interest of the United States is also the interest of the people from which they sprang."[32]

Berle closed the discussion by conceding Davis's "brilliance in debate," although he remained unconvinced. The influence of the Communists was greater than Davis had acknowledged, but Berle insisted that was not the basis of his objection to the ASC; he was simply "old-fashioned enough to believe that the strength of the United States is best exerted and most likely to be increasingly formidable, if Americans are encouraged rather to act as Americans than as hyphenated Americans."[33]

*   *   *

More of a consensus prevailed on how to handle the Serbs, as Berle's instinct for control coincided with Cranston's distaste for right-wing ethnic agitation. After Berle's July suggestion of a meeting between Yugoslav-Americans and government officials, Cranston made plans for such a gathering in Washington. His proposal called for Davis and Berle to address the group, with the latter cautioning them about the divisive effects of their feuds and reminding them of their duty to unite behind their country and its allies. Davis would then urge them to focus on the true enemy and to call a mass meeting "dedicated to the task of consolidating their efforts in the war." The FLD and Cranston would "carry the ball from that point." Cranston was certain that the majority of Yugoslav-American leaders would agree to attend and that the "dissident Serbs would be unable to oppose the meeting successfully." He predicted, "Their program will clearly be branded as opposed to the policies of the American government, and they will rapidly lose their rank and file support unless they come along."[34]

While plans for the meeting moved forward, a number of developments complicated the policymakers' task. One such circumstance involved Yugoslav diplomat Jovan Dučić, suspected of complicity in the Serbs' anti-Croat campaign. Because of Dučić's "activity" in the United States, the State Department recommended that the Justice Department grant him only a provisional, three-month visa extension, "contingent on his good behavior."[35]

Another involved Konstantin Fotić and his official position. Throughout the summer and fall of 1942, the United States routinely elevated several of the missions of Allied governments in exile to the status of embassies to encourage or reward their resistance to the Nazis. Sumner Welles discussed this with Fotić in mid-August, and after an exchange of correspondence, the two governments agreed that Fotić and A. J. Drexel Biddle each would be named ambassadors.[36] Within weeks, the FNB reported that "four prominent Yugoslav-Americans had protested against the anticipated elevation of Minister Fotich to the rank of Ambassador." They included Louis Adamic and Stoyan Pribichevich, and all four asserted in a cablegram sent to London that the appointment "would be contrary to the wishes of all Yugoslav and Yugoslav-Americans favoring a reconstituted Yugoslavia," not a "Greater Serbia." If the appointment were made, the four "would consider themselves absolved of all moral responsibility toward the Yugoslav-Government-In-Exile."[37]

President Roosevelt inadvertently contributed to the ranks of the divisionists as well. In early September, Adamic wrote to Cranston of his concern that the president had referred to Yugoslavia as "Serbia" in a speech the day before. He feared this would cause trouble when the OWI met with the Serbian-American leaders and confided that "Stoyan and I are sick over the whole thing." He was not criticizing Roosevelt, but he wondered "if somebody did not slip 'Serbia' over on him, in the script."[38] He also wrote to Mrs. Roosevelt about how "painfully important" this error was to all of the "nationalities in Yugoslavia" who were so gallantly resisting the occupiers. The president's slip "disposes of Yugoslavia as a state"; this had not only caused an uproar among Yugoslav-Americans, but Adamic feared it might also compromise the resistance effort within Yugoslavia itself. He fully understood how "burdened" the president was, and that this might seem to be "a trifle," but in reality the "matter involves morale of hundreds of thousands of people working in our war plants." He hoped that Mrs. Roosevelt would bring this to the president's attention so that "he will find some simple way of correcting it."[39] The president's solution was simple and ingenious. At a news conference a few days later, the president explained that in his youth he had collected stamps from the area then known as Serbia and that accounted for his error.[40]

A more serious complication involved the publication, by both the ethnic and mainstream press, of attacks on Draža Mihailović. The first story appeared in a *New York Times* article on July 20, 1942, in a dispatch from Ankara, which declared, "General Mihailovitch . . . launched a campaign to stamp out Communist Partisan bands accused of destroying Serbian and Bosnian villages in territory controlled by loyal Yugoslav armies under the General." The Communist press, beginning with the *Sunday Worker,* then accused Mihailović of treason and quoted dispatches from a secret radio station called "Free Yugoslavia," issued "under the signature of the Commander of the Partisan and Volunteer Army, Tito" and which detailed the general's anti-Partisan activities. However, as the FNB soon reported, Mihailović's popularity with the "Slav masses" was too great, and the Communist attacks on him "proved to be a boomerang." The "whispering campaign" attempted by the Communist press in the United States had little success, and most workers concluded that Mihailović "is a fierce Yugoslav nationalist who stubbornly refuses to come under the Soviet orbit and, therefore, must be liquidated by the Soviets." As a result, the Communist press had dropped any mention of Mihailović or the Chetniks and referred only to the Partisans, with every victory by Mihailović attributed to them.[41]

Fotić soon complained to Welles of the "difficulties he was constantly encountering in the United States from Communist sympathizers along the Slovenes and Croatian elements"; he cited the *Daily Worker* article attacking Mihailović as a traitor and a fascist.[42] Simultaneously, *Amerikanski Srbobran* attacked the ministers in New York for living lavishly at government expense, "on Fifth Avenue, where the most successful . . . people in the world live," with monthly salaries of one thousand dollars and clothing allowances that enabled them to "look like gentlemen." This was especially disturbing at a time when Yugoslavia was being starved, its people slaughtered, and their counterparts in America working in the mines for a pittance. The paper called Kosanović the "cicerone of this group"—its "brains"—with Ivan Šubašić merely a "figurehead."[43]

The Berle Committee quickly became preoccupied with the press attacks on Mihailović, with everyone in agreement regarding an unbridled foreign-language press and the need for decisive action." David Karr of the OWI cautioned that "a wide-spread shutdown on such papers would destroy a useful medium," but a "crack down on only a few might serve as an example to others." The committee then endorsed "a stricter control" with the means to be worked out between the Justice Department and the OWI.[44] By early September, representatives of the Justice Department, the OWI, and the State Department had agreed to devise some plan of action, after "ascertaining from the War Department that there is no basis in fact to the report that General Mihajlovic is aiding the Axis forces."[45]

The rancor continued as Serb extremists used the press controversy as part of their "pro-Serbia, anti-Yugoslav argument," while other "Slav circles" viewed the case as one of "character assassination undertaken from Moscow." *Amerikanski Srbobran* not only denounced the criticisms of the Chetniks as false but charged that the Information Center in New York had provided the initial story to the *Daily Worker*. FNB also observed that the story itself had undergone some alteration in the Communist press. The original *New York Times* account reported that the YGIE sanctioned Mihailović's attacks on Partisan bands that had looted Serbian villages. In the subsequent *Sunday Worker* account, these bands became "Patriots," and Mihailović was accused of using supplies furnished by the "occupationists" for his attacks. His inactivity against the Axis forces in the country supposedly had also freed them to fight on the eastern front, meaning that the Chetniks had "openly allied themselves with the Fascist powers." The YGIE, in countering these charges, claimed that Mihailović's wife and children were being held hostage by the Germans, but that he and his forces had "pinned down, for more than a year, around 36 Axis divisions." The *Daily Worker* then extended its criticism to include the YGIE for supporting this "so-called anti-Fascist," prompting the FNB to ponder the "wider implications" of the press campaign. The Federal Communications Commission and the British Broadcasting Corporation had conducted a "careful scrutiny of Soviet domestic and foreign broadcasts" that "failed to disclose a single reference to Michailovich and his Chetnik fighters," while the "Partisan Army" received almost daily mention.[46]

Poole received corroboration of the negative press accounts of Mihailović when he met with Professor Dinko Tomashich, "an ardent Croatian—even fanatical" who had once served as Šubašić's secretary but whose "extreme attitudes" had led to a break between the two men. Tomashich told Poole that "Mihailovich has practically stopped fighting except for some encounters with the 'partisans' who are largely Communist led but not all Communist in the rank and file." Both Mihailović and Milan Nedić had by this time established themselves in Bosnia, "to ensure Serbia the possession of Bosnia, whichever side won in the war." Poole wondered, therefore, whether the accusations against Mihailović might not be at least partially true. Poole discussed this with Cavendish Cannon, who admitted his own misgivings on the same point. Although he had no hard information indicating that Mihailović had ceased fighting the Axis, Cannon knew the Chetniks had received very little in the way of supplies. He surmised that "among people of a somewhat volatile political temperament, sullenness and disgust had set in." The two officials agreed that the United States must not make any public admission of its doubts, but "as experts it was necessary for [them] to keep such a possibility in the back of [their] heads."[47]

The OWI had a similar reaction. On the eve of the meeting with the Yugoslav-American editors, Cranston acknowledged to Davis the "distinct *possibility* that Mikhailovitch is no longer fighting the Nazis," but he suggested that Davis tell the group that, barring better evidence, the United States continued to believe that the Chetnik leader "is fighting on our side against the enemy." Cranston advised that Davis, on behalf of the government, should urge all those in attendance to cease their agitation.[48] Despite their differences over general policy, all of the officials had agreed to tread warily around the Mihailović dispute because of the delicate foreign-policy issues involved.

Before the general meeting with the Yugoslavs, Poole, Cranston, Karr, and Lee Falk, along with representatives from the SWPU and the War Department, met with the editors of two Communist papers published in Pittsburgh: Mirko Markovich, of *Slobodna Reč* and Tony (Ante) Minerich of *Narodni Glasnik.* Cranston had arranged the meeting with the editors to discuss the campaign against Mihailović, in which their papers were the most active. The editors insisted that since June, there had been no indication at all that Mihailović was fighting the Axis, but "positive evidence had come to hand that Mihailovich had turned all his operations against the Partisans and was probably cooperating with Nedich and the Axis." The two also claimed that a virtual civil war raged in Yugoslavia, but that the "people and the real spirit of Yugoslavia were represented by the Partisans." Cranston and Poole agreed that "until recently" Mihailović had been fighting on the Allied side, but there was not yet enough evidence to prove that he had become a traitor. If he had done so, or if he were "fatigued and without hope . . . that would be an occasion for sadness, and obviously the wise course would be to keep the matter quiet and not to trumpet it abroad." The Communist editors had succeeded inasmuch as they had raised questions about Mihailović's contin- ued allegiance and spurred the United States government to investigate the matter. If the allegations proved true, the United States would then decide whether it made sense militarily to make the information public. However, the officials all warned that if, in the interim, the papers continued their campaign against Mihailović, "they would be working harm to the military position of the United States and would be incurring a grave risk that public action of some sort might have to be taken against them."[49]

Poole told Wiley that he saw serious complications in this controversy for both war and postwar policy. The evidence presented by Markovich and Minerich consisted mostly of radio transmissions from the Partisans or from neutral countries; a "principal source seemed to have been the Interconti- nental News Service which is a Communist news service." Poole thought it "plain . . . that the two editors were simply acting in accordance with the Communist Party line as this was being communicated to them." However, Markovich, because of his personal knowledge of and contacts in Yugoslavia, genuinely believed "that the charges against Mihailovich were true." Some of the evidence he presented was also identical to that given to Poole by To- mashich. To Poole, the motivations of the Soviets in inspiring this "embit- tered campaign against Mihailovich" appeared to be that "the Partisans . . . represent the Communist interest in Yugoslavia, though they are admittedly not all Communists," and that the Soviets hoped to establish in Yugoslavia "in the near future, that is in the unconquered mountainous parts, . . . a Yu- goslav-Soviet government." He recalled Louis Adamic's prediction, that if the administration "did not soon succeed in bringing some order and quiet into the Yugoslavia situation in the United States and some clarification of the situation within Yugoslavia, the emergence of a Soviet government in Yugoslavia within the near future was very likely."[50] This focus on the postwar implications of ethnic strife would become Poole's major preoccupation as the Soviets continued to gain influence in central and eastern Europe.

On September 18, 1942, the OWI hosted a group of Yugoslav-American newspaper editors and leaders of fraternal organizations. Berle, who gave the principle address, expressed his usual sentiments: the United States govern-

ment had no interest in European political quarrels, and the future of Yugoslavia "was a matter to be determined by a free Yugoslavia when the war
was won." The recent elevation of the Yugoslav mission to embassy status
was part of a general policy of "tribute to certain invaded countries which
had carried on gallant resistance" and did not convey recognition of "any
particular group within Yugoslavia." The United States supported Mihailović
because he battled the Axis and because it did not have information to show
that he was "doing anything but fighting Germans." Berle urged the editors
"to forget differences and get together as Americans or intending Americans,
fight the war and let European differences alone."[51] In the general discussion
that followed, disagreement among the delegates quickly surfaced, with the
Serbs divided among themselves and Serbs and Croats hostile to one another.
Although the latter hostility was an old one, Cranston demonstrated that the
Serbs had provoked the most recent outbreak by reading portions of *Amerikanski Srbobran* to the assemblage. Eventually, the delegates agreed "to make
every effort to avoid presentation of material, the effect of which would be to
stimulate or intensify discord" in the Yugoslav-American community. However, Branko Pekich, Louis Christopher, and Mladen Trbuhovich resisted an
attempt to adopt a formal resolution to that effect because "it would imply
public condemnation of the Serb representatives and would hold them solely
responsible for a situation in which they felt the Croatian group had at least
an equal share." Eventually, by majority vote, with only the three Serbs in
opposition, the group adopted and signed a resolution pledging to refrain
from anything "which might introduce discord in the ranks of Americans
of Yugoslav descent." Attempts by the dissenters to substitute "Allied" for
"Yugoslav" failed.[52] Cranston later told Davis that he had spoken to the Serbs
after the meeting and they agreed "they would tone it down." All present,
except the named three, believed the meeting "did much to clear the air."[53]

Several days later, Cranston reported to the Berle committee that the Yugoslav editors had "been very quiet" since the OWI meeting. While it was
too early to judge for certain if the initiative had been successful, the attacks
on Mihailović had ceased, at least temporarily.[54] However, despite the assurance the Serb editors had given him that "the pan-Serb and anti-Croatian
program in which they are now engaged" would end, Cranston thought that
their newspaper was "still a bit out of line."[55]

In reality, nothing had changed. In late September, Pekich published a
commentary on the meeting in *Amerikanski Srbobran,* along with a "very
inadequate account" of Berle's remarks, in which he made it appear that Berle
had done little but praise Mihailović and the Chetniks for the "superhuman

strength" with which they battled the enemy. Pekich justified his failure to sign the unity pledge as a gesture of patriotism and loyalty, and he charged that most of those invited to the conference either were not representative of the Yugoslav-American community or were Communists. He admitted that in its sorrow and outrage, *Amerikanski Srbobran* may have exaggerated the details of the offenses committed against the Serbs in Yugoslavia, but the paper had an obligation to bear witness to these "unheard-of crimes." The intent had not been to create tension in America; the Federation and its members had no goal other than victory for America and its allies and for "the legendary Draza Michailovich and his Serbian Chetniks."[56]

What remained of the facade of unity quickly collapsed. Tony Minerich, in an October article written for *Narodni Glasnik,* called for a national meeting of American Croats because the continued attacks of *Amerikanski Srbobran* were "creating disunity among the Croatians in America." Croats, he said, had extended "their brotherly hand to the Serbs, Slovenes and other Slavs of American descent" only to have the Serbs accuse them "of being 5th Columnists and enemies of America." William Boyd-Boich sent a translation of the piece to Cranston with the information that similar articles had been published by Communist Croatian papers in the United States and Canada, "in spite of the pledge made in Washington by Mr. Minerich that he would work for Yugoslav unity." Articles attacking Mihailović had appeared as well, and Minerich denied that he had made any pledges to cease attacks on the general.[57]

The only place where a measure of harmony prevailed was within the Berle committee. The attacks on Mihailović prompted the group to act on a previous agreement to draft a policy concerning "various internecine disputes of foreign committees carried on within the United States," which the departments of State, Justice, War, and Navy, and the OWI would "attempt to carry it out by available means." The resulting statement, circulated among all of the agencies involved, declared it "contrary to the policy" of the United States government to have "foreign interest groups or foreign language publications" issue material concerning the "motives, military activities and policies" of commanders of United States and United Nations forces, or to do so in a way that aided the enemy or interfered with "the military operations of any of the United Nations." Equally contrary to American policy were "organized activities . . . on the part of citizens or alien residents of the United States" that created "controversies between foreign interest groups in the United States," that aided the enemy, or that perpetuated "among persons of recent foreign extraction allegiance to any foreign country or cause."[58] The

Interdepartmental Committee for Foreign Nationality Problems (the Berle committee) adopted the policy statement on September 30, but its members decided to regard it as only "tentative," to give it "no publicity," and to use it only as "a working basis for the Government agencies concerned."[59]

*   *   *

By the fall of 1942, the FNB discovered that Mihailović's new political duties as Minister of War had tended "to divide and even alienate considerable sections of the guerrilla constituency." The strength of the Partisans was increasing, and they were expected to seek "recognition by and representation in the Government-In-Exile."[60] As a remedy, the United States urged the government-in-exile to adopt "a liberal forward-looking policy" and to issue "a declaration of post-war policy envisaging equal economic, social and political opportunity for all." Ambassador Biddle conveyed the message but saw little hope for any change in the policies of the YGIE.[61]

The need for a policy change was clear. In October, Šubašić, stating that Fotić's elevation by the YGIE to the rank of ambassador constituted "treason to Yugoslavia and Yugoslav ideals," announced that he would not tolerate Fotić's serving as ambassador "for a single hour."[62] He planned to sever his ties with the government-in-exile and to retain only his position as Governor of Croatia. He would not reconsider until the YGIE issued "a clear statement of its foreign and internal policies."[63]

Poole met in New York with Šubašić and Kosanović and found that their "consternation and despair . . . have come to something like a climax." They described their country as being torn apart "by men who are its sworn officials and bound in duty and in honor to preserve and sustain it." Kosanović was especially concerned that *Amerikanski Srbobran* had continued its attacks on the idea of a postwar united Yugoslavia, with an ongoing series of pamphlets written by former ambassador Dučić. He had raised this matter with both Momčilo Ninčić and King Peter during the king's visit to make them aware of "the disastrous effects resulting from tolerating such work done by Foreign Office officials." Šubašić intended his recent disassociation from the London government to highlight this danger as well. They also told Poole that copies of *Amerikanski Srbobran* circulated within Yugoslavia, and the people there, unfamiliar with the American "principles of freedom under which the *Srbobran* found shelter," assumed "a newspaper published in the United States must enjoy at least the tacit approval of the authorities." How would the Croatians ever revolt against their occupiers "when they read in a newspaper published in the United States that all Croatians ought to be killed?" The two men hoped the London authorities would act and dismiss Dučić and the other troublemakers but when asked which individual might take this decisive action, they replied "ruefully that they could not think of any one in particular except God Almighty."[64]

While awaiting this divine intervention, the members of the Berle committee decided that since *Amerikanski Srbobran* had not changed its policies, and since Dučić was suspected of being behind the discord, the application of FARA to the Serbs might be appropriate.[65] In mid-November, officials from the Justice Department interviewed Louis Christopher with the intention of discovering if he was working as an agent for Yugoslavia in 1939 and 1940 and thus liable to registration under FARA. He had during that time published a paper called the "American Yugoslav *Reflector*," the goal of which was "to popularize Axis collaborationists (Nedich, Ljotich, etc.) among Yugoslavs in America." Most of the conversation, however, focused on more recent concerns. Christopher admitted that *Amerikanski Srbobran* substituted the word "Serbian" for "Yugoslav" in stories sent to the paper by the YGIE, but said it was a "well-known fact" that the ministers in the Center had sinned first by making the opposite and original substitution. Since the OWI meeting, Christopher claimed that the paper had limited its criticism of the Croats to "about ninety-five percent of what it ought to be;" in addition, Mladen Trbuhovich, who had edited the paper during "the most violent phase of the anti-Croat campaign," had resigned to enter the ministry. Christopher's protests had only a negative effect; one of the officials at the Justice Department told the FNB that Christopher "made a very bad impression on the interviewing committee" who believed he had been very indiscreet "in the choice of words and phrases" he used to describe the YGIE and its ministers.[66]

This dispute penetrated the national media in late November when the *New York Herald Tribune* published a lengthy letter from Ruth Mitchell, former Chetnik and sister of the late General Billy Mitchell. Mitchell claimed that she had served as a Chetnik "intelligence agent" for several months in 1941 but had been captured while swimming in Dubrovnik and imprisoned by the Germans. After her release in 1942, she returned to the United States and became a spokeswoman for Mihailović. In her letter, printed under the title "Killings Laid to Croats," Mitchell charged that the "Croats as a race are engaged in a war of extermination against the Serbs." She repeated all of the Great Serb grievances, from Croatian "treachery" against the government in the spring of 1941 to their massacre of thousands of Serb men, women, and children thereafter. Mitchell acknowledged that some American Croats "are beside themselves with shame, disgust and anger at the behavior of their countrymen" but asserted that none of them had denounced it. This silence harmed the war effort, because it served as the basis for the "unnecessary but perfectly understandable enmity between" Serbs and Croats in America's factories. She disavowed any desire on the part of the Serbs for a "Greater Serbia" but because of the heroism of "Serbia" and "her losses, which are heavier in proportion to population than those of any of the United Nations," the nation had already earned that title and would retain it no matter how "great or small her territory after the reconstruction of Europe." FNB field agent Ivan Ivanovitch reported that Mitchell's missive caused "great indignation" in the Yugoslav community and in particular at the Information Center. He believed that she had "been coached" and was acting as "somebody's Charlie McCarthy—perhaps Ambassador Fotich's or some other Greater Serbian." He also noted that her book, *I Was a Chetnik,* which detailed her service with Mihailović's forces and her capture and imprisonment by the Germans, was about to be published.[67]

After the letter's publication, Peter Klassen of the FNB met with Louis Nemzer of the Justice Department to discuss Mitchell's "ill-advised, untimely, and, because of their virulence, harmful" public lectures and newspaper articles. Fotić had publicly disavowed Mitchell's views; an official from the American Friends of Yugoslavia relief group had pronounced her "deranged" because of her experiences as a German prisoner and has asked that the government take action against her. Justice saw no grounds to do so, particularly in light of her connection to General Billy Mitchell. Taking the same line as Ivanovitch, Klassen related the allegation that the SNDC had contracted to buy "a certain number" of Mitchell's forthcoming book, and Nemzer agreed that proof of such a subsidy would enable the department to act at least against the council. Klassen offered the help of FNB's field representatives in securing evidence, but Poole saw no reason for FNB involvement, telling Klassen was that this was "a matter for OWI [and] State." Klassen's response: "Dynamite Dropped."[68] Mitchell's prominence clearly afforded her a measure of protection.

On the anniversary of the founding of the Yugoslav state on December 1, King Peter, in a rather weak attempt to foster unity, delivered a radio address promising that his country "will rise again" and that all citizens "will be guaranteed the same political, economic and spiritual opportunities of life and action, grounded on an equality of rights for all."[69] The press attacks on Mihailović continued nonetheless, prompting Lawrence M. C. Smith to ask his colleagues on the Berle committee for the State Department's view of the Chetnik leader. Cannon admitted that the general had "not been especially active recently," and appeared to be holding his forces "in abeyance until such time as we can substantially contribute to his effort, thereby making it a major field of action." At that time, the United States would "be in a position to argue forcefully with the Soviet Union that General Mihailovich should receive the support of the United Nations." Mihailović had become an international symbol of resistance "too valuable to be eliminated at this stage, and it will become increasingly evident that, as a military force, he is to be reckoned with." For Berle, this dispute was connected to "the whole question of the foreign-language press and the Communist press, and he asked if Mr. Smith would give consideration to the matter from the point of view of free speech, talk it over with Mr. Cranston, and report to the Committee at the next meeting."[70]

Cranston was not likely to share Berle's conclusion. After a query from Ulrich Bell in the OWI's movie bureau concerning a complaint he had received about the "glorification of Mihailovich in a film called CHETNIK!"[71] Cranston said, "It is my opinion personally and entirely unofficially that a movie glorifying him might turn into a terrible Frankenstein." Mihailović was "probably not pro-Axis"; he fought well at first but began "conserving his forces except for his sporadic attacks on the Partisans ... who are far from being entirely formed by Communists, and who really represent the democratic forces within Yugoslavia." It was also "pretty damn apparent that Mihailovitch is subservient to the Yugoslav Government-In-Exile, which is dominated by Fascists who hope to set up a Greater Serbia after the war." Cranston was certain that "the Russian Government tacitly approves the material intended to blacken" him. "Slavic foreign language groups ... [were] greatly excited over the whole Mihailovitch affair;" but in Cranston's view, they saw him as the enemy and any support given him by the United States against the Partisans would not be well received.[72]

OWI had a more temperate official position. In December 1942, the agency issued an "Information Guide for Foreign Language Press and Radio," designed to enable foreign language editors and broadcasters to serve both their nationality group and the war effort. According to the guide, all editors and broadcasters had a responsibility "to record the progress of the war truthfully and as fully as space and time permit in a way designed to help readers and listeners understand the war and in a way certain to enlist their full support for, and participation in, the war." Certain themes, designed to counter Axis propaganda, should, the guide stipulated, be present in all publications and broadcasts. These included statements that characterized the war as a battle "against dictatorship and for the freedom of people of every race, color and creed," and that reminded everyone that America and the United Nations were working together to achieve victory. Since one of the great dangers facing Americans during the war was "internal dissension," the foreign language press and radio had to avoid nationalistic quarrels and emphasize the need for unity. Yugoslav-Americans, for example, "should unite for American victory," putting aside "narrow nationalism and petty bickers" in the interest of defeating the common enemy.[73]

The OWI's own publications followed these guidelines and continued to reflect the administration's support for the Yugoslav-Government-In-Exile. An OWI pamphlet, *The Thousand Million*, released in December 1942, featured stories on all of the "28 United Nations at war." The section on Yugoslavia began with a verse from "O Serbia" and singled out the country as the only European state to have "become spoil for so many aggressors." The text identified both the Chetniks and the Partisans as resistance fighters but provided only a brief listing of the Partisans as "another guerrilla army" after several lines detailing the Chetniks' exploits of "pitched battles with large Axis detachments."[74]

The mainstream media proved harder to control. As the OWI issued its guidelines to foreign language outlets, Dr. Ante Pavelić, a former assistant to Šubašić who purportedly escaped from Yugoslavia, delivered an address on the Partisans on the *March of Time* radio program. The announcer who introduced him stated that Mihailović no longer led the resistance in Yugoslavia, that a new Partisan army had come into existence, and that Pavelić was going to explain these developments. In his brief speech, Pavelić reported that the Partisans, which included Communists but which were not dominated by them, had approximately three hundred thousand men under arms, engaged in "regular army operations . . . on a continuous front one hundred miles in length" and held "half of Yugoslavia." Mihailović, by contrast, no longer fought the enemy, and his location was unknown.[75]

Fotić immediately protested in a letter to the broadcasters that Pavelić had simply left his post in Berne after the German invasion of Yugoslavia and had been dismissed as a result. He had not escaped and had not occupied the position credited to him.[76] Fotić also met with Berle and with "considerable emotion" discussed Pavelić's claim that the Partisans were now in command of the resistance. He also took issue with a report from the Soviet Union announcing the formation by the Partisans of a government in the town of Bihac in Slovenia. Fotić asked Berle that all of this be stopped, as "it cast doubt on the huge sacrifices the Serbs had already made in this war and were making now; they had made these sacrifices freely and now were being branded as traitors. It all stemmed . . . from Russia," he said, "which had started this propaganda three or four months ago." Berle took the opportunity to remind Fotić that the United States for some time had expressed its concern "lest the growth of the Pan Serb movement and its espousal in some Yugoslav government quarters . . . lead to reactions by the other races in Yugoslavia, and our fear lest outside powers . . . endeavor to fish in waters thus troubled." But he also asked the Justice Department to look over Pavelich's registration under FARA: "It would appear, *prima facie*, that he has pretty seriously violated our laws and certainly has violated our hospitality. My impression is that we ought to exclude him at once. But we ought to do this at the same time we take measures against extremists on the *Srbobran* side."[77]

However, it was the Slovene-American community that produced the most influential publicist for the Partisan cause. The Slovenes, the largest of the Yugoslav-American factions, were initially the least contentious and "tended to play the role of conciliator and mediator in Yugoslav politics in the United States." Yet this group, to which Adamic belonged, became restless on a number of counts, ranging from the enemy alien status of some in their community, to "the recovery of the Slovenian irredenta from Italy and Austria." Like the Croats, the Slovenes were predominately Roman Catholic, but a strong liberal and anti-clerical sentiment, represented by men like Adamic, existed in the Slovene community, and they were active in socialist and union movements in the United States. They had favored the creation of a federated Yugoslavia after World War I and continued to support such a system "in which the Slovenians would balance between the Serbs and the Croats." It was this stance that would eventually propel them into the ranks of Tito's supporters.[78]

Adamic, in an interview with the FNB prior to a December congress the Slovenes had called to formulate their policies, asserted that only Russia supported the idea of a "united and enlarged Yugoslavia." He praised the Partisans and opposed Mihailović because he was part of the YGIE, which was not only unrepresentative but pro-British and anti-Russian. The United Nations, which he condemned for their support of Mihailović, was "drifting without any clear program" other than support for "English Imperialism," and Adamic predicted the result would be postwar civil conflicts such as those that were currently raging in Yugoslavia. He also assailed the State Department and the Office of Censorship for attempting to stop publication of his forthcoming article on the guerilla war in Yugoslavia.[79]

The article to which Adamic referred, "Mikhailovitch: Balkan Mystery Man," appeared in the *Saturday Evening Post* in mid-December. In it, Adamic criticized the government in exile and called for American support for the Partisans.[80] The State Department had registered some objections to the piece, but as the magazine's editor told Adamic, "the censorship people" did not agree and aside from the deletion of "a few lines here and there . . . cut for length," the article would appear as written.[81] Unhappy with the changes, Adamic published the full text as a pamphlet entitled "Inside Yugoslavia" and circulated it to friends and government officials. In this version Adamic was "much more outspokenly contemptuous of the Yugoslav-Government-In-Exile (which he described as "the quintessence of futility")." He also expressed more sympathy for the Partisans and less for the British, and he insisted "more strongly that the Yugoslav problem can be solved only by a clarification of United Nations policies."[82]

Adamic's article earned him the increased attention of the FBI. Earlier investigations of Adamic in 1941 and 1942 in connection with wartime security had revealed nothing of great interest. Tagging him only as a "genuine liberal" who allowed himself to be used by various left-wing organizations, the FBI concluded that Adamic did not profess any "un-American sympathies" and seemed willing to assist the bureau.[83] The FBI ordered the Newark office to close its investigation because no firm allegations against Adamic had been made.[84] As this order was being given, Adamic's article on Mihailović and the Partisans appeared. Adamic's FBI file not only remained open, but the language in it changed, noting that the article had shed "some light upon Louis Adamic's Communist sympathies." Hoover began sending information on Adamic to Harry Hopkins at the White House for transmittal to the president, and to Berle at State.[85]

At their congress, the Slovenes emphasized territorial issues. Affirming that as "Slovenian-Americans, we are an integral part of the American population, our loyalty is to the United States," they also could not "be unmindful of Slovenia and other parts of Yugoslavia" that had been separated after World War I "by secret diplomacy" from the "main body" of the country.[86] Adamic angered Berle by making a speech wherein he said, without any reference to the Atlantic Charter, that the Soviet Union was the only country that "had made any statement regarding post-war Slovenia." Berle could not have been pleased when Cannon reminded him that Adamic's comment was indeed true, "as the Government of the United States has maintained that it will not discuss European territorial problems during the course of the war."[87]

After the congress ended, Adamic and a delegation of Slovene-Americans met with Sumner Welles to present their case for a "free, federated and democratic Yugoslavia" and within it, a "united Slovenia with large autonomy." Welles expressed the government's intent to give "careful and friendly consideration" to their requests but avowed that it was impossible for the United States to make any political or territorial commitments at that time.[88] The perils of receiving such petitions quickly became clear. Within a week, the Slovene delegation told a representative of the FNB that Welles had assured them that the United States government would shortly issue a statement supporting "Slovene and Croat territorial aspirations after the war as a reward for, and an incentive to, their present guerrilla fighting against the Axis."[89]

When the Slovene group met with Poole, they triggered his mounting postwar anxieties. The whole encounter filled him with "foreboding of the pressures which are going to be felt from the foreign nationality groups when the time comes for peace making." The delegation had impressed upon Poole the misgivings rampant in the Slovene community because of the "apparent intimate access to high American officials" of men like Otto von Hapsburg, who represented "unpleasant symbols of a social order from which they had been at pains to escape by migrating to the United States." Poole assured them that the Atlantic Charter continued to represent the war and postwar aims of the United States and that "the peacemakers would not be confronted by prior engagements analogous to the famous treaty made with Italy at London in 1915." The delegation also presented "a quite unreasoned assertion of Slovenian irredentism," asserting that the Slovenes "incorporated into Italy two decades ago must be gathered back now into a Slovenian state." This state would be part of a Yugoslav federation but "not one dominated by Serbian ambition." To Poole, this all represented "an instructive example of foreign politics in democratic dress." While he did not doubt the "sincerity and moving conviction" of the members of the delegation, he felt that their "political aspirations . . . were crudely selfish" and took no account of other groups or causes. Applying reason to a situation that was fundamentally emotional, Poole suggested that a "broad program of public education" carried out through the foreign-language press might make clear the "necessity for compromise in all political adjustments" and "effect a cure of the all-pervasive disease of political parochialism." He recommended this approach to Alan Cranston, since the execution of the plan would fall to the OWI.[90]

∗   ∗   ∗

Much of the parochialism Poole lamented continued to emanate from London. Yet when the king broached the idea of removing Fotić, the State Department preferred that he retain his post—even though he was "to a considerable degree responsible" for the ethnic agitation—and that he adhere to a "definite policy" worked out by his government. The Yugoslav embassy in Washington could not continue to expect American officials to "promote the idea of Yugoslav unity which their own actions have tended to destroy." The State Department agreed that the ministers in New York were probably more representative of Yugoslav opinion than the embassy was, but because they were not fully supported by the YGIE and the entities did not work together, they had become "something of a burden." They too must be brought in line with "whatever unified policy their Government may adopt." Dučić and Bishop Dionisijie "have been definitely objectionable," and the State Department wanted to see the former transferred and the latter brought under stricter control.[91] This instruction carried less weight that it might have; to demonstrate that American concerns did not imply a lack of faith in Mihailović, Welles sent a letter to Fotić expressing the "complete confidence" of the United States Government "in the patriotism of General Mihailovich" whose actions against the enemy "constitute an important element" of the Allied war effort; General Eisenhower dispatched a New Year's greeting to the Chetnik leader as well.[92]

The British exerted more pressure, with Winston Churchill warning King Peter that he did not want the material supplied by the British to be used by Mihailović "to conduct a civil conflict." In the face of clear British evidence of collaboration by Mihailović's officers, however, Ninčić continued to deny that Mihailović himself had any knowledge of their activities.[93] When the king finally agreed to reorganize his government at the beginning of the new year, he dismissed Ninčić, but also announced the "retirement" of the ministers in New York, a move the Croats viewed as another "victory of Fotić and his Great Serb policy."[94] The Pan-Serb faction prevented the cabinet from reaching a consensus on a replacement for Ninčić; as a result, Prime Minister Slobodan Jovanović temporarily assumed both posts.[95]

Jovanović assured Ambassador Biddle that Fotić would be issued new instructions; that Šubašić (whose earlier resignation the king had not accepted) and Dučić would be recalled to London for consultations; and Kosanović would be reassigned to South America. The prime minister also intended to place the Information Center more firmly under the control of the embassy, but he "felt that Fotitch's retention together with the withdrawal of the Ministers in New York would appear in the eyes of the Croat and Slovene and Serb democratic elements such a victory for Fotić that it would only provoke their further ire and opposition in other matters." He also defended Mihailović and demonstrated the unchanged outlook of the Pan-Serbs by asking Biddle to view the Chetnik leader's actions in context: the Croats had first attacked the Serbs; the Serbs had countered, in part with Pan-Serb propaganda; and currently an embattled and besieged Mihailović faced a barrage of attacks from the Communists.[96]

When the prime minister asked Biddle for suggestions regarding the instructions to be prepared for Fotić, Biddle insisted that Fotić work to unify the "Yugoslav refugees in the United States" and "American citizens of Yugoslav descent and origin," and to cease any connections between the embassy and "trouble making" papers such as *Amerikanski Srbobran*. The prime minister agreed, but if he were to convince Fotić of this, he hoped that "the Communist and other opposition press" in the United States (such as *Slobodna Reč*) could "be brought to refrain" from attacks on the YGIE and Mihailović. Jovanović also confided his difficulty in finding a "formula" for "the coordination of action between the various Yugoslav forces of resistance." Neither the Partisans nor the Chetniks would accept direction from the other. Biddle suggested that each should simply agree not to attack the other, to coordinate their activities against the "common enemy," and to defer political decisions.[97]

In an interview with the FNB in early January 1943, Kosanović marveled that the cabinet changes, designed to produce greater unity within the YGIE, had resulted in the dismissal of "those who had worked hardest for a united federal Yugoslavia." This would exacerbate tensions within the United States because Kosanović was certain, as Jovanović had predicted, that *Amerikanski Srbobran* would trumpet the dismissal of the ministers as a vindication of their policy. He emphasized that Yugoslav affairs could not be settled without a recognition of "Soviet interests and of the pro-Russian sentiment of the Yugoslav people."[98]

Kosanović's fears materialized when Fotić met with Welles to express his "tremendous relief" at the recall of the ministers in New York. Fotic identified the ministers as a source of friction, responsible for "false and exaggerated reports concerning the beliefs and activities of Serbs, Croats and Slovenes in the United States being sent to the Yugoslav Government in London."[99] However, Fotić also spoke favorably of the Slovene-American campaign to secure postwar territorial adjustments that would result in Slovenes residing in Italy being returned to Yugoslavia.[100] This latter sentiment Ambassador Biddle attributed to the new instructions Jovanović had given to Fotić, which directed him to propagate the idea of a restored Yugoslav state devoid of "separatist tendencies." The principles of the king's December 1942 speech were to guide all of the country's diplomats in their representations abroad.[101]

Within a few weeks the Yugoslav government modified the effects of some of its changes. The Information Center would be placed under the control of the embassy, but Ivan Šubašić and Franc Snoj would remain assigned to the United States, "with a view to their maintaining contact respectively with the Croat and Slovene elements there." Jovanović saw that as the only way to avoid appearing to favor one group over the other and hoped the United States would impress upon Fotić the need to follow the new directive issued to him. In general, however, Jovanović believed the conflict between the Partisans and Mihailović to be far more crucial than the ethnic quarrels, since it prefigured the "Comintern's efforts to prepare the way for Russian post-war control over the Balkans as far as the Adriatic."[102]

Poole shared these concerns. After the British informed him that supplies would be withheld from the Chetniks unless Mihailović changed his policies, Poole became even more certain that the "confrontation of Soviet Russian and American policy in Central Europe . . . stands out with increasing clarity in the case of Yugoslavia." The United States had undertaken to "rehabilitate" Mihailović, but the State Department, recognizing the "essential relationship" of the Soviet Union "to any solution of the Yugoslav problem," also intended to discuss Yugoslavia with them. The United States hoped that "a common working program in the Yugoslav region" and elsewhere in eastern and central Europe might be reached, Poole reported to Donovan, "though it is recognized that there may exist deep down an irrepressible conflict between these two great members of the United Nations."[103] This had echoes within the United States. The FNB reported that most ethnic papers, whether they supported the general or not, believe that Communist "tactics play an important role in the counterplay between Michailovich and the Partisans"; "pan-Slavism" is abroad in Yugoslavia; and "the 'schizophrenia' of the Yugoslav Government in London renders confusing any attempt to explain, condone, or condemn its policy." In general, surveys of the foreign-language press demonstrated that support for the Chetniks had diminished while that for the Partisans had "steadily increased."[104]

* * *

Legal pressure on the ethnic factions within the United States, either through FARA or a change in the attorney general's more lenient policy toward the press, remained an option for Berle and his colleagues. Cranston was eager to attempt the second alternative, insisting that "the worst foreign language papers in the United States," which were "pro-Axis" or unusually divisive, "be suppressed or barred from the mails immediately." Although the Justice Department remained reluctant to take such action, fearing an unfavorable response in the immigrant community as a whole, Cranston fumed that the "coddling of these papers is senseless" and that "no court would overrule action against a foreign language paper in wartime." He suspected that "outright suppression may be unnecessary" since the Post Office could simply bar papers from the mail at the request of the Justice Department. Actions against the foreign language press would be "more justifiable" than against the English-language press because of the "monopoly position" of the press within the foreign-language community. Only one Yugoslav-American paper made his worst-offenders list: *Amerikanski Srbobran,* which had "waged a long and bitter war against Croatians" while saying little about the Nazis.[105]

Adamic was also a target. *Amerikanski Srbobran* had quickly responded to Adamic's *Post* article with attacks that accused him of being "a professional and paid hater of Serbs" and of involvement in the assassination of King Alexander. Adamic refused to respond on the grounds that it would only make things worse, but he appealed to the OWI to address "the whole *Srbobran* racket."[106] Cranston had little hope of any action, as he told Adamic, even though the paper "has caused me as much trouble as any other paper in the country."[107] Less than a week later, in a letter to another government official, Cranston expressed doubt about further OWI involvement "at this moment into the Yugoslav mess." The Partisan position had received so much publicity in mainstream magazines, such as the *Saturday Evening Post,* that he saw "no reason for us to urge suppression in less important publications."[108]

That left FARA. By the end of 1942, two thousand foreign agents had registered under FARA, with about one-third representing "friendly nations with whom we have lend-lease arrangements." The registration process also had disclosed the existence of two dozen previously unknown foreign political groups. While all professed a desire to improve relations with the United States, the investigations by the Justice Department had shown that desire involved "a considerable effort to sway public opinion behind one or another foreign cause." A series of prosecutions under FARA and other statutes had resulted, culminating in the imprisonment of forty-four individuals, all representing Axis interests.[109]

But could the law be applied to troublesome allies, even if they were as fractious as the Yugoslavs? In late December, 1942, the Interdepartmental Committee discussed the feasibility of a grand jury action for prosecution of Yugoslav-Americans under FARA and agreed that "what Mr. Berle called an 'even-handed' inquiry, bearing equally upon possible derelictions among the Croats and among the Serbs, might have a beneficial deterrent effect upon all foreign factional agitation in the United States." When Poole expressed concern about "the delicacy of the publicity problem" and the danger of an inquiry becoming a "Salem witch hunt," Smith, looking at the issue of "political warfare," asked Poole what effect a prosecution such as Berle described would have in both Yugoslavia and the United States on the willingness of the foreign nationalities community as a whole to support the war.[110]

For Poole, this was the essential question. The war in Yugoslavia, which was in part a civil war, involved social as well as ethnic and national concerns. If the United States continued to support Mihailović, it would find itself on the "Greater Serbia" side of the ethnic conflict and on "the conservative side" of the Yugoslav civil war, with Russia supporting the opposite faction. He did not see how a legal action in the United States would change the situation in Europe, but the prosecution of a leftist publication like *Slobodna Reč* rather than *Amerikanski Srbobran* might influence U.S.-Soviet relations. Legal action was also not the only recourse: the State Department could, for example, refuse another visa extension for Dučić and take action as well against Bishop Dionisije. In general, Poole could not help but be "impressed by what seems to [him] the great disproportion between the size and bearings of the whole situation on the one hand and the relative insignificance of the action mooted in Pittsburgh"; the gains to be achieved and the "danger . . . of complications and unfavorable reactions" were not in balance. If the Justice Department acted, he suggested, it should do so "on strictly legal grounds and . . . not seek political objectives through so uncertain an instrument as a grand jury."[111]

Legal grounds remained elusive. The FBI's investigation of the SNDC's tax returns and bank accounts had not proven fruitful. While FBI informants indicated that a link existed between Fotić and the SNDC, the ambassador enjoyed diplomatic immunity and represented one of the countries whose resistance against the Axis the American press most often featured. As the

Detroit field office, unsure of its ground in a probe involving a diplomat, told Hoover in early 1943, since the SNDC favored the disintegration of the Yugoslav state, investigation of the ties between it and Fotić "might bring about diplomatic complications." Hoover offered no immediate guidance but queried Sharp and his superiors at Justice periodically and rather insistently concerning the status of plans to prosecute the council for failure to register under FARA.[112]

Smith was equally displeased with the pace of the investigation. After yet another Berle committee discussion of "free movements," Smith observed that "the Government is not following an integrated or intelligent policy." Justice was too often called upon to prosecute "at the end of a controversy"—with little information about what had occurred before. One policy should be adopted by all of the agencies concerned, and Smith suggested that a smaller group, from the OWI, Justice Department, State Department, OSS, and the Office of Censorship "meet several times a week to agree on programs, policy, etc." While Berle quickly seconded Smith's comments, David Karr of the OWI countered that all of the foreign-born groups were cooperating with the war effort and that "the difficulty lies with the delicate question of post-war problems and in the pre–Pearl Harbor positions of many." The dispute among the Yugoslavs for example, "is one of ideas and cannot therefore be suppressed." Berle testily observed that if "this particularly inflammable situation is working out, it is largely because of the cooperation of the members of this Committee," and again he warned that "the building up of political pressure groups is a danger; it is becoming a question of public order and of the unhealthy political use of American groups by alien groups and individuals." Poole, seeming to throw his lot in with the OWI, "doubted whether repression would ever be very productive." He continued to see a "campaign of education" using the "magnificent instrument" of the foreign language press as a better alternative. Cranston, seeing an opportunity for his agency to lead, remarked that since "work in this field is primarily the responsibility of OWI," he would check with Davis about better coordination, which he agreed was desirable. Discussion then returned to Smith's suggestion for a smaller subcommittee that would "handle day-to-day problems" while leaving the more important discussions for the larger sessions. Poole thought such a group should have three purposes: "to make intelligence surveys;" "to undertake the necessary repressive measures;" and to "draw up positive programs."[113] Each man's views continued to reflect his agency's specific task: Smith, law enforcement; Berle, diplomacy; Karr and Cranston, propaganda;

Poole, intelligence. Only one point remained constant: the foreign nationalities population was still a problem to be managed and controlled.

As these exchanges took place, the resolve of the Croats to create their own organization to counter the Serbs resulted in a call for a Croatian Congress, scheduled for late February. OWI officials acknowledged that although they had "some doubts regarding it, the only thing that can be done is to endeavor to neutralize it, as it cannot be stopped." Cranston was not yet certain of the extent of Communist influence in the congress, but if the meeting was broadly encompassing, he felt that a government representative should attend. If the group were Communist-dominated, then no representative should be present. The OWI would try to keep the meeting on an "*American basis* (War Bond sales, blood donations, etc.)," but "meetings to promote the sale of War Bonds often serve as an excuse for some of the most scurrilous attacks."[114]

Cranston followed the same line with the meeting's organizers, insisting that their gathering have an "American viewpoint;" avoid detailed discussions of postwar boundaries or forms of government; and refrain from attacks on others who were fighting on the Allied side.[115] But Welles's experience with the Slovenes quickly repeated itself. William Boyd-Boich, who told Cranston that the Croatian Catholic Union would not attend the congress,[116] also informed him that Butkovich was using Cranston's letter to claim he had "free hands" to conduct the Chicago meeting.[117] To Cranston, the letter conveyed neither "favor or disfavor" but only an attempt to show "what bounds we hope the Congress will stay within."[118]

While the Croats prepared for their meeting, the IDCFNP continued to grapple with larger issues of policy. The group adopted Smith's proposal to establish an informal subcommittee that would meet for several weeks on a trial basis, consist of representatives from the Justice Department, State Department, OWI, and OSS, and "exchange current information regarding foreign nationality problems"; report such information and policy decisions to their own and other concerned agencies; and expedite the work of the regular committee. They also broached the idea of putting the IDCFNP on an "authoritative basis" but decided to first solicit from all of the agencies involved a statement of their "jurisdiction or interests."[119]

As each agency set about the task of delineating their jurisdiction or interests, an exchange occurred that reflected the complaints Cranston and Berle made about one another. However, in this case, Poole was the main protagonist, and the underlying theme reflected concerns about communist influence among ethnics. Recording his agency's interests and responsibilities, Poole detailed the "informal but important steps . . . toward closer contact and coordination" the various agencies involved in foreign nationalities issues had undertaken. The first was the interdepartmental committee, "informal and without authority of its own," which "has tended to take on momentum and usefulness" over the past six months. After thus disposing of Hoskins, whose departure for the military neatly coincided with Poole's avowal of the committee's increased utility, Poole took aim at the OWI. The Berle committee had demonstrated both the "reality" of foreign nationality problems and the need for consultation by those working in the area. Smith, in particular, "has for some months been reaching about for a more coordinated approach by the Government to the foreign-nationalities complex" and for "some way to coordinate legal with political action," but he and his colleagues at the Justice Department had been "disturbed by some rather individualistic initiatives in the field of public morale-building undertaken by Alan Cranston of OWI." Cranston's actions disturbed Berle as well, and at the last committee meeting, Berle had expressed the frustration he felt because of the "hindrance" arising from the "divergences in basic attitude between two agencies."[120]

Berle had not been explicit in identifying the agencies or their differences, but Poole was certain that one approach was "the State Department's, or his own, proper emphasis, as he and many others see it, upon the need for expedient action to win the war as contrasted with the more ideological insistence upon principle current among some in OWI (which its exponents interpret as longer-term expediency)." Berle was troubled by how to reconcile "what might be called the old-line American viewpoint and the newer political orientation associated with the epithet 'fellow traveler.'" His remarks had been "forthright but adroit," and Cranston had shown "equal statesmanship" and "refrained from direct issue." The exchanges had the effect of producing a consensus on a number of issues: the foreign nationalities problem ranked first in importance; the procedures and organizations used should remain informal, but "the central position of the State Department should be recognized"; initiatives should be discussed but no action would be taken by the full committee or the subcommittee, only by an individual agency. In the smaller committee meeting, Berle, Poole, Smith, and Cranston had explored the problem of formulating "certain guiding principles," with reference to the State Department's press release of December 1941, which recommended "that American citizens ought to stick to their American knitting" and only "serve as advisors to their foreign cousins." They also had discussed the need for more positive actions to supplement "the negative measures of control and repression which the Department of Justice was in a position to exercise." Cranston, who had "borne the brunt of positive action in the foreign nationalities field," had talked at the smaller meeting regarding the problem of having contacts with officials and organizations "without being drawn into internal politics and accused of taking sides and playing favorites." They had all then looked at the Croatian Congress planned for late February as a case in point. How much involvement should OWI have?[121]

Cranston had had recent experience with the dangers of being drawn into ethnic disputes, the result of a controversy with members of the Italian community. Like the Yugoslavs, Italians in the United States were deeply divided, but in their case it was over the role that former fascists and current communists should play in opposing Mussolini. In January 1943, Carlo Tresca, the Italian anti-fascist editor of *Il Martello*, was murdered in Manhattan. Earlier in the month, FLD radio chief Lee Falk met with Tresca at Cranston's suggestion to discuss the formation of an Italian-American Victory Council, which would be broadly based and involve as much of the community as possible. Ten days after Tresca's murder, the *New York Sun* disclosed Falk's meeting, and soon anti-Communist liberals and socialists in the Italian community were charging that the OWI had encouraged Tresca to accept Communist membership in the proposed council, that he had resisted, and that this had caused his death.[122]

In his defense, Cranston assured Davis that the OWI was "simply trying to unite all Americans behind the war effort" and had never "made any effort to persuade anyone to accept Communists within the framework of the united nationality organizations." The goal of the FLD was to create an organization larger than each nationality group, one that would unite all foreign language groups "in the support of the war on an American basis." The American Slav Congress, comprised of "many of the powerful Slav groups" who "have buried their traditional hates to work side by side" was an example of the OWI's approach. The foreign-language community was interested in the war, but much of that interest was "on a nationalistic basis . . . on a basis of what seems to be in the war for their land of origin." The OWI countered this by convincing foreign nationalities "that victory for America means victory for their lands of origin." Davis accepted Cranston's arguments and used them to refute the attacks leveled in the press and in ethnic and socialist circles against OWI.[123]

When Adamic sent a telegram to Davis denouncing the attacks on Cranston, "a thorough American who is not pro communist in any sense," Davis agreed that the whole story "was so extreme as to be ridiculous for anyone who knows the situation," and he expressed his confidence in Cranston and his staff.[124] Cranston later thanked Adamic for the "swell telegram" he had sent to Davis; it "helped a great deal and I was delighted at the letter he wrote you in response." He told Adamic that he had "found out a great deal about who is who in the midst of all my tribulations. Some 'friends' ducked for cover and I haven't seen them since. If you ever want my right arm, just say so." Adamic referred to that offer when he asked Cranston to take action against *Amerikanski Srbobran*.[125]

The Tresca controversy, which exemplified the kind of initiative that Berle and Poole found so disturbing, never completely faded, but it did little to dull Cranston's animus toward his critics. In his account to Davis of the committee dispute that Poole had related, Cranston adopted a less statesman-like tone than the one Poole assigned him. Cranston asserted that the "considerable divergence of opinion on policy" with Berle originated with Berle's "desire to use foreign born groups in America as a base for the workings of the policy of expediency abroad." This use of "reactionary and often pro-fascist foreign born groups" and the policy it represented "has no business within the borders of America" where "military expediency" was not an issue. Such a policy may have been necessary abroad, but that made it all the more essential at home to "demonstrate that our real faith lies in pro-democratic groups." Cranston considered the formation of a smaller group within the IDCFNP as simply the most recent of Berle's efforts to bring Cranston "into line with his policy." Poole, in endorsing this suggestion, "blundered" by acknowledging that the Foreign Language Divison of the OWI "*has been bearing the brunt of positive action,*" thus enabling Cranston to seize "upon this admission of our central position" and to offer to discuss the issue of closer cooperation with Davis. However, Poole, "obviously following instructions from Berle, who controls him by budgetary methods," had since reversed his previous position by declaring the "central position" of the State Department in the foreign nationalities field. Berle then "went into a rampage against OWI in general and myself in particular." Cranston also bristled at Poole's "fellow traveler" comment, which he told Davis cannot "pass without rebuttal." Although he asserted that Berle's request that each agency submit a statement of their functions was simply "another method of control," he attached one nonetheless, written with "as many verbs stretching into infinity as I could find." He clung to the "faint hope that Berle may fall into his own trap when he tries to write his own statement of functions in this field."[126]

In his written response to Poole's memorandum, which he also sent to

QUESTION OF PUBLIC ORDER · 123

"Adolph" Berle, Cranston agreed on the need for more coordination and the "full and frank exchange of information" that served as a "prerequisite," but objected to the tenor and some of the substance of Poole's account. He was disturbed by Poole's "progress from one sentence hanging a certain policy upon OWI, to another sentence associating this policy with the epithet 'fellow traveler,' to a third associating me with the policy and the epithet. Not even Martin Dies has proclaimed that all of OWI has a 'fellow traveler' complex." Most of what the IDCFNP did concerned American citizens; meetings like that of the Croatian Congress were composed "primarily of Americans" and "their themes and aims should likewise be primarily American." Therefore, "it would seem that action and responsibility in this field lies primarily with the agencies assigned domestic functions, and that the State Department does not hold a 'central position' in the field."[127]

Berle ended this paper war with a gesture of conciliation, informing both Poole and Cranston that the "informal discussion" during which he had spoken of a disagreement between the State Department and the OWI did not "necessarily preclude practical unity of action on questions with which we had to deal." The specific issue concerned the Croatian Congress, "which opposes one of our allies in the war," and whether the United States should recognize it: "Irrespective of the merits of its opposition, it seemed inadvisable to foster a dispute in the Yugoslav community." Restating Cranston's position far more diplomatically, Berle observed that Cranston "is presumably bound by instructions from his superior officers, as I am by the policies laid down by our Department. The apparent difference in policy lies in the fact that the OWI has felt it desirable in the main to encourage or recognize movements of this kind on the ground that they are anti-Fascist; the Department has felt that in general anti-Fascist sentiment should be steered through the medium of the United States Government, rather than through separate race groups, since the latter commonly raise nationalist controversies and are always fraught with the danger of international complications."[128]

Poole adopted a tone similar to Berle's, but he differed more pointedly to assert that the "content of the issues" that exorcize the foreign-language community "are foreign political and therefore tie in with American foreign policy in a primary way." He agreed that "the public interest calls for a frank and full exchange of information among the four agencies principally concerned" but was certain the "closer collaboration we now [have] in view" will accomplish that.[129]

When the Croatian Congress (which had sparked this debate) took place, it did so without the kind of government participation that had characterized ethnic gatherings in the past. Yet according to the FNB, the delegates appeared to follow Cranston's admonitions. The meeting was "markedly pro-Russian" but avoided "the extremes of Croatian separatism on the one hand and overweening Communist orientation on the other." Speakers celebrated the Partisans, were all "strongly pro-Slav," and often mentioned "the debt of Slavs to Russia," but there was no "direct attack on Mihailovich." Adamic, contrary to expectations, did not attend. Šubašić and Kosanović were very visible, but the delegates laughingly dismissed Šubašić's plan to send a cable to the king reminding him of his duty to promote Yugoslav unity. As a result, Šubašić now doubted that he had authorization to accept the king's invitation to journey to London for consultations on Croatian issues. The resolutions adopted at the meeting asked the United States to take action against "disunity campaigns"; condemned those Yugoslav officials who worked "against Yugoslav unity"; and endorsed the "union of Serbs, Slovenes, and Croats" into a single Yugoslav state. The congress created a permanent organization, the National Council of American Croats, with Croatian-born violinist Zlatko Baloković as president and Butkovich as one of the vice-presidents.[130] Despite Šubašić's concerns, many Croats considered the election of Baloković to be a victory for Šubašić; Baloković had so little political experience that he seemed likely to simply follow Šubašić's orders.[131] FNB analysts also commented on Šubašić's "skillful political guidance," which had made the congress "an expression of opposition to Greater Serbianism."[132]

In late February, the Berle committee, perhaps in response to the rancor that its earlier decision had caused, amended its request for statements of "jurisdiction and interests" and agreed to allow the representatives from each agency to simply ask their superiors for a description of their "functions, activities and programs." A similar request would be made to agencies not on the committee but with an interest in foreign nationalities issues. The letter dispatched asking for this information reflected the victory of Berle and Poole in the earlier skirmish with Cranston by stating that Berle served as ex officio chairman of the committee because all of the activities of government agencies in the foreign nationalities field "have a direct effect upon the foreign relations of the United States or may be affected by the foreign policies of the United States." For this reason, the committee considered the State Department to "occupy an important position in this field." The full committee also directed the subcommittee to draft a new statement of policy, using the State Department's press release of December 10, 1941, as a guide.[133]

It fell to Poole and Cranston to "draft a statement of attitude on the part of U.S. government towards foreign political situations in the U.S.," a development Poole welcomed as an opportunity for the two "to get things started in right direction."[134] In their deliberations, which also featured continued attempts to clarify each agency's role and responsibility, Poole advised Cranston, as he had Smith, that in a democracy, "division and conflict, so far as it is peaceful," was not an issue. The question was how to keep this "essence of democracy . . . within measure" and how to maintain "unity . . . in the conduct of the foreign relations of the United States" so that the country "can still be enabled to appear and act upon the international scene as a single and not a divided personality." The answer, Poole reasoned with consistency, was that the Department of State fixed "the lines of American foreign policy"; the Department of Justice administered laws designed "for the internal security of the country"; the Office of War Information distributed information, built up morale, and "through its Foreign Language Division" channeled "into established lines of policy the foreign political dynamisms to be found within the population." The three must fully exchange information and coordinate policy and build upon the "good beginning" of the IDCFNP.[135]

By mid-March, the two men had agreed on a statement of responsibility for each agency and on another regarding foreign nationalities and foreign politics. The first expanded on the definition of the duties assigned to the OWI by Poole but included the FNB as well. The OWI, through its Foreign Language Division, had responsibility for "clarifying the origin, issues and progress of the war for aliens resident in the United States, foreign born citizens, and those among first and second generation Americans who speak foreign languages or who maintain ties and interests in their lands of origin, and to gain their maximum support for and participation in the war effort." The FNB, using its contacts with foreign nationality groups, would gather information on "political attitudes and trends among them" and report its findings to other relevant agencies. The second statement explained that in order to protect the free exchange of ideas while safeguarding American security, the government expected alien diplomats to understand that they "must carefully refrain from any intrusion whatever into the political life of the United States." American citizens had an obligation to "maintain at all times an American outlook as distinguished from an outlook shaped instead by national interests that are inimical to the best interests of the United States." Accordingly, associations designed to "promote particular national interests abroad" should be lead by "non-citizens" and must conform to the restrictions required by the government.[136]

Cranston sent these drafts to Berle and Smith, with the suggestion that the second, "once agreed upon, be officially released and that its substance be reiterated in appropriate public utterances."[137] Although two or more of the subcommittee members met for lunch during the ensuing weeks, there is no record of any meeting of the IDCFNP after that of March 17, where Cranston reported the completion of the drafts.[138] In late April, Poole sent his slightly different draft of the foreign nationalities statement to Smith, saying that he could not agree to the copy sent by Cranston "without some further adjustments." He continued: "As I said to Alan, I am particularly fearful of any attempt to make a statement of this kind the vehicle for an expression of American foreign policy in general."[139]

Berle apparently agreed: he had, on March 23 dispatched a confidential report on "free movements" to all diplomatic and consular officers in other American republics, Canada, Egypt, Algeria, and England. The report reiterated the existing policy and outlined "recent developments" in certain cases. Berle encouraged diplomatic posts to continue to send information to Washington on the development of free movements but cautioned them that while "there is no objection to displaying a friendly interest in such movements and their leaders," nothing should be done "which might be construed as an indication of support, even though unofficial." The experience of the past year had shown that free movements had little practical use because of divisions within the groups themselves and made little contribution to the war effort. The "personal ambitions" and postwar political agendas of the leaders of free movements caused them to promote their own interests rather than the "broader national unity of American citizens of foreign descent." Berle warned that two trends within free movements bore special notice: attempts to form a "union of all factions within each nationality group" and to join all free movements into "one over-all anti-Axis union." In nearly every case, the impetus for both came from Communist organizations or leaders and could be traced back to August or September of 1942, indicating that all of these attempts may have been directed "from a common source." The first tactic enjoyed the most success with the American Slav Congress, which "strictly speaking was not a 'free movement' but because of its utilization by similar elements, and its tendency to become a political pressure group, is included in this report." The ASC was said to be permeated with Communist elements and to have "promoted the holding of meetings by American citizen groups, particularly of Yugoslav descent, which have taken sides in the controversy raging over General Mihailovitch and the partisans, and for and against a post-war united Yugoslavia."[140] The other groups Berle highlighted were genuine free movements with varying degrees of left-wing influence, but none of them involved an American ally, as was the case with the supposed sponsoring agency of the ASC.

* * *

After more than eighteen months of belligerency, the issues facing the agencies involved with foreign nationalities had become even more intractable. The Yugoslav government-in-exile could not heal the divisions among Yugoslavs, and the Allies could not control the Yugoslav government. By the spring of 1943, the foreign policy aspects of the Yugoslav-American conflict and of the issue of free movements in general led to the apparent triumph of the State Department's policy of control over the attempt to promote and manipulate ethnic activity favored by the OWI. Cranston had failed to effectively channel the ethnics' behavior, and the contacts he had with ethnic organizations had embroiled him in controversy. Berle was able to take advantage of this, and of the clear connection between American foreign policy and free movements, to simply reiterate the department's objections to the involvement of American citizens in foreign political intrigue. His circular dispatch also reflected his own objections to ethnic activity and his penchant, common to others in the field, to see members of foreign nationalities groups as dupes, particularly of left-wing entities. The IDCFNP, having achieved little coordination, ceased to function but Berle had gained his main objective: the State Department had prevailed over its rivals and succeeded in defining American policy. However, the favoritism shown by the United States to one faction in the Yugoslav dispute, which increased the agitation on the other side, rendered that victory of little practical consequence.

4

To Bully a Conscientious Little Paper

By the spring of 1943, Alan Cranston's policy of encouraging ethnic activity designed to unify diverse groups had been supplanted by Adolf A. Berle's strategy of controlling and discouraging "race movements." Yet neither approach had a history of significantly reducing the divisions within America's ethnic communities. The Yugoslavs remained a case in point. A new organization, the United Committee of South-Slavic Americans, was formed in the summer of 1943, but its pro-Partisan stance enraged the Serbs and seemed to confirm Berle's fears of Communist influence in America's foreign nationalities communities. The administration's inability to control ethnic divisions within the United States was matched by the Allies' failure to convince the Yugoslav-Government-In-Exile (YGIE) to free itself of dominance by the Serbs. The British campaigned for a change in Allied policy that would force King Peter's hand, with the United States as a reluctant participant. At home the Congress reduced the options available to deal with ethnic tensions by severely curtailing the activities of the Office of War Information (OWI). The Justice Department also eliminated the Special War Policies Unit (SWPU), and although the Foreign Agents Registration Act (FARA) unit survived, it had fewer resources at its command. However, the FARA unit and the Foreign Nationalities Branch (FNB) soon moved to the forefront of foreign nationalities policy as internal security and foreign policy concerns intensified.

* * *

In early April 1943, King Peter spoke again of the need for unity among the resistance forces fighting in Yugoslavia, but his own cabinet remained divided, afflicted by what the British described as "the flounderings of the Yugoslav Government." The British believed the king was "intelligent and mentally active," but he lacked an "able Prime Minister or even an able adviser" and thus was unable to cope "with the complicated jealousies within his Government."[1]

Ivan Šubašić, who had delayed his trip until after the Croatian Congress, arrived in London for consultations that same month. Konstantin Fotić was there as well, but Ambassador A. J. Drexel Biddle advised Washington that their arrivals had not produced the controversy he had anticipated. The Ban had made "a special effort to appear reasonable," although the king observed that Šubašić's diabetes caused his behavior to be erratic and "consequently he was apt to antagonize on a given day the very people [whom] he might have brought round to his views on the previous day." Fotić quickly returned to Washington with instructions that he absent himself from the Serb National Federation (SNF) meeting planned for later in the year and that he advise Bishop Dionisije to refrain from any provocative behavior. Biddle reported that both the king and the prime minister had been concerned over Šubašić's presence at the Croatian Congress and they did not want the government identified with any additional controversies.[2]

Yet no substantive change in the embassy's policies occurred. In Fotić's absence, Yugoslav *chargé d'affaires* Vladimir Rybar complained to Berle that broadcasts by members of the Yugoslav Information Service had been censored and that the effect was "to prevent the Yugoslav broadcaster from setting out the nationalist Yugoslav view," which "left the way open to the so-called Partisans, supported by the Communists." The list of statements struck by the censor included the claim that Draža Mihailović had the "full confidence" of the Yugoslav people; and that anyone who speaks against Mihailović is "Hitler's agent."[3] Fotić pursued Vladimir Rybar's complaint upon his return from London, vowing "to make an issue of the Yugoslav policy in British and American radio propaganda." He would appeal to President Roosevelt, if necessary, "not to let Government agencies come under the influence of . . . Croat or radical ideologists who are aligned against Michailovich." In a rather indiscreet conversation with a newsman, Fotić said that Serbs would never accept the Croats again as "partners" unless they "expiated their crimes."[4]

Fotić had no reason to fear a change in American policy. As Berle told De-Witt Clinton Poole, "the problems of Central and Eastern Europe could not be worked out on the basis of current agitation among political refugees." The United States had to have "as free a hand as possible" and to take as much account as possible "for the wishes of the peoples and the realities of the situation as these might be disclosed when we came to have direct access to the situation." Showing a grasp of both practical realities and Roosevelt's outlook, Berle said that for the time being, the "United States must be clear of commitments" while maintaining the "principles of the Atlantic Charter" and assisting the Soviets "up to the gullet."[5]

Adherents to the Partisan cause had a different view of American policy. Louis Adamic told Poole in May that, in conversations with a variety of Slovene and Yugoslav-American editors and community leaders—virtually all of whom were "traditional democrats"—he had encountered a high level of criticism of American foreign policy. Specifically, the people to whom he spoke had asked who was behind the anti-Partisan sentiment of the OWI and why Berle seemed so sympathetic to those with "reactionary purposes." Adamic claimed that a Yugoslav-American radio broadcaster in San Francisco had been told by the OWI "not to boost the Partisans" because of a complaint made against the broadcaster by Ambassador Fotić. Bringing party politics into the equation, Adamic warned that at first the criticism he described had been directed at the State Department, but now the target was the president; Slovene-Americans were usually Democratic but their support for that party might be diminishing.[6] The FNB's analysis of the Slovenian press confirmed that "the majority of Slovenian opinion does not support the London government in exile."[7]

Poole interviewed Šubašić after he returned from his ten-week stay in London and portrayed him as "a man bewildered" by what Šubašić described as "the spectacle of a group of ministers deliberately destroying the country and the government which they ostensibly serve."[8] Although the king seemed to Šubašić to be sympathetic to the "Yugoslav idea," he would not accede to Šubašić's request for access to his budget as governor of Croatia, explaining that the Serb members of his cabinet had threatened to resign if he distributed the funds. While these conversations with the king were cordial, Šubašić's talks with Prime Minister Jovanović had been "candid and bitter." When the prime minister assured Šubašić that he had ordered Fotić to avoid any support for the Greater Serbia campaign, Šubašić refuted him with evidence of continued attacks by *Amerikanski Srbobran* on a united Yugoslavia. To Poole,

Šubašić held out only the hope that the British would support the king in a reorganization of the cabinet.[9]

Poole coupled this with an account of a conversation a "friend" of the FNB had with Fotić; he feared that the two interviews, taken together, presented the "picture of approaching crisis." Fotić, with his own interpretation of the stalemate Šubašić described, claimed that a "Croatian plot" existed, which "with the aid of British official pressure" was designed to cause a change within the YGIE that would result in Croatian dominance. If that failed, the two Croatian ministers in the United States would resign and become part of an opposition government, a "so-called Yugoslav National Committee" with Šubašić as its representative in the United States. Fotić was preparing a memorandum on this to present to Sumner Welles in which he would emphasize "the ill effects which such a crisis, befalling at this time, might have among Yugoslav elements in the United States." When asked by his interlocutor about the "chauvinistic editorial policy" in *Amerikanski Srbobran*, he responded with the usual catalog of charges against the Croats. However, Fotic also seemed to confirm his guilt by hinting that he had hidden from the editors of *Amerikanski Srbobran* even more "devastating evidence against the Croat Ustashis."[10]

The anticipated crisis occurred when a variety of issues, including British pressure on the YGIE to relocate to Cairo; the Yugoslav cabinet's objections to the king's proposed marriage to a Greek princess; and the still unresolved quarrels between Serbs and Croats led to the resignation of Slobodan Jovanović in mid-June. The Croat members of the government then pressed their demand that one of their own serve as ambassador in either London or Washington and that the king approve the budget for Šubašić as governor of Croatia. The new prime minister, the elderly and pro-Serb Milos Trifunović, whose government would last for less than two months, did little but issue a cabinet statement that called for the restoration of a united Yugoslavia; the reversion of those areas "which have a purely Yugoslav character" but which were currently under "foreign and hostile domination;" and "a more or less federal solution which would permit the Serbs, Croats, and Slovenes to collaborate with each other in the realization of their common political aims without renouncing however their ethnic individuality."[11] The king followed this with a broadcast praising the efforts of all resistance fighters, without regard to the "temporary name" under which they were fighting.[12]

The British, increasingly frustrated by the YGIE's failure to take substantive measures to produce an effective and unified resistance, decided to increase the amount of aid furnished to the Partisans. The British continued to aid the Chetniks, on the condition that the arms supplied should be used only to fight the Axis; the Partisans were also asked to agree to take no action against the Chetniks except in self-defense. The British liaison officers stationed with each group would make sure that these conditions were met.[13] The British also pressed for the removal of Fotić, but the United States continued to prefer the status quo. To Cavendish Cannon, the rumored replacement was so "partisan Croatian" that "it would be a calamity to have him as Ambassador." According to Cordell Hull, Fotić was the only "element of continuity of pre-1941 Yugoslavia in the Government" in addition to being "probably the most capable man in the Yugoslav Government" at that time.[14] In the end, no change occurred. The new Yugoslav prime minister, diplomat Dr. Božidar Purić, "a schoolmate and intimate friend" of Fotić's, allied himself with the Greater Serbia faction, which remained the main force in the government. Mihailović and Fotić retained their positions.[15]

* * *

In the United States, press accounts about the Partisans began to replace the usual publicity about the Chetniks, much to the dismay of the State Department's Division of European Affairs. In 1943, Adamic published a book, *My Native Land,* which clearly favored the Partisans and reviewed the history of the war in Yugoslavia as a crusade by the young to create a new world. He wrote of Mihailović with more sadness than anger, as a man of the past who had become a dupe of the British and the unprincipled men who surrounded the "boy-king" in London. He acknowledged Tito's Communism but portrayed him essentially as a heroic dissident, challenging the reactionaries in power. Adamic's attacks on Fotić were bitter and intemperate; in a chapter entitled "The Yugoslav Nightmare Invades America," he held Fotić responsible for the ethnic turmoil in the United States.[16]

In the June 1943 issue of *Fortune,* Stoyan Pribichevich, whose views the FNB had solicited the year before, also published an article favorable to the Partisans. Acting European Affairs Division head Ray Atherton criticized it as an example of the "line" followed by both Pribichevich and Adamic: that of "energetic opposition" to the YGIE. Although this piece was "rather less violent" than earlier articles, it featured the usual attacks on the king's "hopelessly ineffectual" government and credited "without reservation" reports about the Partisans "[that] most people studying this question with real objectivity consider grossly exaggerated." After extensive discussions in the spring of 1943, the division concluded that although the effect of publications highlighting the clashes between rival resistance groups "would be deplorable" because they would leave the "lasting impression . . . that the Yugoslavs are fighting each other," the State Department "could not properly request that they be withheld from publication." Adamic, who was "in the forefront of the Yugoslav disputes," was a particular problem because he had "copiously contributed to the disunity in the Yugoslav element." Atherton further discredited Adamic by repeating charges that his critics in the Slovene community were circulating: that his activities appeared rooted in "great personal ambitions" and his two-way passage concept had attracted "chiefly . . . those who think they could make something out of it personally."[17]

Nonetheless, Adamic continued to play a major role in Yugoslav-American affairs. By the summer of 1943, discussions in the Croat and Slovene segments of the Yugoslav-American community concerning the formation of a new, all-Yugoslav group came to fruition. Adamic, Zlatko Baloković, exiled Yugoslav politicians Šubašić and Kosanović, and the leaders of various Serb, Croat, and Slovene groups formed what eventually became known as the United Committee of South-Slavic Americans (UCSSA). Initially comprised of the Serbian Vidovdan Council, the Slovenian American Council, and the Council of Americans of Croatian Descent, the new organization's stated intent was not to divide further the Yugoslav-American community but to unite all Yugoslav-Americans in defense of the Yugoslav state and to counter what its leaders saw as the divisive propaganda of the pan-Serbs.[18]

Initially, they had trouble uniting themselves. During the organizing meeting in June, the Croats present objected to the original name proposed, The United Committee of American Jugoslavs, on the grounds that "almost no Croat Americans" thought of themselves as "Jugoslav Americans," and such a title therefore would insure "no Croat following." The group then became known as the United Committee of Serbs, Croats, and Slovenes, although that changed within a few weeks to the UCSSA after Bulgarian and Macedonian groups had been invited to join.[19]

Poole compiled a sketch of Baloković, the self-described "Paderewski of Yugoslavia," who viewed himself "as a spokesman for Slav-Americans and even for the Slavs of Europe." Baloković championed the reorganization of the YGIE, a postwar federated Yugoslavia, and "a Yugoslav understanding with the USSR." He had contempt for Mihailović "for temporizing with the fat politicians in London" and praised the efforts of the Partisans, but his associates did not "as a rule hold too high an opinion of [Baloković's] political sagacity." Adamic, "a person of some consequence," had described Baloković as "a thin neurotic egotistical person who likes to talk a great deal and who does." Others had expressed the fear that the Communists "might find him readily adaptable as a front." Poole surmised that he would exercise influence, however, because of his artistic reputation, his considerable fortune, and his close ties to Šubašić.[20]

Neither Šubašić nor Kosanović attended the United Committee's organizing conference, which the FNB attributed to a letter dispatched by Fotić "conveying what the Ambassador described as State Department disapproval of their participation at American meetings and gatherings." Adamic had been absent as well but agreed to accept the presidency of the committee.[21] Whatever the actual cause of his absence, Šubašić later told Poole that when Croatian-Americans had asked his advice about the resolution passed by the Croatian Congress in February, which called for "the creation of a joint committee of all Yugoslav groups in America," he had stressed his status in the United States "as a guest." He advised that the Croatians meet with United States officials to ascertain that their plans were in accord "with the interests of the American nation and its official policy."[22]

This was not the case. When the UCSSA held its first official meeting in early August in Cleveland, delegates sent greetings to the Partisans and dispatched a telegram to President Roosevelt supporting Yugoslavia's claim to the land in dispute between Yugoslavia and Italy.[23] In the first issue of its *Bulletin,* edited by Adamic, the UCSSA condemned "those ministers in the Yugoslav Government in London, past and present, and those officials of the Yugoslav embassy in Washington, who have been active in divisive propaganda" designed to achieve "undemocratic ends in Yugoslavia." The United Committee would "demand and continue to demand that the Great Powers make it possible for the Balkan peoples to become masters of their own countries and their economic and cultural life." To those ends the committee would support the war effort and cooperate with the OWI and the State Department. However, the group would also strive to inform Americans about the significance of problems in the Balkans and to secure the support of the American government for the Partisans.[24] A later edition of this same publication condemned the Trifunović government by stating, "It couldn't possibly be worse." The king's rule was a "dictatorship" and the premier was "reactionary, . . . cynical, opportunistic"; the entire group "represents nobody" and answers only to "young Peter."[25] Without a change in Allied policy, the reputations of Great Britain and the United States as defenders "of constitutional democracy in Europe will disappear" and the people of Yugoslavia "may conceivably turn from fighting the Axis to fight their invading government."[26]

The State Department saw little positive value—and a measure of ideo-logical danger—in the United Committee. As Cannon observed, the group "may appear to be a step in the right direction," but its "undercover" intent "is to direct the movement along Leftist lines, in opposition not only to the Yugoslav National Defense Council and the Serbian National Federation but also to three fairly active Croatian organizations." In short, "this looks like just one more militant organization in the American-Yugoslav field, under cover of a pretended unifying group." In its resolutions, Cannon noted, the group made no mention of support for Mihailović but voiced "its admi-ration of the Partisans and the Army of Liberation." Baloković had been "rather violent in his denunciation of the Yugoslav government in exile and the Embassy in Washington," but Adamic, about whom American officials knew a good deal, appeared to be the main force. Other delegates to the or-ganizing conference included journalists with ties to the communist press and Butkovich, "who recently caused some excitement by his ... broadcast, organized by the OWI, in which, curiously, he took a line for Croatian sepa-ratism which was about as extreme as the Serbianism ... he and others of this group pretend so piously to deplore."[27]

The FNB report on the UCSSA had more balance and context. The agency characterized this "South Slav *'front populaire'* ... as a counterpart of and support for the popular front which the Partisans are deemed by these Ameri-cans of South Slav extraction to stand for in the homeland." The UCSSA aimed to secure American support for Tito's National Anti-Fascist Liberation Council, formed the year before in Bihac, which had a liaison with Allied military forces. Adamic admitted freely that Tito was a Communist but in-sisted that many of his followers were simply leftists. In its press release, the UCSSA expressed its commitment to the unity of all South-Slavic Americans and its support for the war efforts of the United Nations and for democ-racy and self-determination in the Balkans. The Committee also pledged to work with government agencies such as the Office of War Information, the Office of Strategic Services, and the State Department, and to support the president. Nonetheless, the FNB expected the Communist press to give the new organization a great deal of publicity.[28]

*   *   *

With the creation of the UCSSA, the need for policymakers to find more effec-tive instruments to curb ethnic tensions seemed even more urgent. Attempts by the Justice Department to use FARA to rein in the Serbs continued to find little success as the FBI's field offices failed to substantiate any violations by the Serbian National Defense Council (SNDC) of either the Registration Act or the Voorhis Act.[29] Other agencies involved in foreign nationalities issues provided information to assist with a FARA prosecution, but much of the evidence, since it originated with parties to the dispute, was of questionable value. In early May 1943, Poole sent a letter to Lawrence M. C. Smith and to Cannon—"but to no one else"—enclosing a paper he had received from Ante Pavelić. Pavelić, whose radio broadcast the year before had enraged Fotić, detailed a number of conversations the ambassador was supposed to have had since his return from London in April with a variety of Serbs and Serbian-Americans. In these discussions, Fotić had spoken of his opposition to British demands for a unity government because this would spell "the end of Serbianism." When Fotić met with the editors and contributors of *Amerikanski Srbobran,* one source reported to Pavelić that Fotić had urged moderation; another than Fotić had instructed those present to intensify the paper's campaign against the Croats. In any case, Pavelić advised that the "Serbian campaign will continue, probably will be pursued with more bitterness." Poole, with his usual balance, concluded that *Amerikanski Srbobran* represented "about the sorest spot at present in the foreign nationalities field," and while "it would appear that in effect the Foreign Agents Registration Act is being violated . . . diplomatic questions intrude as well." However, since Kosanović claimed to have positive proof that Fotić paid members of the staff of *Amerikanski Srbobran,* Poole offered to pursue this if the State Department or the Justice Department wished him to do so.[30]

The involvement of Pavelić and Kosanović as sources of information against the Serbs highlighted the foreign policy implications of the Yugoslav-American controversy. By June, the FNB reported that the Greater Serbia agitation had "taken on a definiteness and determination which are capable, if only by their untimeliness, of causing reactions harmful to American and United Nations interests." The spokesmen for the Greater Serbia cause had begun to enumerate "the territories which they believe should go into the making of the new Serbia," and to declare that any union with the Croats, who were depicted as fascists and murderers, was impossible. Their attachment to Mihailović, as a Serb fighting the Communist Partisans, had "put them into a position that [was] not only anti-Partisan but also anti-Soviet Union." Since January, the propaganda in the paper, using religious differences and the prewar demands of the Croats for more autonomy, had emphasized "the impossibility of reconstituting Yugoslavia . . . and the consequent necessity and justification for a post-war Greater Serbia" under the rule of King Peter. Attacks on Šubašić and other former ministers in New York were also features of this phase of the campaign, along with new and refashioned atrocity accounts.[31]

As the FNB filed these reports, FARA section attorney Charlotte Slavitt and staff analyst Alexander Dragnich were also studying the Serbs, and their conclusions resembled those drawn by Poole and the FNB. Evidence of legal culpability in the *Amerikanski Srbobran* case consisted either of charges made by pro-Yugoslav papers, or *Srbobran's* own statement, following Fotić's return from London, that the anti-Croat documents it printed had recently come to it from "the most trustworthy sources." Without more proof than that on hand, Dragnich and Slavitt agreed the government could make a convincing case against neither a federation with an excellent record as a benefit society nor a paper that had consistently supported the war effort of the United Nations and the Red Cross and campaigned for war bond purchases.[32] Hoover, meanwhile, added a more political slant to their assessment: although he identified the paper as "outspokenly pro-Serbian and anti-Croat," it also was "anti-Communist" and "vigorous in its efforts to bring about the establishment of a strong and independent Serbia and to eliminate the possibility of the Communist control of the country of Yugoslavia."[33]

After reviewing the material on hand, FARA unit chief James R. Sharp agreed that *Srbobran* waged a "vociferous pan-Serbian campaign for a separatist and independent Serbia," relying heavily on documents apparently created in Axis-occupied Yugoslavia and smuggled out of the country. This "propaganda" featured attacks on every entity except the Serbs, with special emphasis on the "treachery" of the Croats, and it affected more than a million people in the United States of Croatian extraction. Available evidence pointed "fairly clearly" to Fotić, Jovan Dučić, and Bishop Dionisije as the guiding forces behind *Amerikanski Srbobran*. However, "direct proof of agency of *Srbobran* for these foreign principles [was] at best circumstantial, although proof of collaboration with them [was] unquestioned."[34]

A few days after Sharp drew these conclusions, Slavitt submitted a "Summary of Evidence" memo on the Serbs, even though she had not completed her "principle memorandum" of the case against *Amerikanski Srbobran*. She also attached a historical summary, prepared with Dragnich, which, while factually accurate, downplayed the emotional and irrational elements of ethnicity in order to emphasize the political dimension of the Serb-Croat conflict. She and Dragnich contended that much of the interwar political conflict in Yugoslavia centered on "a common struggle for democracy by all the people against the ruling clique," with Maček's Peasant Party working to unite all of the ethnic groups against the dictatorial policies of the central government. In the United States, "self-seeking Croats and Serbs" had de-picted this conflict as "a nationalist struggle of one people against another." Most of the South Slavs in the United States had so little experience living together that they "were ready to believe the worst concerning each other." The representatives attached to the Royal Yugoslav Ministerial Mission in New York all supported the Yugoslav ideal and were members of political parties that historically had opposed the dictatorial policies of the govern-ment. The government in London, though divided, embraced the Greater Serbia position.[35]

Although Dragnich had collaborated on this historical summary, he dis-agreed with the conclusions Slavitt drew in the evidence summary that ac-companied it, particularly her contention that the material in *Amerikanski Srbobran* was *designed* to incite conflict between Serbs and Croats in the United States. To Dragnich, "the intent is not to provoke Serbs in this coun-try against Croats in this country, even though it may result in that, but rather to get the Serbs sufficiently interested to help the Serbs in Serbia at-tain a separate and an independent state." The YGIE was divided, but Fotić had the support of the king; for Dragnich, this raised the question of which government was instructing Fotić or supporting the *Amerikanski Srbobran*. He also objected to Slavitt's charge that *Amerikanski Srbobran* compromised American unity by inducing the "allegiance of Serbs to Serbia." The paper sought "to get Serbs to think of themselves as Serbs and not as Yugoslavs"; the effect might have been "detrimental to American loyalty," but that was not the aim of the policy.[36]

While these debates continued, the Foreign Language Division announced that Elmer Davis had charged *Amerikanski Srbobran* with being largely re-sponsible for the conflict between Serbian and Croatian Americans. Davis delivered his "indictment" of the paper after SNF president Samuel Werlinich wrote to him on the eve of the federation's national meeting, reminding Davis that he alone of the SNF leadership had been willing to sign the pledge of unity in Washington in September 1942. Since he was under criticism for this, he asked Davis for the government's current views on the policies followed by the SNF and its paper. Davis responded with a review of the concern with which the government had monitored the policies of *Amerikanski Srbobran*, with its "violent attacks upon all peoples of Croatian extraction and their clergy, its strong anti-Catholic articles, and its veiled efforts to defend the Quisling Nedich who supports the Nazi regime in Serbia [which often has] the effect of aiding the Nazi campaigns of intolerance and race hate, and are damaging to the American war effort." The resolution Werlinich signed had obligated him to follow the policies of the American government "in working for unity of all Americans, regardless of national or racial extraction." Davis was confident that Werlinich's actions "represented the spirit of the American Serbs" who had elected him to lead them. The "unconquered people of Yugoslavia" have made great contributions to the war effort, and any domestic "strife between these groups endangers the common cause." Anything that Werlinich can do, such as "the stand" he had taken in the past by signing the unity pledge, "is greatly appreciated."[37]

Although Davis's action seemed typical of the more aggressive tactics favored by the OWI, it actually represented another example of the consensus that existed on the policy to be followed with the Serbs. Davis had acted in concert with his peers, circulating his letter of condemnation in advance to all of the agencies involved in foreign nationalities issues in order to secure their approval, which all had given.[38] However, the broadside did not have the effect Davis had intended. Ruth Mitchell, as honorary chairman of the SNDC, immediately denounced Davis for his "simply outrageous" letter that had been filled with what she called "thinly disguised threats" designed "to bully a conscientious little paper" run by "as loyal Americans as exist." She then proceeded, unconsciously, to demonstrate what Davis had so objected to by charging, "There is hardly a Croat-American who has not a relative fighting bitterly *against* us." Yet the OWI remained "*strictly pro-Croat,*" and FLD head Cranston identified "himself with the Serb slanderers." Such policies aided the Germans and weakened Mihailović, "their arch-enemy in the Balkans." The OWI had fallen "for the great Croat hoax of the 'partisans,' who in fact fought almost exclusively against our Allies, the Serbs." Mitchell was especially critical of the ties between Cranston and Louis Adamic, "a proclaimed pro-Croat and Serb-hater" who "obviously aspires to control the Balkans as a Croat-Communist Commissar." In short, it was Davis and his organization "who have aided and abetted the German game in America" not *Amerikanski Srbobran*.[39]

In his response, Davis reminded Mitchell that the United States recognized the government of Yugoslavia and not that of Greater Serbia, only to have her fire off a telegram claiming the Serbs did not use that term to denote "forcible inclusions of unwilling people" and that its use was "in itself enemy propaganda."[40] The exchange ended with Davis's denying all of Mitchell's charges of bias "with no confidence that it will persuade you, but a confidence that it can be supported by the record." His office reflected the policy of the United States, which was that Yugoslavia be reunited and that all crimes be punished. Adamic, who was "neither a Croat nor a Communist," did not guide the policy of the OWI and "would be greatly surprised if he heard that [he did]." Davis restated his commitment to have all Yugoslavs work together in a common effort.[41]

This plea had little effect as both sides continued to complain about the other to officials they perceived as sympathetic. Fotić soon told Berle that a Communist paper was using Davis's letter to campaign for communist delegates, which the paper referred to as "Roosevelt delegates," to the convention of the SNF, but the ambassador received little comfort in exchange. Berle observed that the papers in question were American, "printed by and for American citizens." This demonstrated how dangerous it was "to involve American citizens in controversies based on foreign political disputes" and why the United States objected to "foreign influence exerted on Americans of European extraction, and in a foreign language."[42]

At virtually the same moment, the "very earnestly pro-Yugoslav" Kosanović contacted Poole concerning the "possible participation" of American officials in the SNDC Congress, Kosanović cautioned that it "would be most undesirable" for any American official to be present at the meeting, which he also viewed as unrepresentative since it had only two thousand members out of an American Serb population of more than one hundred thousand. He also alerted Poole to the Serbian church's publication of *The Sufferings of the Serbian People,* which he claimed was a "repetition" of all of the atrocity stories published by *Amerikanski Srbobran* in the past. Since an American cleric had written the preface, Kosanović feared that Yugoslav-Americans would think the book had "an official American seal of approval."[43]

When the SNDC met in Chicago at the end of June, the administration kept its distance from the event. The SNDC sent a message of greeting to the White House and a request for aid to Mihailović on the occasion of Vidovdan, but Cannon decided that since "the organization has repeatedly rejected all advice from official quarters to cooperate in the war effort, this telegram is not acknowledged."[44] Mitchell and Werlinich attended but Fotić did not, and the FNB speculated that he did not appear to be still associated with the group. Mitchell delivered the main address to the assembled three thousand delegates, wearing what she said was a Chetnik uniform, and during her talk, released her correspondence with Davis. As honorary chairman of the council, she also read a proclamation denouncing the Yugoslav Information Center in New York and the YGIE, the latter for not properly representing the Serbs. Given these events, the FNB thought it likely that Werlinich would be ousted by "extremists" at the SNF elections in September.[45]

Werlinich's position proved to be as precarious as the FNB predicted. In a July board meeting of the SNF, Werlinich defended his correspondence with Davis by saying that he had no idea the OWI would make it public. Although the board accepted this, its members also criticized him for signing the unity pledge in September 1942, and the majority insisted, over Werlinich's objections, on sending a delegation to Washington to explain the Greater Serbia cause. *Amerikanski Srbobran* later printed resolutions of the board that attacked OWI for "maligning, damaging, and insulting the Serb National Federation," and for "breach of promise" in publishing the Werlinich correspondence. Werlinich signed these resolutions but told the FNB that the more hard-line Louis Christopher would no doubt succeed him as head of the SNF and that the "pan-Serb clique" was keeping the issue of Davis's letter alive to insure their election victory.[46]

These developments caused Sharp to cast doubt on the efficacy of the Davis letter, which had had the effect of giving the "pro-Serb crowd," who used it "as a rallying point," even more power. Ruth Mitchell had been brought "to the forefront of the Greater Serbia campaign" and Werlinich seemed sure to be defeated in his bid for re-election. The controversy, Sharp pointed out, also seemed to have "brought the pro-Serb argument into the English-language press." On the positive side, he said, "There is only the feeling that the writing and publication of the letter may cause *Srbobran* to be somewhat more cautious in the future than it has been in the past" but that "cannot yet be estimated." In general, the letter had not accomplished its goals.[47]

Davis had also made the OWI a party to the ethnic dispute. An FBI intelligence survey of August 1943, which characterized the Serb-Croat dispute as one of "attendant polemics and verbal pyrotechnics," concluded that "neutral sources are inclined to believe, according to reports, that the OWI's allowing itself to be so naively drawn into the factional dispute between the Serbs, Croats and Communists on a partisan basis, has certainly done nothing to alleviate the explosive condition of disunity which exists among these groups and which condition has for some months past been a matter of some concern to various governmental agencies."[48]

The meeting at the State Department between the delegation from the SNDC and Loy Henderson, Chief of the European Division, and Cavendish Cannon, who supervised Balkan affairs in the division, seemed to bear out these criticisms. The encounter did not go well; the delegates had left behind "in a taxicab the memorial which they had proposed to submit" and had to promise to send another by mail. In addition, "Miss Mitchell ... talked without abatement," and despite a complaint from one of her own colleagues "still seemed to be unable to restrain herself." She finally took to "whispering in the ear of one of the State Department officials while the other members of the delegation endeavored to proceed with their presentation to the disengaged official." In any case, the "nub" of their presentation consisted of "a complaint against OWI."[49]

Foreign Nationalities Branch informants later revealed that the editors of *Amerikanski Srbobran* and the officers of the SNF actually were divided over their course of action. The federation feared that the government would move against the paper, and they were looking for a way to "extract" themselves from the position in which "the vituperative columns" of *Amerikanski Srbobran* had placed them. Support in the Serb-American community for *Amerikanski Srbobran* rested on the paper's appearing to have "government approval or at least non-interference," and they were anxious to retain that image. The SNF believed that Great Britain, anticipating a United States withdrawal from the area after the war, was shifting its policy to favor Russian power in the Balkans. The Serbs had decided to pursue a policy of exposing the Soviet threat and depicting the Serbs as crusaders "for democracy against Communism." A Greater Serbia thus would be depicted as "the sole Balkan military bulwark against Russian aspirations." The Serbs hoped this policy would find favor in Washington and relieve the pressure against them.[50]

It did not. After Bogdan Radica, a Croat who represented the Yugoslav Minister of Propaganda in New York, reported to Poole that the anti-Croat material appearing in *Amerikanski Srbobran* came to the paper from the Yugoslav press attaché in London, his claim became a new focus of the SWPU investigation. Chester Lane requested that the FBI obtain from the Office of Censorship information on "cables or other communications between" persons in Great Britain and the editors of the paper, as well as members and officers of the Executive Boards of SNF and the SNDC. He attached a list of the relevant names and requested that all be placed on "the National Watch List for a period of sixty days" and that any intercepts received be sent to him.[51]

In early August, Slavitt submitted a brief to Sharp of "new evidence" derived from conferences in New York with Kosanović, Šubašić, and Radica. These included the Yugoslav government budget promised by Kosanović to Poole, which listed the monies available to Fotić from open and confidential sources. Open sources showed that Fotić paid a monthly salary to a variety of people who wrote for the paper or for other publications or who served on the federation council. Such payments, according to Slavitt, rendered the recipients agents of a foreign principle under FARA. Fotić allegedly also had an "undisclosed confidential payroll" for which he refused to provide an accounting; Radica had seen this payroll list and could quote sums and names from it, but had no copy. All three also provided oral evidence of Fotić's pan-Serb activities, much of which they or others had presented before. Slavitt drew conclusions from these accounts, but her proof was questionable. Radica, for example, charged that Fotić rewrote embassy releases, substituting "Serbia" for "Yugoslavia," and removing criticism of Nedić. Slavitt then claimed that articles in *Amerikanski Srbobran* "extolling" Nedić as a savior of Serb lives followed these incidents, which she believed lent "substance" to the charges against Fotić. Proof of Mladan Trbuhovich's charge—that Fotić had ordered the paper and the federation to advocate a pan-Serb rather than a Yugoslav stance and that Fotić had orders from the YGIE to furnish the paper with anti-Croat documents—consisted of two pages of the so-called "Danckelmann Memorandum." Trbuhovich said Fotić had given this to Branko Pekich to publish; the text bore handwritten corrections that Slavitt thought "may yield further evidence." She also reviewed the activities of other individuals such as Ruth Mitchell, her claims regarding her involvement with the Chetniks, and her support of the Greater Serbia movement.[52]

Slavitt closed her report with a number of final recommendations. She advised that the Serbian National Defense Council be stripped of its permit to collect war relief, which would deny the council and the paper any claims to "official" support that might impress "gullible Yugoslavs." She also asserted that Ruth Mitchell should be required to register under FARA because of her own claims of "being a Chetnik under the command of General Mihailovitch." Slavitt was certain that enough evidence existed to make a decision on prosecution of the Serb organizations; her previous principle memorandum had recommended "a grand jury investigation as a means of obtaining further direct evidence for conviction." If prosecution was deemed inadvisable, she recommended that Mitchell, along with the officers and editor of the council, the federation, and *Amerikanski Srbobran* be called to Washington to discuss their liabilities under FARA. She also advised, "most respectfully," that if prosecution was not to occur, the case "be shelved except for merely cursory surveillance." All of the evidence available, she concluded, "is available now"; to "codify and re-codify information serves only an abortive end." There was enough information in hand to demonstrate violations of FARA; the leads Slavitt had furnished could, in a short time, "be developed into real evidence and proof adduced." With a veiled reference to Elmer Davis, she said that public rebukes of Mitchell and the other Greater Serbia "foreign agents" had produced only "defiance and vituperative abuse." Unless more official action were taken, their "future line" would simply continue that pattern "with accelerated virulence" as the opportunity for influencing the peace replaces the exigencies of war.[53]

Lane had anticipated Slavitt and invited Werlinich to Washington to discuss "the present controversies within the Yugoslav community."[54] He and Hoover also discussed the lines of investigation to be followed concerning Ruth Mitchell, with Lane suggesting that "her sources of income" be probed and that the bureau also attempt to secure information concerning her claim of imprisonment by the Germans.[55]

Before the meeting with Werlinich took place, Dragnich, looking at the Serb issue in a wider context, again dissented from the brief Slavitt had submitted. Her evidence, he said, derived from three men who had repeatedly "incurred the wrath of *Srbobran*" and from whom one could not "expect objectivity." He considered the only sound recommendation to be the revoking of the SNDC's war relief permit, which would undermine the council's prestige and "deprive it of the chief argument for existence." Prosecution, by contrast, "would yield small benefits" while providing the group with a nationwide platform. Much of what *Amerikanski Srbobran* printed was true, and it was easier to demonstrate that than to prove the council had violated FARA or that those violations "stood in the way of our war effort." Dragnich also saw little proof that "the foreign connections of this group [were] in anyway tied up with the Axis." Echoing Adamic's insertion of partisan political issues, he warned that anti–New Dealers in the press would use action against the Serbs to attack the administration or to try to prove that the intent was to aid the Communist forces in Yugoslavia. He offered the hopeful speculation that the individuals in question might be willing to register under FARA out of fear that action might be taken against them; if they did, that alone would carry out the intentions of the act: "to disclose to the public the source and substance of the propaganda which they are disseminating."[56]

When Lane and the FARA staff met with Werlinich, Sharp explained that the intention of the meeting was to discover "who *really* had been responsible for the policies of *Srbobran* in the course of the past year or so." Werlinich denied any knowledge of the FARA staff's prior meeting with Christopher and said the latter had never discussed it with the federation board. He also appeared "vague" when asked about Dučić or his role in the formation of the SNDC or Ruth Mitchell or *Amerikanski Srbobran*'s sources of information. While a majority of the delegates to the upcoming convention opposed him, Werlinich offered the hope that if a copy of FARA, along with a letter from Justice, were sent to the membership, they would understand that he "was not to blame for the attitude of the American Government" and that the government disapproved of *Amerikanski Srbobran*. Sharp agreed to furnish him a copy of the act, as he had for Christopher. Dragnich thought it fitting that the government would assist Werlinich with "whatever weapon we can give him" on the slim hope that he could still defeat Christopher and Pekich at the upcoming convention.[57]

Extremism continued to prevail, however, as *Amerikanski Srbobran* launched attacks on Davis and Cranston. The paper denied that the United States government objected to its policies and those of the SNF by insisting that the "temporary office" Davis headed did not speak for the other agencies involved and that it was his organization that was a source of concern. The ideology of the OWI was "totally strange" to that of American democracy, and Cranston was pressuring "other national, democratic groups" in addition to the Serbs, "to force them to collaborate with Communist and revolutionary elements." The paper also claimed that the resolution that the leaders of the SNF had refused to sign in September had consisted of a denunciation of Mihailović.[58]

This pattern continued at the SNF convention in September. According to the FBI's report of the meeting, Werlinich had support for his re-election from "the Liberals and the Communists," but the nationalist faction used the Communist endorsement, coupled with a charge that he was "conspiring with OWI" as proof of his betrayal of the Greater Serbia cause. Werlinich, "anticipating typical Balkan intrigue" came prepared to argue his case, but failed in his attempts to present correspondence from Davis and the Justice Department that indicated the government's continued disapproval of the policies of *Amerikanski Srbobran*. He lost his re-election bid by a vote of forty-one to sixty. The victors, president Louis Christopher and the continuing secretary Branko Pekich, were the primary fanatic proponents of the Greater Serbia philosophy. After the meetings, which featured speeches labeling all Croats and Croatian-Americans "as fascists and fascist-apologists," Christopher privately declared that the SNDC would now "play the principal role in Serbian politics in" the United States, and "Serb nationalist propaganda" would be even more evident. In a letter written a few days later and intercepted by the FBI, Pekich described the meeting as "strictly Serbian in the true sense of the word from the first day to the last." The politics of the Serbs had triumphed and "as a result of his wretched stand, Volinich was finally liquidated."[59]

During the convention, a controversy also erupted over the "ceremonial and symbolic christening" of a bomber named the "Serbian Chetnik," a move the FNB described as designed to illustrate "governmental and army" support for the Chetniks and "by extension, approval of the anti-Yugoslav, pro–Greater Serbia campaign" of the paper.[60] The agencies involved in this study again demonstrated their ability to cooperate in the face of this latest Serb provocation, but the failure of their efforts also revealed the lack of coordination on ethnic issues that prevailed throughout the government.

In the spring of 1943, Edward B. Hitchcock, chief of the Foreign Origin Section of the War Saving Staff of the Treasury, exchanged correspondence with Pekich on procedures for raising funds to purchase enough war bonds to name a bomber "Serbian Chetnik."[61] In June, Dragnich alerted his superiors to an announcement in *Amerikanski Srbobran* that Hitchcock was scheduled to speak at the Vidovdan celebration in Chicago. Given the "public rebuke" administered to *Amerikanski Srbobran* by Elmer Davis and the paper's attack on Davis's right to "define American policy," such an appearance by an American official "[did] not seem prudent."[62] After a conversation with Bradford Smith, acting chief of the FLD, who agreed that it would be "extremely unfortunate if the Treasury should appear to give official sanction to the Serbian National Defense Council," Lane took the matter to J. H. Houghteling of the War Services Staff of the Treasury.[63] Lane confided that the Justice Department "had under consideration the question of seeking an indictment of some of the officials of the Serbian National Federation, for violation of the Foreign Agents Registration Act" and advised that the appearance of Hitchcock would be an "embarrassment" to all of the agencies involved. Houghteling immediately agreed to cancel the appearance, regretting that he had no facilities "for securing information regarding the background of foreign language groups." After a discussion of how best to word the cancellation, Houghteling sent the following telegram to the Serbs: "Regret that due to conflict Mr. Hitchcock has been recalled to Washington and will be unable to address your meeting. Please tell your members that buying bonds is the best evidence of unity." As he told Lane, he chose the word "conflict" deliberately.[64]

In early July, Davis, mindful of Houghteling's comment about his lack of resources, requested of Berle that some mechanism be created by which the War Department and the Treasury Department would "clear any future dedication of airplanes with other agencies particularly interested in the political or general public aspects involved." Berle's double-edged reply assured Davis that the State Department was "aware of the use which various foreign language newspapers and associations have made of contacts with various agencies of the United States Government in claiming such contacts as proof that this Government favors their activities," and that the War Department and the Treasury Department would clear these matters with them in the future. He thanked Davis for his offer of assistance from the FLD in furnishing "evidence on the use of pseudo-patriotic activities designed to further foreign interests."[65]

The immediate Serb problem remained since the federation planned to christen the bomber at their annual convention. Cranston turned to the War Department, informing the relevant official that the federation "has followed certain policies not in the best interests of the war effort." The SNF was using the bomber campaign to "discount" the OWI's objections to their behavior by demonstrating that the "War Department, and thus the entire American government, actually approves" of their actions. Cranston said that it "would be extremely unfortunate if the organization was thus able to imply that it had American sponsorship for its present policies." Although the official assured Cranston that he would make certain that the bomber was not named after the Chetniks, the federation completed the christening ceremony of a model, announcing that "somewhere in California" the plane, "paid for in war bonds by the SNF was being readied for flight." Cranston quickly asked that the War Department issue a statement disavowing the group's actions. The OWI then released the War Department's "explicit and blunt denial" of all of the federation's claims.[66]

Pekich protested "this mistreatment" to Davis and Treasury Secretary Henry Morgenthau. He presented his correspondence with Hitchcock and an account of a meeting during which Pekich "presented to him an official record of purchase of bonds" and Hitchcock authorized "the necessary arrangements for a ceremony for christening of bomber." Pekich claimed to "know, as an absolute fact, that there are certain individuals in the OWI whose ill-concealed prejudice against Americans of Serb descent is very apparent" and that this "prejudice" interfered "with the faithful performance of their duties." Davis sent his regrets that he could not interfere in the matter.[67] However, the OWI dispatched a letter of complaint to the Treasury Department protesting the "ill-planned, strictly independent policy" the War Saving Staff had followed toward foreign language groups, which had negated the more "constructive efforts" of the OWI.[68]

*　　*　　*

The actions the OWI took toward the Serb Federation represented something of a last hurrah for the organization, which by the summer of 1943 was in danger of extinction. Throughout his tenure, Davis waged constant battles with other agencies who saw little value in the work of the OWI or who sought to do the task themselves. Tensions also existed within the OWI itself: liberal employees who had been hired by MacLeish repeatedly clashed with the more conservative corporate executives who came to the OWI after 1942. Davis, who was, as George Creel said, a genial man who tried to make the best of things, found that "his capacity for compromise" was no match for these divisions. Harmony became even more elusive in the winter of 1943 when Gardner Cowles Jr. reorganized the OWI's domestic branch and gave new responsibilities to staff members with media and advertising backgrounds who wanted the OWI to project "a more benign side of the war." Within a few months a number of writers reacted by resigning and informing the press that the OWI had become "an Office of Bally-hoo," dominated by "high-pressure promoters who prefer slick salesmanship to honest information." Cowles also eliminated the OWI's Bureau of Intelligence, even though it had secured useful information about the foreign nationalities community through its public opinion research.[69]

At the same time, Congress, dominated by a conservative anti–New Deal coalition, used the war as an excuse to dismantle more and more of Roosevelt's domestic programs. The OWI had always been under suspicion, with Republicans claiming its domestic branch was simply a re-election vehicle for the president. Roosevelt, with so many other battles to wage, made it clear that defending the agency was not a priority. After hearings that featured attacks on the agency's publications, graphics, films, and Davis's own supposedly left-wing politics, Congress left the domestic branch with an appropriation equaling less than a third of what it had requested (2.7 as opposed to 8.8 million dollars). Davis considered this a token funding that allowed the domestic side of the OWI to survive, but as nothing more than "a media-oriented co-ordinating agency" for government and the communications industry. The Congress also specifically enjoined the OWI from preparing or publishing any kind of literature for public distribution within the United States, and after June 1943 all releases were "filtered through commercial channels."[70] To justify these actions, the Congress made a variety of accusations against the OWI. In general, they found the agency guilty of "poor administration . . . employment of too many aliens . . . issuance of propaganda on strictly domestic issues . . . [and an] unusual number of deferments from military service of eligible men."[71] One congressman, who persistently referred to the OWI as the "Office of War Interference," praised Davis as a man of "integrity and reliability" in his chosen field—but labeled him "a complete failure" as an administrator.[72] Many of the more specific accusations against the OWI grew out of a House committee investigation of the Federal Communications

Commission (FCC), chaired by Edward E. Cox of Georgia, and involved the work of the Radio Section of the Foreign Language Division and its head, Lee Falk. The Cox Committee claimed that the OWI and FCC pressured radio stations to "dismiss personnel by holding the threat of license suspension over their heads"; that the OWI attempted "to force upon radio stations a pro-Russian or an arbitrary OWI slant"; and that Falk used the division to secure publicity for himself and employment for his friends.[73]

Cranston had previously bragged about his division's clout in purging radio stations of Nazi sympathizers, and in its defense, the OWI asserted that most of the committee's findings involved pro-Axis broadcasters. The radio industry itself, through the National Association of Broadcasters, had recognized the danger these stations posed to national security and in 1942 had formed a "self-regulatory committee," the Foreign Language Broadcasters Wartime Control. Lee Falk had served as a liaison between this group and relevant government agencies. Since the code of practices issued by the Wartime Control group specified that anyone who had not cooperated with the war effort in the past should not be employed by the industry, station personnel were asked to voluntarily submit fingerprints and statements of their personal history; this material was sent to the FLD, which forwarded it to the FBI "with requests for pertinent information on individuals concerned." Final decisions "on retention or dismissal of individual broadcasters" remained with the managers. At the industry's request, the FLD maintained a file on those dismissed to prevent other stations from hiring them. These policies had been modified in the fall of 1942, when, after consultations between the OWI, the Attorney General, the FCC, and the Office of Censorship (OC), only the latter had been given the "complete power to remove personnel from the air." The OWI had, since that time, dealt only with the OC or the Department of Justice and not directly with the radio industry. The OWI insisted that the other allegations against it were equally unfounded, and the OWI remained "proud of its record of having helped to preserve foreign language broadcasting in the United States and in helping foreign-language stations make a vital contribution to the war effort without jeopardizing national security."[74]

Cranston also tried to convince the Congress of the FLD's importance to the war effort. The foreign nationalities population, concentrated in "heavy industry and critical war areas . . . represent a crucial body of public opinion, and of military and industrial power." Axis propaganda targeted this population, and the FLD, operating in twenty-eight languages and distributing "information to clarify the progress of the war and to gain maximum participation" of all foreign-language groups, constituted, Cranston said, "the principle means of countering this Axis propaganda with truth." The work could not "be done in English" since many in the foreign language community did not speak it. If the FLD did not exist, "Goebbels and all his mouthpieces" would enjoy a monopoly on information distributed in these communities.[75]

The division's output was as significant as Cranston claimed. In just one month in the fall of 1942, the FLD, using the translating services of the OWI's overseas branch, distributed stories and features to more than two dozen foreign language papers. The division also supplied radio programs to foreign language stations, and its programming surveys showed that "approximately 95% of all public service broadcasts devoted to the war effort [originated] in the Foreign Language Division of OWI."[76] However, to the Congress, it was that kind of influence—from an agency they saw as suspect—that was at issue. By this stage of the war, Nazi propaganda was not as great a concern as it had been in 1941; more traditional fears about left-wing radicalism had replaced it.

Cranston himself was also a Congressional target because of the Tresca case and because of his work with the Common Council for American Unity. After press reports that cited Cranston's opposition to alien registration as proof of his Communist affiliation, Cranston asked Read Lewis for help in refuting the charges.[77] Lewis obliged, pointing out in his letter to the House Appropriations Chairman the origins of the Common Council in Creel's World War I committee; its close ties to the government, both through its work and its board of directors; and Mrs. Roosevelt's position as "honorary chairman of our National Committee." He detailed the work done by Cranston and the Common Council in connection with alien registration and the cooperation with the Justice Department that had occurred at the time, arguing that this would not have been possible "if the original opposition of the Common Council to alien registration had been motivated by Communistic sympathies."[78]

But the battle was lost and Cranston asked that the OWI no longer seek one of those controversial draft deferments for him from Selective Service, but instead allow his local draft board and "national manpower needs" to decide his status. In 1941, while working for the Common Council, Cranston had believed himself eligible for a deferment, because his work had "considerable value to national defense," and also because of his "wife's dependency." By the fall of 1943, no doubt in light of congressional charges,

Cranston agreed it advisable for the OWI "to keep requests for deferment down to an absolute minimum." He had been planning to seek induction in any case, as soon as he had completed the "large-scale revisions in the work of the Division necessitated by our reduced budget." He was certain that he could be replaced by others on the FLD staff, people he had trained and were "fully competent to take over."[79]

Significant changes also occurred at the Justice Department, as the result of a reorganization plan developed by Solicitor General Hugh Cox. Although the FARA section ultimately survived, the SWPU did not, despite the best efforts of Smith to save it. Lane had sensed, as the war policies unit prepared its budget estimates in 1943, that "[Attorney General] Biddle . . . began wondering just what kind of a juggernaut he had on his hands." The Special War Policies Unit had been Jackson's creation; Biddle had never monitored it closely, and suddenly he realized "how many non-lawyers there were on staff." When Biddle appeared before Congress to testify on his budget request, "he was not particularly helpful in answering questions about what the Special War Policies Unit was doing" and could not explain the unit's purpose or accomplishments. Lane then realized that "we weren't going to continue to enjoy the full support of the Attorney-General which we had had before."[80]

The issue was joined when Cox suggested that the foreign-language activities of the unit be reduced and its functions divided among the Criminal Division, the FBI, and other areas in the Justice Department. Smith protested that "curtailment in effect is an abandonment of essential operations" and a step that would "be exceedingly unwise, if not dangerous." The translators and analysts serving the sections dealing with foreign- and English-language publications, foreign agents, and subversive organizations were part of an "integrated operation" and their elimination would render the unit "ineffective." Convinced that Cox knew nothing of the history of the unit and did not understand that criminal prosecutions were the least desirable tactic to pursue in this area, Smith painstakingly explained how the unit functioned. His basic point was that the "integrated program" of law enforcement currently in existence dealt "with actual or potential violations of law" and used "administrative and non-prosecutive legal sanctions" to end violations of the law, with "expensive, cumbersome" criminal investigations undertaken only as a last resort. Coordination with the OWI, which operated "at the level of domestic morale" and with the Office of Strategic Services (OSS), which treated the "foreign political aspects" involved, provided "a consistent and integrated approach in a field demanding consistency." The unit thus achieved its goals "through other agencies or other units in the Department which are serviced by us (often without credit or recognition)."[81]

To Smith, the importance of the unit and its personnel to the department could not be questioned, and he tried to make clear how vulnerable the Justice Department would be without the SWPU. In dealing with sedition and the "domestic right" ; with "the foreign-language press and non-enemy foreign agents"; and especially with "Communist and other leftist groups," the unit was able to act and save the department from charges of "neglect in a field of great public and congressional interest." Through its administration of the Foreign Agents Registration Act, which had been transferred to the Justice Department from the State Department because of "public criticism," the expense of prosecution—made even more complicated by "considerations or foreign policy or reciprocity"—had been avoided and registrations secured in large part "from the knowledge of our analysts, and from information secured by reading the foreign language press." The problem had not diminished. Increasing numbers of people within the foreign nationalities community were "foreign-controlled or connected" and were "directing programs for political groups abroad." The unit had been working closely "with Mr. Berle, Mr. Cranston of OWI, and Mr. Poole of the OSS" to coordinate activities in this regard.[82]

In his review of the activities of the unit's work with the foreign-language press, Smith asserted that while his unit had reluctantly assumed the responsibility of "reading the press for other government agencies," it had since become their principle source of information. Smith was careful to emphasize that the unit did not conduct general surveillance of the foreign-language press but targeted "only specific papers and groups for specific reasons." The most careful attention was focused on those papers with suspect content, or which acted on behalf of free movements, or foreign agents or organizations, while others were just sampled or scanned. This had resulted in action against a number of papers, including *Amerikanski Srbobran,* again in cooperation with the OWI and OSS. Such actions against a fairly limited number of publications resulted in beneficial changes at other papers. Congress had not had to enact legislation, and the danger posed by the foreign language press, though still a factor, had diminished. The FBI could not perform this task, since it was "an expert analytical job based on an understanding of the political activities of the groups involved." Smith was certain that the termination of these activities by the unit would result in public and Congressional criticism.[83]

Smith also challenged Cox's assumption that a separation of enforcement from analysis led to inefficiencies which could be remedied by moving the Unit's functions to the Criminal Division; he considered it crucial for all of the activities of analysis and enforcement to be integrated under a single director within the War Division. Sounding like Jackson, Smith said it was particularly important that any section administering the FARA not be placed in the criminal division, "because of the stigma which would then be attached to registration" and because of the violence that would be done to Congress's intent that the law be one designed to secure disclosure rather than prosecution. Although he was transferring out of the unit to work on Lend-Lease, he urged that the present personnel be retained under Chester Lane, an "excellent lawyer" with "long experience" in registration issues.[84]

Smith's arguments saved only FARA. In late August 1943, Biddle announced a reorganization of the Justice Department, which included the abolition of the Special War Policies Unit and the reassignment of its functions. The administration of FARA remained within the War Division, but other functions of the unit, such as those related to sedition, were transferred to the Criminal Division or abolished. Biddle explained that these moves were part of the general reorganization of the department begun the preceding year as a result of "the tremendous increase in the Department's war duties and responsibilities."[85]

As the OWI was being decimated and the SWPU dismantled, Poole saw both the need and the opportunity to increase his group's responsibilities. He and Berle agreed that the FNB's press analysis had to continue and that the State Department might well look to that agency to replace the material no longer available from Justice. In October, Poole met with officials at State to discuss the timing and content of the kind of material the FNB could provide; all agreed that the FNB would keep the State Department apprised of "new developments" but avoid "the reiteration of well-known themes."[86]

Poole could easily follow Berle's directive, since he had shifted his focus and that of the FNB almost entirely from war to postwar issues. His interviews with prominent Yugoslavs reflected this change in emphasis. When he met in August with Šubašić, who Poole said was "worth listening to as a 'grass-roots' political thinker representing Balkan opinion of a substantial sort," they discussed the progress of the war, the future position of the Soviet Union, and the fate of the Balkans. Šubašić advised that since the Soviet Union had sustained a great deal of war damage and would maintain a "national weakness" for some years, its policy would be defensive, though there "would be aggressive features certainly, such as characterize any good defense." Stalin, he said, "was an Asiatic . . . a stranger to Europe" who "judged all men by what they did, not by what they said." Stalin "distrusted" the European powers but had "a little more confidence" in the United States because it "was farthest away." A small power such as Yugoslavia, in its relations with both Germany and Russia, would have to be reasonable and make itself "as important as possible economically to both sides," but should also join with other South Slavs in a "confederation for their common defense."[87]

Poole also met with Stoyan Gavrilovich, the new head of the Yugoslav Information Center, who provided "an interesting analysis of the whole situation in terms of the social-political struggle which the Allied military commanders [would] find inside Yugoslavia whenever they . . . [arrived] there at the head of forces of invasion." The point Gavrilovich repeatedly made was that the war had simply interrupted the internal political and social struggles within Yugoslavia that had been extant for decades. The Serbs in power consisted of a dozen "oligarchic" families and were determined "to hold on to power at home at all costs." Although the leadership of the Partisans was Communist and "very friendly to Russia," the majority of the followers were simply "liberal" or "democratic" and typical of those who had always dominated Croatia and opposed the ruling Serbs. Yet, Gavrilovich saw neither faction as the solution to the question of who should rule after the war. If the Serbs, with the support of the Allies, regained power, it "would most certainly mean the end of Yugoslavia as a federation." If the country fell under the influence of the Soviets, which would result in an extreme "democracy" held together by a strong central "leadership," a federation would prevail. A more favorable possibility would be the emergence of "a liberal agrarian democracy" represented by the Peasant Party of Vladko Maček. The monarchy "was indispensable as an institution," even though the present king "had no serious intellectual interests . . . diverted himself with loose women," and planned an "unfortunate" marriage.[88]

From these remarks, Poole drew several conclusions that sustained many of his earlier convictions. As he had once told Smith, the struggle within Yugoslavia was not only an ethnic one, but it also involved "still unresolved social re-adjustments precipitated by the emergence under war conditions of the many against the few, markedly in Serbia." Any solution supported by the Soviets "would be radically different from anything that the United States and Great Britain would naturally support" and a "new 'East-West' confrontation" would likely result, "comparable to that looming for Germany." With an eye on the deliberations of the Allies, Poole warned that any "prior commitments" made "may turn out to be commitments to one side in a civil strife" and should be undertaken only "with great care."[89]

* * *

In late September, the Yugoslav-Government-in-Exile, in response to British pressure, relocated to Cairo, and the king signed the budget for the Ban of Croatia. To Šubašić, the king's action confirmed the status of Croatia as an "autonomous" commonwealth within Yugoslavia and served as a necessary prelude to Šubašić's return to his people. The YGIE also closed the Information Center in New York and transferred its activities to Washington, an action very much desired by the State Department. Those members of the center who were close to Kosanović, "a most ardent opponent of the Greater Serbia element," were not moving to Washington, and Gavrilovich had also declined the offer to do so. The FNB viewed this as proof of the continued strength of the Greater Serbia philosophy within the YGIE. Šubašić, however, remained optimistic, hopeful that "sound democratic leadership" could prevail both in the United States and in Yugoslavia.[90]

In a radio address delivered from Cairo, the king expressed his sadness at the continued "insufficient harmony" among Yugoslavs but insisted that his people were "one family" and that they understood that "a strong united and stable Yugoslavia is an absolute necessity." However, in asking all of his countrymen to work together, to "obey General Draza Mihailovic and the other leaders and organizers of your resistance to the enemy and refrain from internal struggle," he showed his government's resolve to recognize only the Chetniks by name.[91]

As the FNB provided detailed analyses of these developments, Poole encouraged his staff to view Yugoslavia "as a great human drama," played by three ethnic groups "drawn together by racial affinity" but "set against each other, by history and religion." The Croats, because of their experience under the Austro-Hungarian Empire, had "the mentality of an oppressed minority." The Serbs, "proudly independent . . . a bit primitive . . . and not apt at Government except by military dictatorship," had dominated Yugoslavia since its inception. The Slovenes added their own historical experiences to this already "complex cross-set of sentiment and passion." The monarchy had been the only unifying force in Yugoslav history; any discussion of the country must take place against the historical background and current condition of the dynasty governing it. To Poole, that picture revealed a young king with a "neurotic mother" and a Greek fiancé, who was being manipulated by Serb army officers who now spoke of throwing him aside because his life had made him "more Yugoslav than Serbian."[92]

Poole analyzed Adamic with the same sympathetic eye, and drew a portrait similar to that of Carey McWilliams. In his account of an interview with Adamic late in 1943, Poole carefully laid out the contrasting views of Adamic circulating in Washington (tool of the Communists versus necessary counterweight to Great Serb agitation) and then dramatically related their conversation. To counter Adamic's assertion of the need for the South Slavs to "cleave to Russia," Poole offered a vision of Great Power cooperation, buttressed by the example of agreements reached on a variety of issues at the recent Moscow Conference. After recording Adamic's assertion of Great Britain's past imperialism in the Balkans, Poole inserted a passage from one of Adamic's books as if to show how long and deeply held was Adamic's negative view of the British. In Adamic's fear that the United States would return to an isolationist position after the war and that "anti-Soviet" and anti-Slavic opinion, so prevalent among American officials, would warp United States foreign policy, Poole detected "the inferiority complex of the immigrant 'Bohunk' as Adamic has described it in his book." Yet Adamic, as "a reporter," expressed views that had "some currency." He admitted that he favored a "Sovietization" of the Balkans, but defined that "as a reordering of social and economic life by a welling up of grass roots democracy through local committees or Soviets." To Poole, this did not mean that Adamic favored a Communist system, but that he was not afraid to cooperate with Communists and believed that "Communism was not wicked in itself, though utopian perhaps." Poole concluded that Adamic was "certainly no Bolshevik" but "a humanitarian and his dreams and his thinking lack anything like political precision"; Adamic simply "supported the underdog," the Slavic people, whom "he knows and whom he feels to have suffered uncounted years of oppression." He viewed the Partisans as incorporating his ideas and claimed that "80 percent or more of the Yugoslavs in the United States wished to lend their devotion and material aid" to Tito's cause.[93]

Whatever the motivation, Adamic and *The Bulletin* of the United Committee continued to attack the YGIE, its personnel, and the Serbs who supported it, with often inflammatory language. In October, Adamic connected Fotić to the fascists "No. 1 Serbian Quisling" Milan Nedić by pointing out that the two men were first cousins. He also claimed that the YGIE maintained contact with Nedić in the hope that he would be "prepared to do a Darlan" for them when the Allies invaded. He reprinted any and all articles critical of the government-in-exile from sources as diverse as *The Economist,* *New Statesman,* and the *London Tribune.* The overall theme was always that the "real Yugoslav government . . . the mighty political entity of the whole people's movement toward freedom" was Tito's National Anti-Fascist Liberation Council.[94]

At least one of Fotić's allies was nearly as critical as the American and ethnic press. The British, having secured the move to Cairo, insisted that Fotić be recalled because he "was the symbol of the pan-Serb movement; that this was making trouble in the country; and that they wished to restore the balance by eliminating Fotitch as the principal remaining symbol of an oppressive doctrine." Berle, who conducted most of the discussions with the British on this issue, adhered to the State Department's policy of stability over change and countered that Fotić had ended "the agitation proceeding from his Embassy" under pressure from the United States. The year before, after the administration had negotiated an agreement between "the Croats, supported by the Communists, and the Serbs, supported by the Embassy" for each to cease attacking the other, Fotić had complied, but the Croats, "urged by the Left Wing press" had not. If the United States did as the British requested, Berle wrote, it "would be assumed to mean that the British Government, or we, or both of us, had at length decided to favor the partisan group." The British denied that was the intent of the request; they sought only to "restore a balance between the two forces and not to favor one against the other."[95]

The United States did what it could to stem the tide of opposition to the YGIE. At the end of October, the Post Office issued a stamp honoring Yugoslavia, as part of a wartime series called "Overrun Countries Commemoratives." In its press release, the OWI detailed the invasion of Yugoslavia and its people's resistance but did not name any one group of fighters or politicians. Yet, the copy's praise of the Yugoslavs and the "glorious fighting traditions of their ancestors," as well as references to German reprisal policies, conjured images only of the Chetniks.[96]

However, a change was in the offing. When Churchill, Roosevelt, and Stalin met for the first time at the Tehran Conference in late November, Churchill proposed official recognition of and increased aid for the Partisans. He was aided in this by American OSS officers who had assumed liaison positions with Tito's forces and who confirmed reports of the more effective resistance to the Axis being mounted by the Partisans.[97] Publicity in the United States also continued to favor the Partisans. In October, *Newsweek* had presented a "fairly complete and authentic picture" of Partisan control in Nazi-occupied Yugoslavia, based on an Associated Press correspondent who had reached one of the Partisan headquarters in the countryside. He reported that although the Partisans were largely Communist, there were many non-Communists in the ranks. He also stated that the Chetniks "have been almost completely inactive in the last few months."[98]

Newsweek followed this with a sketch of Chetnik and Partisan activities and estimated that Mihailović had a force of twenty thousand while Tito had eighty-five thousand to one hundred thousand soldiers and that "the operations of each are roughly in proportion to their numbers." The author disclosed that King Peter had recently instructed Mihailović to increase his attacks on the Germans, because it was clear to the king "that Tito was pulling ahead in the race for British-American public favor." Mihailović had not heeded this advice and continued to make only "quick stabs" against the enemy while awaiting Allied action.[99] In early December, *Life* published the first photographs of the Partisans. The pictures showed a force of men, women, and children while the captions depicted the Partisan movement as including everyone from Communists to conservative democrats to Roman Catholic priests.[100]

At virtually the same moment that the Allies convened in Tehran, the Partisans almost negated this favorable publicity by declaring their year-old Anti-Fascist Council for the National Liberation of Yugoslavia (AVNOJ) to be the acting government of the country. Dr. Ivan Ribar, a well-known prewar politician, headed the regime; Tito, as acting prime minister, retained the title of Marshall in command of the armed forces. AVNOJ repudiated the authority of the Yugoslav-Government-In-Exile, in part because of its support for the "traitorous" Mihailović, and called for elections to decide the eventual fate of the king and his ministers. The Partisans also made official their intent to create a federal state once they gained power.[101]

The reaction of the State Department to Churchill's plans and Tito's actions was not a positive one. Berle told Hull that abandoning the Serbs "would . . . be considered in many quarters as simply a bitter act of treachery." A better course would be a "friendly solution" of the Partisan-Chetnik dispute, and while that seems "extremely difficult," if it does not occur, "the Mikhailovitch group will eventually either disintegrate, or go over to the Germans; and in the end its leaders will be massacred." Fotić, "the ablest man left in the Yugoslav Government in Exile" could perhaps be used as "the medium" for a settlement.[102]

The time for the course Berle suggested had passed. After discussing the Yugoslav question with his allies at Tehran, Roosevelt agreed to assist the Partisans militarily, but with the stipulation that the decision carry no political implications. In the wake of these developments, the JCS and OWI proposed that the United States "present news regarding Tito's government factually," without any speculation about his relations with the YGIE, and refer to the Partisans as "the Yugoslav Army of National Liberation." The State Department, following the president's lead, refused; Hull directed that "we must not refer to Tito's 'government' as such" and noted that it had not been recognized by any of the Allied governments. He agreed that speculation concerning Tito and YGIE should be avoided, and while "Yugoslav patriot activities throughout Yugoslavia" should be emphasized, the term "Partisans" should not be mentioned.[103]

The YGIE adopted a more extreme position. The king condemned Tito's actions, and Božidar Purić called the Partisan movement the "bastard child" of the Soviets.[104] The Soviets praised the creation of AVNOJ and announced their decision to finally send a military mission to the Partisans.[105] Churchill looked for a middle course, hoping that he could mediate between the king and the Partisans by suggesting that the king agree to dismiss Mihailović—against whom the charge of collaboration was "irrefutable"—in return for a Partisan agreement to recognize the monarchy.[106] The British anticipated that this might cause a government crisis, but the successor regime might be more willing to reach an accord with the Partisans.[107] American policy remained constant; Hull reaffirmed his country's resolve to deal with "the resistance forces from the point of view of their military effectiveness, without . . . entering into discussions of political differences."[108]

Šubašić thought it a mistake for Tito to have proclaimed a provisional government in what was still essentially a military area, but the king's intemperate denunciation of it was even more "devastating." Ivan Ribar's government may not be "broadly representative," but "it did issue from the people," and for the king to speak as he did against his own people "was a piece of political stupidity." Yugoslavia now had no government that inspired confidence, and Šubašić feared "the future of the dynasty . . . to have been hopelessly compromised." Kosanović was equally astounded by the king's action, but his view of the Ribar government, which he considered "progressive" and non-Communist, was more favorable than that of Šubašić. Kosanović advised Poole that it could develop into an "organ with which Allied military forces could cooperate when they came on to the territory of Yugoslavia."[109]

The Soviets' embrace of Tito did not trouble either of the Yugoslavs. Tito's prominence, they told Poole, was "a Yugoslav phenomenon, a natural outgrowth of Yugoslav developments, and not a creation of Soviet Russian or Communist enterprise"; if Tito attempted "to set himself counter to Machek and the Croatian Peasant Party, he would be quickly overborne by the weight of peasant conviction and loyalty." However, each of the Yugoslavs despaired of the ability of the government-in-exile to create a viable or representative regime.[110]

*   *   *

By 1943, the fifth-column fears that had gripped the country in the early days of the war receded as the American people united behind the war effort. Ethnic political activity had not decreased, however, and political factions within the United Nations continued to compete for power. The declining fortunes of the YGIE and the increasing stature of the Partisans troubled American policymakers who feared the postwar growth of Soviet influence. The creation of the United Committee promised more rather than less ethnic agitation, but by the end of 1943 the government had fewer resources at hand to deal with ethnic issues. Concerns about communism had strengthened anti-radical sentiment within the Congress, leading to charges against Cranston and the OWI that crippled the agency. Cost-cutting measures caused the demise of the SWPU, and although FARA survived, its abilities had been curtailed. Only the FNB remained fully active in the foreign nationalities field.

5

A Wordy Civil War

With only the Foreign Nationalities Branch (FNB) and the Foreign Agents Registration Act (FARA) section of the Justice Department active in the foreign nationalities field, no agency remained to encourage or channel ethnic sentiment to the extent that the Foreign Language Division (FLD) of the Office of War Information (OWI) had under Alan Cranston. By 1944, the work of the FLD, now much reduced in size and scope, centered on general war campaigns such as anti-inflation and antiwaste drives[1] and involved routine consultations with foreign-language stations and war-bond committees targeting the foreign born. In a review of activities for March 1944, Constantine Poulos, who had succeeded Cranston after his departure for the military, reported that the American Fat Salvage Committee had praised the work of foreign nationalities groups in their campaign, and the FLD had, through its press releases, "plugged this phase of the American war effort on the home front." The efforts of the FLD in promoting racial harmony had also been acknowledged through an award given by *Variety*.[2]

To no one's surprise, Poulos resigned from the OWI in May. In a letter to Louis Adamic, he complained that since the advent of "new administrators" in January, "we have been beating our heads against a stone wall in trying to continue the job that Alan Cranston started and carried through for two years. We were sniped at and gnawed and trimmed and pestered until there was absolutely nothing else for us to do." The OWI had declined to appoint his successor from within and had instead hired an outsider, who Poulos predicted "will do exactly what we have avoided for 2 1/2 years—that is to play the game of the embassies here in Washington." In his letter of resignation, Poulos said that he originally had joined the OWI and the FLD to accomplish three objectives: to insure that the foreign nationalities population fully understood "the issues of the war in order that they could wholeheartedly participate in it"; to provide information that would prevent ethnics from being "misled and betrayed by some of their own selfish self-appointed leaders"; and to avoid the mistakes of the Great War that had "made the foreign-born in this country and their children the victims and scapegoats of postwar hysteria." While the OWI had succeeded in the past, Poulos no longer believed that these goals could be achieved under OWI's "present policies."[3] The "present policies," as Poulos's successor described them, called on the FLD to "promote official government war information authorized for domestic distribution and official government program information to the foreign language population through the foreign language press and radio." This work would be done in English, with absolute "impartiality" and under the slogan "Informed citizens are good citizens."[4]

Of the goals Poulos enumerated, only the second still had currency, but without the war as a focus. The shape and political coloration of the postwar world and its bearing on the internal security of the United States had taken center stage. As the war entered its final phase, mobilizing the ethnics to produce and serve gave way to the need to enforce limits on their ties to foreign entities and their attempts to influence American policy. Changes in Allied policy toward Yugoslavia and the rancor they produced within the Yugoslav-American community gave these tasks a special urgency. By the end of 1943, the dominance in foreign nationalities work of FNB (which monitored the ethnics and their views of foreign developments) and the Justice Department (which enforced FARA) reflected these developments. The FNB, although preoccupied with the growth of Soviet power, provided a useful service to policymakers; but the reduction in the FARA section's staff, coupled with the political contacts made by one of the Yugoslav-American groups it pursued, rendered its work ineffective.

*   *   *

In the ethnic communities of the United States, news of Tito's formation of a government had "arrived like an Act II climax in the dramatic feud" between the supporters of the Partisans and Chetniks. The Serb press was particularly alarmed, as Serbs faced the "prospect of isolation" because of Tito's action and that of the Allies at Tehran. While *Amerikanski Srbobran* was cautious in its remarks about Tehran, it blamed current events on its usual enemies: the OWI, "the mercenary known as Louis Adamic," and "the traitorous Croat exiles" in Great Britain.[5] The Serbian National Defense Council (SNDC) carried on this theme in its new English-language publication, the *American Serb*, which, with an eye toward the Foreign Agents Registration Act, announced that it was financed by "voluntary contributions" and that no foreign government or entity contributed to it. The FNB saw the paper's tone as "temperate" compared with *Amerikanski Srbobran*.[6]

The American Slav Congress (ASC) weighed in as well, but in support of the decisions made at Tehran. Although the congress had not previously involved itself in international disputes, its leaders called a meeting for late January to deal with "the Yugoslav, Czechoslovak, Polish and Russian situations." The FNB anticipated that although the ASC had so far "spoken with an American accent," the tone of this meeting might feature more of a Soviet influence.[7] Its prediction proved accurate when "Communist elements . . . won a crucial round in the internal struggle for control" of the organization. For the first time, the congress, which had always had the "semblance of a Pan-Slav movement directed from the Kremlin," took positions favored by "the Communist-led bloc" of delegates on a number of controversial issues. These included the dispatch of greetings to Stalin and Tito and a resolution of support for the decisions reached at Tehran. Since Judge Blair Gunther, an "active Republican," and president Leo Krzycki, "an old-time socialist and present-day militant New Deal Democrat," retained positions of influence within the congress, the FNB concluded that the Communists cannot be said to have completely captured the ASC. However, the Serb National Federation (SNF) had withdrawn its participation, charging the ASC had become a "tool" of the Communists and of radicals such as Adamic. Adamic, in fact, did not attend the congress; Zlatko Baloković represented the United Committee of South-Slavic Americans (UCSSA) and his own National Committee of Americans of Croatian Descent.[8]

The UCSSA also celebrated the events in Yugoslavia. Adamic, in the early January issue of *The Bulletin*, conveyed his "opinion" that the formation of the Tito-Ribar government "had occurred with the approval of the big Allies." He stressed the multi-ethnic nature of the cabinet, ticking off how many members from each ethnic group were represented. He also provided biographical sketches of the leadership; Tito's, curiously, made no specific reference to Communism and identified him only as "the leader of the underground before the war."[9] The next issue of *The Bulletin* carried an article by Sava Kosanović, described in an introduction as "one of the few truly democratic Yugoslav politicians in exile." He criticized American news accounts and editorials that depicted "the problem of Yugoslavia" as "the problem of Serbo-Croation Relations," because they adhered to the "old line" designed to discredit the idea of a unified Yugoslav state. Serbs and Croats had worked together for years to oppose dictatorial governments and were doing so again in the ranks of the Partisans. Kosanović called on the Allies to drop their political "reserve" and to support the Partisans both politically and militarily.[10] Adamic made the same point in a telegram to the White House and in meetings with State Department officials.[11] Some concerns did exist; the liberal Croatian press, for example, voiced its "uneasiness" at the failure of the Tito-Ribar government "to mention Dr. Machek's Peasant Party" or the king. By late January, the FNB also detected an "almost completely defeatist" mood among Yugoslav diplomats in the United States. Ivan Šubašić had become increasingly concerned with the absence of any role for Vladko Maček and the Peasant Party. Kosanović remained more optimistic, but he believed that Tito, since he was not a Serb, could not serve at the head of a Yugoslav regime. DeWitt Clinton Poole also conferred with Yugoslav diplomat Stoyan Gavrilovich, who was no longer on the payroll of the Yugoslav-Government-In-Exile (YGIE), which he called "a stench in the nostrils of honest men." His mindset was as bleak as that of the others, and although he described himself as "pro-British," Gavrilovich believed that only the Soviet Union could solve Yugoslavia's problems. For Poole, who saw Gavrilovich as a "coldly intellectual servant of the Foreign Service," such a statement "was the most telling demonstration yet encountered of the hold which victorious Communist-cleansed Russia seems, for the moment at least, to have taken on the imagination of frustrated Europeans." Poole found it especially interesting that Gavrilovich did not ascribe "any conviction of good intentions" to the Soviets and attributed three goals to their policy: security for their frontiers; a "general situation" in Europe that would further enhance their security; and a "grandiose plan of national aggrandizement" which included the "whole Eurasian continent" in the name of "a people's government." Poole, in what had become a familiar device, recounted this to his readers "to make vivid the power which the Russian idea seems more and more to gain over the minds of the defeated of Europe. . . . Perhaps talk of this kind is not more than a challenge to America, but that is not the impression it leaves."[12]

In late February 1944, Churchill, in reporting the decisions made at Tehran to the House of Commons, delivered the "first official, although indirect, accusation against Mihailovich." The Chetniks, Churchill confirmed, had "made accommodations" with the Axis and had more or less ceased to fight the enemy. The Partisans represented a "far more formidable" force, waging a "wild and furious war" against the Germans, holding "in check no fewer than fourteen out of twenty German divisions in the Balkan Peninsula." The Partisans were Communist in origin, but as the Partisan "movement has increased in strength and numbers, a modifying and unifying process has taken place and national conceptions have supervened."[13] Fotić attributed Churchill's changed policy to the selfish recognition that the Soviets, not the Americans or the British, would be first to liberate eastern Europe, and his hope to make the Partisans "at least as friendly toward Great Britain as toward Russia."[14]

Ethnic reactions to Churchill's remarks ran the usual gamut. Like Fotić, the leaders of the SNF believed they were betrayed by the British but voiced their continued faith in the United States.[15] In general, "Croats, most Slovenes, and pro-Tito Serbs" praised the speech, while "pro-Mihailovich adherents" deplored it.[16] Adamic approved of Churchill's remarks, but in a conversation with Poole he warned that unless the United States followed suit, it "[will] have forfeited leadership" in this area to the British. Adamic "deplored the lack of positiveness in American foreign policy" and predicted that the failure of the United States to become more active in Europe would have "results which would be adverse to almost everybody." The government already appeared to be "just dropping out in Yugoslavia" in favor of the British, who lacked the "moral prestige" enjoyed by the Americans. British policy toward the Partisans would be much more effective with American support, and Adamic intended to exert what influence he had at the White House and the State Department to secure a statement from the United States government similar to Churchill's. With regard to Russian policy, Adamic agreed that the Soviets desired governments "friendly to Moscow," but what Russia did in Yugoslavia depended on whether American policy "proved to be alive or dead."[17]

The British still hoped to broker an agreement between the monarchy and Tito that would give the King Peter a role in the postwar government, and they invited the king and his prime minister to London for talks in March. The king took advantage of the visit to marry his fiancé, Princess Alexandra of Greece, declaring after the ceremony: "I mean to return to Yugoslavia with my wife; the marriage strengthens my position; I am now my own master."[18] The king's mother and the king's government had opposed the marriage, believing it to be inappropriate during wartime and fearing that the effects in Yugoslavia would be detrimental.[19] Peter tried to alleviate this by emphasizing that although German on her father's side, both Alexandra and her mother had "Greek blood," and that both the king and his bride were the "great-great-grandchildren of Queen Victoria." The wedding, "a very simple" affair, took place in the Yugoslav embassy in London, with Peter annoyed at the "conspicuously absent" Churchill but heartened to learn that a "large cheering crowd had gathered outside the Yugoslav Embassy in Washington" on hearing the news of the nuptials.[20]

The reality was somewhat different. Tito, in a radio address in January, had declared his supporters' universal agreement that the king and his government were "not to be allowed back in Yugoslavia" lest they "bring intrigues with them" and "sow discord among our peoples."[21] American diplomats reported that "considerable disapproval" greeted the news of the king's marriage in Serbia and that it had "not increased his prestige or popularity."[22] Reactions within the United States were similar. By May 1944, an FNB survey showed that all of the Yugoslav-American papers, except *Amerikanski Srbobran*, had reacted coolly to the king's marriage.[23]

After talks between the king and the British, Šubašić emerged as the leading candidate to head a reorganized Yugoslav government. Although he continued to speak of his "devotion" to Maček, the British sensed that Šubašić "might not follow Machek unreservedly in case an open conflict developed between Machek and Tito." Such a break seemed likely if the Communist Croatian press in the United States was any guide. *Slobodna Reč*, in an article printed in April, quoted Partisan radio broadcasts that listed Maček as one of the signatories of the Tripartite Pact and included him among the enemies of the Partisan movement. Tony (Ante) Minerich, editor of *Narodni Glasnik*, told a representative of the FNB that "the pro-Partisan Croatian-Americans are committed to a policy of discrediting Machek, indeed of charging him with treachery." This was causing a breach within the Croatian community in America, since members of the Croatian Fraternal Union of America (CFU) and the pro-Partisan National Council were supporters of Maček.[24] However, Churchill considered Šubašić to be the only Yugoslav capable of forming a government that would be broadly based and not "obnoxious to the Partisans," and he asked President Roosevelt to find the Ban "and put him on an aeroplane as early as possible."[25]

Although King Peter had agreed to see Šubašić, he dispatched a long letter to Roosevelt complaining of the pressure the British placed on him to abandon Mihailović and to seek an accommodation with Tito. If he dismissed Mihailović, he would be a "traitor" to his people and to his army; what Churchill asked of him was "murder, under disguise of my personal suicide." The king insisted the Yugoslav people had repudiated Tito because he was the "representative of international communism," and that his support consisted of less than "a quarter of one percent of the population of Yugoslavia." The king begged Roosevelt to intervene. Roosevelt passed the letter on to Cordell Hull, asking if he would "prepar[e] a nice personal letter from me to the King of Yugoslavia? It can start off, 'Dear Peter,' as I have always treated him as a sort of ward." The reply, signed by the president but probably prepared by Cavendish Cannon, expressed sympathy for the king's views and his efforts to bring harmony to his country, but it criticized the advisors and officials who served him for not always showing "the wisdom necessary to achieve these ends." Mihailović, a "fine soldier," should not have been asked to take on governmental responsibilities but only to exercise "his excellent talents in the field." Roosevelt suggested that the king rely on the "wise counsel" of Šubašić and acknowledge that the strength and support of the Partisan movement was much greater than the government in exile had admitted. Even though the interest of the United States in the Balkans was less than that of the Soviets and the British, the president "treasured the friendship of the Yugoslav people" and sent "every good wish for [the king's] welfare and happiness."[26]

The correspondence between Peter and Roosevelt coincided with the receipt by Roosevelt of a letter from Tito, sent via the Office of Strategic Services (OSS). Tito expressed his gratitude for American support, as his forces struggled to rid Yugoslavia of its "criminal occupiers" and to bring "true democracy, equal rights and social justice to all nations of Yugoslavia." He attacked the deeds of the "home traitors" such as Mihailović, but he promised victory over the enemies of "all the Allies." The White House also sent this letter to the State Department for a reply, with Roosevelt requesting that the responses to both be sent at the same time, since, as he said, "I don't want to cross wires." The letter to Tito, also drafted by Cannon, thanked Tito for his assistance to American airmen and promised "more effective assistance" through the Allies, but it made no mention of political issues. Since "there has been no abatement in the conflict between Tito and the Government" recognized by the United States, the head of the military mission to the Partisans rather than the president signed the letter, lest a personal message from Roosevelt to Tito "serve further to complicate the unhappy Yugoslav conflict."[27]

As Šubašić prepared to meet the king and at last play the conciliatory role Poole had recommended two years before, Adolf Berle encouraged Poole to "remain in personal touch" with him, in part so that the Ban's departure for London "should not seem to take place under exclusively British auspices."[28] On the eve of his journey, Poole found that Šubašić had lost even more of his optimism about his ability to work with Tito because of attacks in the Communist press on Maček and his Croatian Peasant Party. Šubašić had appealed to Croatian-American leaders "to counter with every means at their disposal" the anti-Maček campaign, with the result that the agitation among Yugoslav-Americans "is thus loaded anew with explosive." As "a Slav and a Russophile," Šubašić expected to cooperate with Moscow, but Poole theorized that his conviction that the Soviets stood behind the anti-Maček campaign had caused him to look more closely to the United States and Great Britain to counter what Šubašić now perceived as a "Tito-Moscow" threat to a postwar democratic regime. If a new government were to be effective, Šubašić told Poole, both Tito and Mihailović had to be relieved of any political role in it. Fotić must be removed as well, and the "liberal and progressive nature" of the government's program made clear. For Poole, the whole issue constituted "one more maneuver of Soviet Russian foreign policy" manifesting itself in the United States. The previous campaign in the communist press against Mihailović and the current one against Maček constituted "a cautionary yellow light at the intersection of Russian policy with Yugoslavia." The Soviet crusade to destroy Maček and transfer his followers to Tito had received wide acceptance among Yugoslav groups in the United States, and Poole cautioned that current attempts to reorganize the YGIE to include Šubašić might be adversely affected.[29]

Officially, the United States remained committed to Mihailović, but the Justice Department and the Immigration and Naturalization Service (INS) were prepared to make favorable comments about at least some leftist allies. The "I Am An American" radio broadcast of May 1944 featured a "Mr. Marchan" discussing conditions within the Yugoslav community. After explaining the linguistic and religious differences among the three major groups, Marchan declared "there is harmony in the Jugoslav community in Chicago" as all worked to defeat "Hitler and his Nazi bandits." When the narrator asked if "the superb example of General Draza Mihailovich and his Chetniks have inspired the Jugoslav peoples of Chicago," Marchan replied in the affirmative, claiming that Mihailović had "Croatians, Slovenes, and Serbs fighting side by side." During a later discussion of Poles and Slavs, Marchan spoke favorably of the recent "Congress in Detroit" where "perfect harmony prevailed." After expressing regret that the Russians were not represented on the broadcast, Marchan said that "we can't talk about Slavs today without looking with admiration and hope to the Russians and the Russian Army." The narrator agreed that an appropriate way to end the program was with a "tribute to our Russian allies, whose example inspires all of the United Nations to greater sacrifice and greater efforts."[30]

In fact, little harmony existed within the Yugoslav-American community. By the spring of 1944, the Serb-Croat dispute had assumed the proportions of "a wordy civil war," intensified by the presence of newsman Ray Brock on one side and Adamic on the other. Brock, formerly the Balkan correspondent for the *New York Times* and author of stories "unqualifiedly in favor of Mihailovich and of the Serbs," had become a spokesman for the Greater Serbia cause, referring to himself as a "press agent for Mihailovich and his Chetniks." Brock's position on Tito was clear, as this exchange during the question-and-answer period after one of his speeches shows: Question: "Who gave Tito the rank of general and where did he come from?" Brock's answer: "Joe Stalin gave it to him. He [Tito] came from a cellar in Zagreb." The FNB surmised that the Serbs welcomed the presence of an attractive speaker such as Brock, since the general public's support for Mihailović had declined. The "pro-Yugoslav" side of the dispute continued to be represented by Adamic, who, although "not a Communist . . . is inspired by romantic social radicalism and an idealistic devotion to Soviet Russian leadership." Strain was evident within the United Committee, however, caused by clerical elements who feared the "Sovietization" of Slovenia, and by others who found Adamic's "political romanticism difficult" or his personality overbearing.[31]

Adamic also remained a favorite target of the Serbs. In late 1943 and early 1944, the Navy Department came under attack from the Serbian community for including copies of Adamic's *The Native's Return,* written in the 1930s, in its distribution of reading materials to ships and naval stations. Criticism centered on the last seven pages, which concerned Adamic's impressions of his visit to Yugoslavia to see the family he left behind when he came to America. He had written movingly of the "plain people" of the region but had referred to the royal government as "part of the post-War political gangsterism in Europe." Were the regime not supported by the West, "the people of Yugoslavia would have swept it into the Danube and the Sava long ago." To Adamic, the Russian Revolution had saved Russia "from falling prey to the hounds of European imperialism," a fate not enjoyed by Yugoslavia and its neighbors, who were "now squirming in the clutches of international finance capital." The only salvation was for these countries "to overthrow their present racketeer rulers," form a federation, and "in some mutually satisfactory way, attach themselves to the USSR." Only through the "aggressive liquidation of backwardness, personal greed, and the whole class of people" who have made their fortunes at others' expense, could Yugoslavia progress. Adamic had also praised the "Slavic vitality" that "created New Russia . . . the most solid state in the world, firmly hooked to the future." He was certain that a war was near, and while such destruction was "horrible to contemplate," if it led to "general upheavals on the part of masses everywhere," it would be "desirable." Millions were "dying a slow death in Europe, anyhow," and even the chaos that would follow a war "before the forces of true social progress could be organized" would be preferable to the current peace "with its gangster diplomacy and racketeer methods of government." He closed with a prediction, only half of which came true, that America and Russia would be the two most important countries in the future and that "America will have to go Left." These passages were in the original edition but had been removed from subsequent editions at Adamic's request and were not in the volumes sent out by the Navy. The Navy made reference to the deletion in its response to the Serbs and said also that any memoir "is subject to the charge of inaccuracy and bias," but that members of the navy "were considered competent to recognize such portions which may obviously be propaganda." To deny this book to the armed forces "would, however, be a denial of one of the freedoms for which they fight."[32]

In April 1944, the strains within the United Committee took their toll; Adamic "suffered a nervous breakdown" and resigned as president of the UCSSA. Baloković, Kosanović, and Frano Petrinović, a wealthy Croatian businessman who supported Yugoslav causes, expressed "some relief" to Poole since Adamic's "excesses or indiscretions" of speech had identified the UCSSA with Communism in the minds of many. To Petrinović, such a charge was especially distressing. By contrast Poole assessed Baloković, calling him "a highly successful concert violinist, deriving from genteel stock in Croatia," but long a naturalized citizen, as "definitely on the Left" but "somewhat naive politically." His wife, an American heiress, appeared "to find leftist ideas congenial and exciting." Poole was hopeful that Petrinović, who impressed him as "a man of large consequence and of balanced judgment" would exert "a steadying influence" on the committee.[33]

In the Yugoslav-American community, the FNB found that Adamic's resignation had been anticipated and aroused "little comment." While illness played a role in the resignation, the contacts of FNB field agent Carl Butts added a different dimension, reporting that the United Commitee's reputation for leftist tendencies also concerned Adamic and further prompted him to step down. Most Slavic leaders thought of Adamic as ambitious and self-serving, and they therefore felt that "he would quite logically step out of any organization when it either ceased to fulfill or endangered the requirements of his own aspirations for leadership and prominence."[34] In its announcement of the resignation, *The Bulletin* cited only Adamic's health and his doctor's orders that he desist from the "strenuous work" that had impaired it for some months. The publication promised that he would return to his duties when he recovered.[35]

*　*　*

Although Poole's concern about the growth of Soviet power affected the tone of his reporting, he and his staff continued to provide thoughtful and accurate analyses of conditions within the Yugoslav-American community. Poole told Berle that since the changes at the OWI and the Justice Department had taken place, there had been an "increasing demand by the State Department" for FNB material and "a corresponding demand in the OSS" for distribution abroad. This "had not really been foreseen at the outset" and was "gratifying." Berle, probably sensing that Poole wanted an endorsement of the branch that would insure its survival after the war, simply agreed that FNB material would be "of great help to the men serving in the field." Nonetheless, Poole, aware that the State Department never supported FNB's creation and had little interest in its longevity, continued to emphasize the foreign-policy aspects of the FNB's work. He told Berle that the Branch's material "was being held a little more strictly to OSS and the State Department and the Military agencies" but with "a careful selectivity" with regard to the little that was sent to the OWI and the Justice Department.[36]

The FARA section at the Justice Department also worked on foreign nationalities issues, but Poole doubted its effectiveness. In late April 1944, he confided to Berle his concern, based admittedly on "informal and somewhat casual contacts," that "the higher officers" of the department lacked "any lively interest" in the FARA, and viewed its enforcement as "a bit of a nuisance" to be left to "men of secondary rank and authority." Yet the result was not neglect, because, he said, the "officers feel the need to establish a record," particularly since the attorney general was preparing his first report on administration of the act. The act was "highly political," and it needed to be administered with "clear political insight and discriminating judgment"; anything "merely routine or legalistic or prosecutorial" would do far more harm than good. Since the law involved primarily "considerations of foreign politics," Poole speculated that it had not been wise to remove its administration to the Justice Department from the State Department. He had no doubt that Berle was aware of all of this, but since Poole's work brought him into contact with the law and its administration, he hoped that Berle could bring the matter to the attention of "some higher officer" in the Justice Department so that the "delicate political aspects" of the act could receive greater attention.[37]

Poole's general assessment of the FARA section, as least with regard to Yugoslav-American organizations such as the Serbian National Defense Council and the United Committee, was fairly accurate. FBI field offices and FARA analysts continued to investigate whether financial ties existed between the SNDC and the Yugoslav embassy, or if Fotić or Jovan Dučić, even though the latter had died in the spring of 1943, had directed the propaganda efforts of *Amerikanski Srbobran,*[38] but proof on all counts remained elusive.

The methods used by the section closely resembled those of a criminal investigation as Biddle authorized the examination of current bank records and tax returns for individuals connected to the SNDC.[39] James R. Sharp, in sending Hoover a list of names in reference to the SNF, *Amerikanski Srbobran,* and the SNDC, requested that the "official and personal bank accounts of the below named Yugoslav officials be discreetly checked since September 1943 and currently monitored for records of payments made to the active foreign agents" connected with the organizations named. Sharp speculated that payments were made from "sizeable lump sums" withdrawn in cash or on checks payable to these officials, and that the money was then dispersed to the "agents." The FBI should therefore give "special attention" to the withdrawal of such "regular sums."[40] When J. Edgar Hoover asked Sharp whether the bureau should "preserve certain records of telephone communications" between the headquarters of the SNDC and various other sites, "including the Yugoslav Embassy in Washington," Sharp answered in the affirmative and added that it would be "of particular importance to know the identities of persons involved in such long distance calls."[41]

Hoover did not seem pleased with the task. He complained to James P. McGranery, Acting Assistant Attorney General in the War Division, "that an enormous expenditure of investigative time" involving "agents in ten cities covered by six different field offices" would be involved, and that "the results that might be obtained" would not be "commensurate with the investigative effort expended." Hoover requested advice as to the value of the inquiry and said that no action would be taken in the meantime.[42]

The political questions involved became more complicated as *Amerikanski Srbobran* shifted its focus in light of the altered status of the Partisans. The previously dominant "anti-Croatian line" changed into a denunciation of Nazi and Ustashi policies, without the usual "blanket condemnation of

Croats," and the "anti-partisan theme" became "the major propaganda line" in the paper. The "pan-Serbian line" which had been used to justify the creation of an independent Serbia, was now used in opposition to the Partisans, with the paper claiming that Allied recognition of the Partisans ignored the guerrilla struggles of the Chetniks, and that this struggle entitled the Serbs to a dominant position in the postwar Yugoslav state. Alexander Dragnich concluded the Serbs realized that the possibility for an independent Serbia no longer existed; as a result, Mihailović and his forces now were depicted as agents of the Yugoslav government fighting for the "liberation of the Yugoslav state." *Amerikanski Srbobran* called the Partisans "Communists, international bandits, Croat-Ustashi, etc." and criticized the Allies, especially the British, for extending supplies and recognition to Tito's forces.[43]

Given these issues, the FARA section decided that relief activities might be a more fruitful, if equally tangled, area of investigation. The response in the foreign nationalities community to the war effort, coupled with that of the population as a whole, had led to the existence of more than seven hundred competing relief agencies by 1942. One of the first to assist the Yugoslavs was the American Friends of Yugoslavia, formed in April 1941 under the leadership of Frank Polk, who had served as undersecretary of state in the Wilson administration. The Friends sponsored a relief agency, the United Yugoslav Relief Fund (UYRF), which was chaired by the head of IBM. To bring some order into the field in general, the administration had created a War Relief Control Board in 1943, which had in turn established "one principle agency" called the National War Fund, "with which other smaller societies" could affiliate. Members of the National War Fund shared in the monies "allocated for war relief by local community chests." The board had the power to grant or withhold licenses for relief work, and it encouraged smaller groups to merge or to create single agencies to represent a particular country or cause. The board also refused to grant permits for relief work to political organizations. However, as the FNB observed, it was on the "issues of organizational independence and freedom to promote foreign political views that elements in some foreign nationality communities have made their most stubborn resistance to simplification and control." America's ethnics, the FNB said, "seem to feel conscious of no disloyalty to their American allegiance in concerning themselves busily . . . with the political affairs of their lands of origin" even if in doing so they "advocate" governments "opposed to the principles of democracy." As a result, "war relief [had] become a principal arena in the United States for discussion and agitation of foreign political questions." In many instances, "where such political differences . . . pose a question of national life or death, all attempts to achieve unity in relief work have been obstinately blocked."[44]

The Yugoslavs were a case in point. Branko Pekich told the FBI in June 1942 that the federation had collected fifty thousand dollars, which had been used to send food parcels to Yugoslav prisoners of war via the Red Cross. "Croatians or Serbian radicals" complained that the money should have gone to Mihailović, but since "there is no commerce [or] financial intercourse between the United States and Yugoslavia," this had not been possible. After July, the federation ceased its relief work, and the permit of the SNDC became operative.[45] At the end of 1942, Ruth Mitchell and the SNDC asked that one half of all relief funds designated for Yugoslavia be given to the council for distribution. She claimed that the other Yugoslav agencies spent too much money on administrative costs, or had not cooperated with the Serbs, or had raised less money than the Serbs. Her main argument however, was pan-Serb: "The money most generously contributed by American Serbs and by many American admirers of the Serb fighters was given for the Chetniks and General Mihailovich's fighters who are pure Serbs. It is only fair and proper that it should be handled by American Serbs for Serbs."[46]

This attitude remained constant. In August 1943, the SNDC filed papers with the War Relief Control Board in order to retain its relief permit, first granted in the spring of 1942, as part of the National War Relief Fund. The documents listed Ruth Mitchell as honorary president, Michael Dučić as president, and the organization as a "patriotic and educational" one. The Serbian people continued to need relief because of "the greatest torture" and "well formulated plan of . . . national extermination" to which they had been subjected. While the SNDC did not oppose relief for the country as a whole, the majority of assistance should go to the Serbs; the other nationalities had not "suffered the agonies of war to the extent which was the lot of the Serbs." Croatians, due to their state's collaboration, have "received good treatment from the Axis Powers," while Slovenes have been deported to Serbia and "there burdened the already suffering Serbs." Despite the SNDC's "extreme leniency and our just cause," its attempts to work with the American Friends of Yugoslavia, designated by the Control Board as the primary Yugoslav relief agency, had proved so difficult that the Serbs had continued to work individually.[47]

Political complications intensified in October when Adamic wrote to Hull requesting "the necessary license or authority" for the United Committee to collect relief funds for the Partisans. He pledged to restrict solicitations "to South-Slavic Americans who support our Committee" and not to compete with other relief organizations. Weeks of delay then ensued. After Adamic complained to Poole that the UCSSA's request to collect relief for the "liberation forces" in Yugoslavia had not been granted, Poole advised Berle that the hesitancy exhibited by the department "may be warranted" since many Yugoslav-Americans were "frightened by the 'Communist' color of the United Committee." This had mixed results. At the end of November, the division of Foreign Activity Correlation chastised the European division for the delay in sending Adamic's letter to the proper relief authority but also noted that Adamic should be told that relief committees were to "have no political affiliation." By December, members of the United Committee discovered that a permit had been denied them "because of the prior position of the American Friends of Yugoslavia and the Croatian Fraternal Union."[48]

It was not until the fall of 1944 that the Control Board extended temporary recognition to the War Relief Committee of South Slavic Americans, on the understanding that it would soon merge with the UYRF. Although James Brunot, who headed the Control Board, knew that this action had generated "uneasiness and alarm" in the Yugoslav-American community, he was disturbed when the CFU and other more conservative Croatian and Slovenian organizations announced they would not cooperate with the South Slavic Committee, on the grounds that any monies raised would be "channeled primarily to the Partisans."[49] By December of 1944, however, the CFU and one of the Slovene groups had reversed course and begun to work with the South Slavic Committee, but only to outfit a Yugoslav relief ship, which had been requested by the Yugoslav Red Cross.[50]

Since government regulations prohibited relief organizations from engaging in political activities, the SWPU decided to look at a "few" relief organizations to ascertain if they should be asked to register and "whether such a result is a desirable one."[51] By March 1944, when the president's War Relief Control Board dispatched a circular letter reminding relief groups that regulations allowed for the "revocation of registration where political action or propaganda is combined with relief collection,"[52] the FARA section had decided that relief activities, when combined with political action on behalf of a foreign principle, warranted registration under FARA. The unit then pursued both the Serbs and the United Committee, vigorously but fruitlessly, for years.

Sharp, Dragnich, and Charlotte Slavitt first met with Serb National Federation (SNF) head Louis Christopher to discuss the Justice Department's position that since the Serbian National Defense Council (SNDC) "engaged in political activity in conjunction with its war relief collections," it was liable to registration. Christopher resisted; the Serbs' attorney, Richard S. Kaplan, did not believe they were subject to the act. Sharp countered that by Christopher's own admission, his organization collected funds for "Serbian war sufferers," who certainly qualified as "people outside of the United States," and therefore was acting on behalf of a foreign principle. The council cannot deny that it engaged in political activity; in answer to the War Relief Control Board's request for its publicity material, the council had responded that its publicity pertained to its "cultural and educational work" rather than exclusively to relief purposes. Christopher did not dispute this, and the conversation then turned to the mechanics of registration, but Christopher continued to contest the fairness of the law. At one point he noted, in a comment that clearly defined the ramifications of FARA, "If the law is so broad that if you smile at a diplomat then you must register, then apparently we must register." When he asked if the UCSSA was also registering under the act, Sharp replied in the affirmative, which was at best a premature assurance.[53]

To buttress the unit's case, Slavitt prepared a list of charges detailing the political activity of the SNDC and the "divisionist anti-Croat, anti-Yugoslav, pan-Serb propaganda" circulated by it, which was "exclusively political propaganda and totally divorced from any solicitation of relief contributions." The council also collected and dispensed so-called "administrative funds" that it had not listed in its monthly relief reports and that consisted of dues paid by its members. In addition to this failure "to report donations received to defray administrative and operating expenses," which violated the regulations governing relief, the council had not reported the funds expended for purposes other than relief.[54]

Sharp, Dragnich, and Slavitt next talked with Dr. Vladimir Rybar, Counselor of the Royal Yugoslav Embassy, concerning compliance with FARA. After a rather fruitless and contentious discussion about the embassy employees who were registered and who were not registered—and why—Sharp asked if any newspapers or organizations were on the embassy payroll. Rybar answered emphatically in the negative. Sharp countered that compensation did not have to be involved for the act to be applicable: a person or organization that published material obtained from the Embassy could be subject to registration. Sharp also advised that diplomatic status would not safeguard a person from prosecution, but Rybar refused to discuss this, insisting that as a diplomat he was responsible only to his own government and to the State Department.[55]

The SNDC proved uncooperative as well. Rather than register, the council soon informed Sharp that it was a "body of American citizens of good standing," representing "patriotic Americans of Serbian descent," and did not consider itself an agent of any foreign principle. To avoid registration under FARA and to comply with relief regulations, it had "decided to limit its activities to the patriotic and humanitarian field."[56] Sharp doubted the Serbs self-denying pledge and asked the FBI to "obtain evidence of continuing political activity by the Council as well as evidence of past activity."[57] FBI field offices then collected copies of *Amerikanski Srbobran* and articles written by the late Jovan Dučić to ascertain if evidence "of control of the policies of this paper by members of the Yugoslav Government-in-Exile or other foreign principles could be found."[58]

The ensuing investigation, which followed a circular path and threatened to exceed the FBI's resources, as well as the time of FNB and FARA analysts, validated Smith's concern about the FBI's lack of expertise in such matters. In early April, the Pittsburgh field office sent a copy of *Amerikanski Srbobran* with an article attacking General Dušan Simović to Washington for translation. The article appeared to be "written in a style used in Yugoslavia and . . . the language used therein is not the normal language used by writers" in the paper. The special agent in charge requested that an FBI translator review the article to ascertain if it "may have come from a foreign source." Hoover answered that the department did not have the necessary expertise and that the letter had been sent to the War Division. He also asked who had expressed the view about foreign authorship. The agent replied that the translator in his office thought the "wording and expressions" were written in an "old country" style but could not prove this was the case.[59]

Dragnich, who received the material from the FBI, continued to rely on parties to the dispute and on information they had previously given to Slavitt and the FNB. He asked the latter to consult with the editor of *Amerikanski Srbobran* to verify information from Kosanović, who said that a military attaché at the Yugoslav embassy had written the articles critical of Simović for *Amerikanski Srbobran*. Kosanović thought it possible that *Amerikanski Srbobran* editor Mladen Trbuhovich had retained copies of articles written by Dučić, since he claimed he could prove that Dučić's writings had determined the political positions taken by the paper. Kosanović also repeated the claim that the YGIE had ordered Fotić to "play down the Pan-Serb idea and to stress cooperation and federation in Yugoslavia," but that American Serbs had expressed annoyance with Fotić for now asking them to reverse a course he had previously pressed them to follow.[60]

The FNB could not ascertain who wrote the Simović article; the staff at the paper would only say that it was prepared by "one of our friends from the outside."[61] Hoover, repeating the information from Dragnich that had now been circulated through a few more layers of bureaucracy, informed the special agent in charge in Pittsburgh that he had received a communication from the FARA section indicating that "various pro-Yugoslavs have stated that the details in the article" could have been known "only to the Yugoslav Embassy in Washington" and that the writer had taken part in the March coup.[62] Despite several weeks of effort, nothing concrete or actionable had been gained.

At the same time, the SNDC, as part of its resolve to concentrate on relief activities and thus avoid registration under FARA, decided that the publication of the paper would be taken over by a new group, the American Serbian Cultural Association, which received no "funds of any kind" from any foreign government, and copies would be sent regularly to attorney Kaplan's office. Kaplan admitted to Sharp that some of the people in the organization may have "gone overboard with reference to ideologies" but that they were prepared to follow his instructions to avoid additional problems.[63] When Kaplan asserted that the SNDC had ceased any activities that may have made it liable, Sharp boldly replied that the department could prove that persons on the payroll of the Yugoslav government had helped form the SNDC, and that "information used as a basis for propaganda came from individuals on the Yugoslav Government payroll." These actions violated FARA; the Council's limitation of these activities "does not mean that the Department does not insist upon disclosure of past activities."[64] Kaplan, having clearly absorbed the worldview of his client, later told Slavitt that Croatian members of the YGIE were using "state jewels" to finance the "cost of the dissemination of anti-Serbian propaganda," and that "Louis Adamic is responsible for the Department of Justice's pressure upon the Serbs to register. Louis Adamic is Mrs. Roosevelt's whitehaired boy."[65]

Had Kaplan challenged Sharp, the latter would have been hard pressed to provide the proof he claimed existed. In late June 1944, the Pittsburgh FBI field office reported that all of the 1942 issues of *Amerikanski Srbobran* had been checked to ascertain if Dučić admitted in print that he had been sent to the United States by the YGIE to organize the SNDC, but no such admission had come to light. The translator thought that several articles appeared to consist of propaganda, but he had not had time to translate them. Articles in the English language *American Serb* also appeared to be "purely propaganda," and the field office provided excerpts that illustrated the political activity of the SNDC, including denunciations of attacks on Mihailović as "an atrocious lie" and the claim that information praising the Partisans came to the United States from "Axis owned and controlled radio stations." Throughout the report, the FBI agent noted that no single article served as proof that the paper was a propaganda organ but that the publication in its entirety conveyed that fact. The last paragraph was more explicit: "[F]rom reading this paper one would get the opinion that the Serbian people are doing everything they can to help the war effort but are not getting a square deal from the American Government. Further, that the pro-Serbian Cause is a just and right cause." A reader in Washington found this unacceptable: in the text, this paragraph is bracketed and the words "opinion" and "delete" are written in the margins and "opinion" is also underlined.[66]

Despite their political differences, the United Committee's position on registration was similar to that of the Serbs: a majority of the members of the UCSSA's executive committee were "extremely reluctant or unwilling to see the Committee register as foreign agents." In words that echoed those of the Serbs in the SNDC, Adamic protested that committee members did not view themselves as "foreign agents" but as "[part of an] American organization which, as such, is interested in the future of the South-Slavic peoples." They saw most of their work as "purely American," and Adamic cited their record in selling war bonds, for which they had received a commendation from the Treasury Department, as a case in point.[67]

The usual meeting between the FARA staff and the United Committee leadership soon followed. To buttress the government's case, Dragnich amassed information regarding the "foreign connections of the United Committee," which included contacts with and financial support for a United Committee of South Slavs in London, headed by Dr. Boris Furlan, a former cabinet minister in the YGIE who was assisted by two individuals who, according to Dragnich, were "probably still on the payroll of the Yugoslav government." The UCSSA in the United States had also recently elected Kosanović and Šubašić as honorary members. Both of these men were "paid by the Yugoslav government-in-exile, but neither of them had much in common with the individuals who control that government."[68]

When Adamic and Baloković met with Sharp, Slavitt, and Dragnich, the two men argued that the UCSSA had done much more than Fotić to rally the South Slavs behind the war effort and to sell war bonds. Sharp "expressed appreciation" for these efforts, but since the UCSSA "engaged in political activity [on] behalf of a foreign principle," it had to register under the act. Adamic and Baloković insisted they had no contacts with Partisan forces and were supported by their member organizations and by voluntary contributions. The funds they had sent to their counterpart in London had been for the publication of pamphlets in support of the Partisan cause. Sharp again explained that registration did not carry with it any judgment about the activities an organization involved itself in, other than that they were performed on behalf of a foreign principle—in this case the Partisan army. Since the UCSSA was also engaged in political activity, an exemption for relief collection would not apply. Like Louis Christopher before them, Adamic and Baloković finally admitted that, as Sharp explained the law, their organization was liable to register, but they cautioned that their members would continue to object to the designation of "foreign agent." To make this more palatable, Sharp agreed to compose a letter for distribution to the membership explaining the requirements of the act and attaching a copy of Biddle's previous press release emphasizing the fact that "pro-Allied propagandists were as much subject to the Act as anyone" and that registration carried no "stigma."[69]

The Justice Department originally claimed that the United Committee had to register because it was serving as an agent for the Partisans and the South Slavs. While a "strained interpretation" of the law might also depict the UCSSA as an agent of the London United Committee, Slavitt had advised against this, in part because the UCSSA connection to the Partisans was sufficient to require registration. After receiving an intercepted cable from the Office of Censorship—one Adamic had sent to the London Committee discussing additional financial and information exchanges—Slavitt reversed herself and decided that this group could be considered a foreign principle as well. She therefore amended the draft of the letters prepared for Sharp to send to the members of the UCSSA to include this additional charge.[70] A friendly exchange of letters then took place between Sharp and Christy George Peters, the attorney representing the UCSSA, about the mechanics of registration for the UCSSA and its members, including Šubašić, Kosanović, and Petrinović. However, in light of the illnesses of both Adamic and Baloković, the organization secured an extension of the registration deadline to May 10, 1944, the date requested by Peters.[71]

A week before that deadline, however, Baloković informed Sharp that while he had recovered and become acting president of the UCSSA, Adamic, who had resigned his post, was "seriously ill and his illness is expected to be a prolonged one." Šubašić had been summoned to London, and the remaining members of the committee had decided that "the purpose for which the Committee has been formed will be destroyed by its registration" and by the requirement that all of its printed matter "bear an inscription that the Committee has registered" as a foreign agent. Baloković also made several points that highlighted the problems inherent in the law and its application to groups such as his. First, he found it ironic that the government of the United States was doing more to help Tito and the Partisans than the UCSSA could ever hope to do, but that the Committee and its members, in attempting to accomplish the same objective as the United States, "[had] become 'agents' of a 'foreign principle!'" Second, exemptions existed under the law "where the foreign principle is a friendly government and such government requests of the United States exemption of its agent from registration." Tito could not avail himself of this, although his government was "a de facto government"; however, the UCSSA was not connected with it, and to say otherwise "would . . . be swearing falsely." He would be happy to furnish the Justice Department with any information it may require, but he could not believe that the Congress intended the FARA "for the elimination and destruction of the activities of a body of American citizens" such as the UCSSA. Most significantly, Baloković understood the attorney general's intent when he explained that the act carried no stigma, but he still complained that "no matter how tactfully, gently and eloquently we try to explain to the man on the street the meaning of the Attorney-General's above mentioned statement, to him a foreign propaganda agent is just a foreign propagandist and nothing else, and in his but simple soul a foreign agent is necessarily, more or less, a public enemy."[72] Sharp insisted again that they register, but he extended the deadline until May 22 to allow them time to reconsider their stand.[73]

A few days before the new deadline, Baloković and Petrinović met with Sharp and his staff. Baloković—playing the political card that Adamic had used previously—warned that registration might so offend the membership as to effect the coming presidential elections. In any case, the UCSSA board had recently voted down Adamic's proposal that they register and had voted to disband rather than do so.[74] Baloković's veiled political threat caused Sharp to write to Edward J. Ennis, acting head of the War Division, on May 24, 1944, for advice on how to proceed. He cited Baloković's statement regarding the dissolution of the UCSSA as an alternative to registration and also his contention "that efforts would be made to invoke Senatorial and State Department assistance against registration." Sharp still believed that registration was required, and he expected the State Department would concur, but suggested that an alternative was a reconsideration and withdrawal of the registration request "if justification exists" to do so.[75]

As Sharp's request circulated, the attorney general issued his first full report on the implementation of FARA in June 1944. In the six years since the original act had been passed, forty-four foreign governments had operated "information centers or propaganda offices" in the United States. Since the amendments to the act in mid-1942, 420 statements had been filed with the department; 240 of those covered propagandists of foreign principles. A total of 121 foreign agents or agencies have been indicted under the law since 1938, mostly representing the interests of the Axis. Seventy-nine convictions or guilty pleas have been secured. The amount of propaganda directed at the United States, which included everything from radio broadcasts to exhibits to posters to motion pictures, indicated the importance that foreign interests attached to the views of the American public in general. However, it also illustrated the attempts made to influence that one-quarter of the population born abroad or born in the United States with at least one foreign-born parent. Biddle regretted that propagandists pay "too little regard" to the "adverse effect" this material "may have upon the process of assimilation of foreign groups in the United States, upon the unity of our citizens, and upon other vital American interests or relations."[76] The major Yugoslav-American organizations, which were not among those registered, would have added their own regret: that their own government, as much as any foreign propagandist, saw fit to label them as something other than American.

* * *

The fortunes of the United Committee seemed to improve during the summer of 1944. King Peter relieved Mihailović of his post in the cabinet and asked Šubašić to form a new government, to work "with all of those elements in our country who are actively resisting the enemy." After talks with Tito on Vis, an island in the Adriatic Sea where he had been evacuated by the British after a German attack on his headquarters,[77] Šubašić agreed to designate Tito's Partisans as the only "official armed force" in Yugoslavia, and AVNOJ as the only "political authority." Šubašić also announced that the seat of government would move from Cairo to London, and he informed Fotić of his (Fotić's) "retirement."[78]

Berle viewed these events and the role of the United States in them with some skepticism. The Germans' near-capture of Tito provided further proof to him that the "huge reputation of Tito's army has of course largely been a fiction of the British and Russian publicity." Šubašić has thus been elevated "just at the time that Tito was being substantially eliminated," which made Šubašić "a powerful figure in Yugoslav politics" who might be able to achieve "some unity" with the Serbs. Berle assumed that the British, "who had bet their entire stake on Tito, were probably forcing the ban forward to fill the gap." He said, "I suppose they knew of Tito's flight before we did." The

United States now had "a half interest in a Balkan Prime Minister—and this although our general instructions are to keep out of Balkan politics."[79]

Berle's assessment of both Tito and Šubašić were off the mark: Tito remained the more powerful of the two, and Šubašić found unity elusive. The king's fate had been left unresolved in the talks and Mihailović and his forces quickly refused to accept Šubašić's authority or the agreement he had negotiated. The Chetnik leader, speaking as head of the "Central National Committee of the Kingdom of Yugoslavia" issued a statement from "the Free Yugoslav Mountains" in late July 1944, claiming that Šubašić and the Partisans represented only a "small minority" of the people of Yugoslavia. Šubašić could not use that base to build a united government; any attempt to do so would only create "discord" which "surely cannot have been the intention of the Crown nor could it serve the interests of our Allies." The Chetniks pledged their allegiance to the king but refused to be bound by the acts of the Šubašić government.[80] Fotić agreed, informing Cannon that he would not recognize the new government. He had not formally resigned, but he intended to remain in the United States to do all he could to publicize the situation in Yugoslavia. While Fotić promised to do nothing that would "embarrass" the American government, Cannon surmised that Fotić's status "may present complications."[81] That danger eventually passed. Fotić had refused to resign because, under Yugoslav law, the dismissal of an ambassador required "the signatures of two other designated cabinet members besides the Premier." Šubašić was the only member of the new government and had no cabinet officers at the time. After Šubašić formed his government—and via a "direct communication" with the king—Fotić surrendered his post.[82]

Most members of the Yugoslav-American community approved of the recall of Fotić and the subsequent formation by Šubašić of a new government, but *Amerikanski Srbobran* did not. The paper turned against King Peter and predicted that he would either be "written off as negligible" and sent into exile, or would not be "taken seriously by the Serbs . . . who view his capitulation to the Croats as a British gun-in-the-back-action." The SNF called on the king to turn the government over to Mihailović or at the very least, "release the Serbian people from their oath to the crown." Croatian nationalists criticized the new government as well, and they considered both Tito and Šubašić, as Croats, to be traitors to the Croat ideal of an independent homeland.[83] By early August, articles condemning the Šubašić government as an illegitimate and unrepresentative "sham" appeared regularly in *Amerikanski Srbobran*. FNB suspected the articles, written under the name of "Politicus," were the work of Fotić.[84]

The United Committee matched the Serbs in rhetoric, but theirs celebrated the new government as a "triumph for all democratic forces" and "a complete rout" for the reactionaries; the "sinister figures" of Mihailović and Fotić "have been dumped into the ashcan of history." Kosanović had been named minister of interior in the new government, and *The Bulletin* published transcripts of interviews he gave over the BBC and in New York. In the most inflammatory of these, Kosanović took issue with a statement Fotić had made calling the new government unrepresentative because it did not include any "Stock-Serbs." Kosanović dismissed this, saying, "I hate the Nazi theory of racism, no matter where it appears." He was a "Stock-Serb," as was the king, and anyone who rejected the new regime and its appeal for unity "is for Hitler."[85]

Although Fotić was now "just another refugee," Berle and Poole agreed that the FNB should continue to meet with him and "pass on to the State Department whatever of interest might be gathered from the contact."[86] In a subsequent talk with the former ambassador, who had joined Mihailović's Central National Committee, Poole found his fears about the appeal of the Soviet Union confirmed in even this most unlikely quarter. Fotić "exhibited that faith in Russian dynamism which has become the commonplace of European political thinking." He believed that "the British hold . . . was slipping" and that the Soviets were waiting until "the British position deteriorated further." To Fotić, the answer to Yugoslavia's future clearly "lay with Moscow"; even Mihailović stood ready to cooperate because, although "anti-Communist," his people were not "anti-Russian." Fotić doubted that the Soviets would "give any further serious support to Tito" and predicted they would back Mihailović, who was "firmly ensconced in the Yugoslav mountains" while Tito "was on an island in the Adriatic."[87]

Berle, possibly nurturing the same hope but mindful of the need for a free hand in making policy, recommended to Poole that since the "Serbs were a factor of prime importance," Poole, while remaining in friendly contact with Fotić, should tell him that "the current situation was a very delicate one" and that the United States could not take any "positive action" at this time. The United States held "a good opinion" of Fotić and understood the importance of the Serbs "in any Yugoslav solution," but the administration believed that Fotić could best serve his own interests by "keeping as quiet as possible" so as not to prejudice "possible future developments."[88] Fotić, with "sincere appreciation," disclosed that he had already decided to pursue "a course of great moderation." He also assured Poole that he was not the author of the Politicus articles that had appeared in *Amerikanski Srbobran* and that he had counseled leaders of the American Serb community against "attempt[ing] to carry foreign political issues over into American partisan politics."[89] While reassuring, this admission also appeared to confirm the information Kosanović had given to Dragnich concerning Fotić's role in the ethnic quarrels.

Although Fotić had promised to be moderate in his activities, he also thought it essential to state the "Serbian-Mihailovich case" to the American public.[90] His opponents had the same resolve. In mid-September, *Slobodna Reč* printed a message sent by Tito to the UCSSA over his "Free Yugoslavia" radio station, in which he thanked the committee for its work in attempting to unify "the Yugoslav peoples." He compared their efforts to those of the "home traitors" in Yugoslavia who had established contacts with men like Fotić, who sowed division in order to "deceive the American public as to the real truth about events in Yugoslavia."[91]

* * *

The question Sharp had raised about the United Committee's liability under FARA remained unanswered as Laurence A. Knapp, who "had a good record in the State Department," replaced Sharp as head of the FARA section. With this change, Poole and Berle agreed that "the FARA business would probably go much better in the future than in the past."[92] Initially this was not the case with either the Serbs or the UC. In late July, Slavitt presented a summary of the Serbian case to Knapp before her own transfer out of the unit. She limited herself to violations of FARA, even though she believed that the people and organizations in question had violated a host of other laws, ranging from the Espionage Act of 1917 to the Neutrality Act of 1939. There was little new in her report. Ambassador Fotić remained the "chief foreign principle" in the case, but the evidence collected against him, she said, "in large part has been circumstantial." However, recent FBI reports had provided "more direct and admissible evidence of foreign principle control," and Slavitt believed that evidence, coupled with a "few witnesses turning state's evidence," could produce "an immediate indictment." In addition to Fotić, other "foreign principles" included Dučić, Bishop Dionisije, and (more broadly) Mihailović and "the people of Serbia"; the SNF, *Amerikanski Srbobran*, the SNDC, the American-Serbian Cultural Association, and the primary individuals leading them were all "unregistered foreign agents."[93]

The FBI did not appear as certain of the value of its information. A report on the Defense Council prepared for the quarterly intelligence summary for August 1944 concluded that while some of the officers of the Defense Council had admitted the foreign authorship of a number of articles printed in *Ameri-kanski Srbobran,* no direct proof of this or of Fotić's direction existed. In an unchallenged display of opinion, the report concluded that the members of the council were not "subversive or un-American" and only worked out of a "sentimental attachment which they still feel for the welfare of Serbia."[94]

The FBI also had not produced much useful information on the UCSSA, but the reasons differed from those involving the Serbs. In investigating the UCSSA, the FBI focused on its ties to the Communists, rather than on its liability under FARA. In April 1944, for example, the New York FBI field office stated that informants identified the UCSSA "as Communistic because of [the] pro-Communist attitude and pro-Sovietization stand taken by Louis Adamic." However, although the released document is heavily censored, the detailed presentation of informants' views on Adamic and the UCSSA were mixed. Some saw Adamic as a socialist rather than a communist and as a man who had opposed the policies of the YGIE for some time. To others, the UCSSA was indeed pro-Partisan but anti-Communist; like Šubašić, the UCSSA saw support for the Partisans as a way of opposing the YGIE. Most attributed a great deal of personal ambition to both Adamic and Baloković. Although some of those questioned by the bureau stressed the natural sympathy that many Slavs felt toward Russia, the FBI report quoted extensively from *Daily Worker* articles to indicate the support shown for the UCSSA by the Communist press.[95]

Hoover was more certain, asserting that the UCSSA had been "infiltrated by Communist elements to such an extent that it might well be designated as a Communist front organization." It was "apparent" from its activities and propaganda that the UCSSA was "functioning as a pressure group for the purpose of aiding in the 'Sovietization' of multi-national Yugoslavia." Hoover expected the field offices in New York and San Francisco to continue their efforts and to give "preferred attention" to investigation of the UCSSA.[96] Hoover followed this theme in a report sent to the attorney general, describing the UCSSA as serving as a propagandizer for the Partisans and the cause of the "Sovietisation" of Yugoslavia. The recent resignation of Adamic did not occur for reasons of health but because of pressure exerted on Adamic by his "literary backers."[97] Hoover sent the same information to Berle and to military intelligence but included an additional paragraph which read: "As additional relevant information is received concerning the United Committee of South-Slavic Americans, which consistently adheres to the Communist Party line, and which is apparently operating as a Communist pressure group among Yugoslav Americans, it will be made available to you."[98]

However, the case remained stalled because Baloković had made some valuable contacts. His wife, the former Joyce Borden, was a good friend of Esther Lape, who was an intimate of Eleanor Roosevelt's. In mid-May, Lape asked Mrs. Roosevelt if she could see the Balokovićs, because "Zlatko" wanted to tell her how the FARA was being "abused" to force people such as he to register as foreign agents simply because of his attempts, and those of Adamic, to unify Yugoslav-Americans working in defense plants. Mrs. Roosevelt agreed to the request and saw the couple at the end of May in New York.[99] After the meeting, Mrs. Roosevelt wrote to Francis Biddle, saying that she had seen Baloković, who was replacing Adamic as head of the Yugoslav Committee, "and I think it is important for you to see him." Biddle replied the next day that he had written to Baloković "to ask him to come to see me the next time he is in Washington."[100]

On May 31, Mrs. Baloković sent Mrs. Roosevelt a memorandum on the United Committee and another detailing the military and medical supply needs of Tito. The latter, signed by Sava Kosanović, charged that the Partisans were being denied vital supplies and relief because the outlets responsible were controlled by the government-in-exile or other anti-Tito forces. Organizations such as the United Committee could not step in because they were not authorized to collect relief funds. Mrs. Roosevelt sent the supply memo to President Roosevelt, and while it made its way through the War Department, she sent the Balokovićs the response she had received from Biddle.[101]

In the statement on the United Committee, Baloković wrote eloquently of the dangers he saw in the Foreign Agents Registration Act. His organization represented "the overwhelming majority of Americans of Yugoslav descent" in the United States and in its work sought to "combat the vicious propaganda of a small but active group of Serbian chauvinists whose divisive tactics were actually interfering with the war effort." Their efforts to promote unity had been successful, despite pan-Serb activities that were "unfortunately encouraged by the Yugoslav Government-In-Exile and its Ambassador in Washington." The UCSSA consisted of "American citizens having no connection with any political party or government agency in Yugoslavia or elsewhere, receiving instructions from no one, and receiving no money . . . from any foreign source." Yet the Justice Department insisted "that the committee must register as an agent of a foreign government." The United Committee's investigation of the use of FARA in other cases had convinced them that the law was being used "by someone in an attempt to prevent these individuals and organizations from expressing their opinions—a manifest infringement of the right of free speech." Baloković insisted the stigma attached to the term "foreign agents" amounts to "intimidation, and the endless red tape in which organizations become involved, after registration, causes them in many cases to cease their activities and disband." Members of groups such as the UCSSA were simply attempting to "strengthen the democracy" of the United States and to "extend the blessings of democracy to the various countries from which they or their parents have come." For the government to hinder them, Baloković said, seemed to be "a conspiracy against American democracy itself."[102]

The committee also feared that the registration campaign could be a plot by the president's enemies, designed to cause the "little people" who supported him to lose their "deep faith" in Roosevelt and their counterparts in Europe to doubt that America remained a "symbol of hope and justice." Baloković used as an example a number of "prominent democratic leaders from Europe" who have had to register and preface their speeches and articles by declaring: "I am registered with the Department of Justice as a Foreign Agent. The United States Government does not assume any responsibility for my work." Since these people "represent the most active fighters in Europe against the Germans," he expected "the enemy will make good use of this situation for anti-American propaganda." In the end, Baloković cited a number of examples of actions taken by the Justice Department against companies that distributed material from or relating to the Soviet Union and that again appeared designed to prevent "the exchange of news as well as cultural intercourse between" the United States and the Soviet Union.[103]

On June 14, Mrs. Baloković reported to Eleanor Roosevelt on the meeting with Biddle, which she attended; she and her husband and Ennis and Biddle "had quite a long talk" about FARA, and she, "being a 'mere' woman" had told them "exactly" what she thought of the measure. They had heard nothing more about their group's registration, but she advised Mrs. Roosevelt that "the Department of Justice is continuing to pursue many other similar liberal organizations. I hope they can be stopped before really serious domestic and international complications develop."[104]

None of this swayed the FBI, an agency which, in any case, viewed acquaintance with the First Lady as more suspect than not. In late June 1944, the Boston field office sent a pamphlet to Washington, entitled "The Yugoslav Struggle through American Eyes," that had been published by the UCSSA in May and sent to a local high school. The field office believed that "the Bureau might be interested to know that such literature is apparently being disseminated among high schools." The material was far from subversive. The pamphlet consisted of reprints of articles on the Partisans and on the war in Yugoslavia from military and civilian publications; the articles by John Talbot and Stoyan Pribichevich, some of which were interviews with Tito, had been "released by the Office of War Information." In the interview with Tito, Pribichevich and Talbot were identified as "Allied correspondents." Although Tito made a brief and contemptuous reference to the "treason" of the Chetniks in this piece, he stated that his postwar plans consisted of the resolve to create "a nationally equal Federal Yugoslavia" and "a truly demo-cratic Yugoslavia" on terms of "closest friendship and collaboration" with the members of the Grand Alliance. In another article, where Pribichevich wrote of seeing "my old country" for the first time in twelve years, an insert in the text identified him as "the son of a former Yugoslav Minister of the Interior who opposed the late King Alexander's proclamation of dictator-ship, passed two years in prison and died in exile in 1936." The pamphlet as a whole consisted of the kind of romanticized war stories that could be read in any mass circulation magazine. Pribichevich repeatedly described Tito's appearance in heroic terms ("splendid blond, wavy shock of hair," "finely chiseled face of an American Indian," faithful dog "Tiger" at his feet, etc.); Staff Sgt. Ralph Martin, who would later become a Mihailović defender, re-counted the bravery of ordinary Yugoslavs (the "dancer" who "now prefers the machine gun," the "eight-year-old kid" who yearns for the front) who were united in their determination to fight the Axis. A few of the articles concerned the experiences of Allied airmen rescued by the Partisans and they also spoke glowingly of the bravery of the young people ("fighting babies" in the words of one) and of the equal role played by women in the Partisan army.[105]

Slavitt was far less concerned about the United Committee, and her con-clusions in that case were very different from those she had drawn about the Serbs. She identified the United Committee as the "chief oppositionist group to the pan-Serbian, pro-Mihailovich crowd" but their only liable ac-tion seemed to be that the group, via its *Bulletin,* "disseminates pro-Partisan propaganda." She emphasized the time and effort that had been expended in investigating the committee's case, which at that point still stood with Sharp's request to Ennis for guidance on how to proceed. Slavitt offered only the hope that with the Partisans now represented in the Yugoslav government, the United Committee might dissolve and that "some overall Yugoslav Gov-ernment Information Service will take over a united, unifying, pro-Yugoslav public relations program."[106]

Dragnich's conclusions were similar. The evidence in hand against the United Committee consisted mainly of intercepted cables from Adamic to

Vladimir Velebit and other Yugoslav officials pledging the United Committee's support and asking to be put into direct communication with "Tito's headquarters." The contacts between the UCSSA in the United States and the United Yugoslav Committee in London had increased to the point where the London organization had become the UCSSA's "most important foreign connection." The UCSSA also distributed to the Slavic press in the United States and Canada articles published by the Partisans in Yugoslavia. Yet Dragnich saw no point in pressing the UCSSA to register, even though "the facts in the case substantiate the requirement of registration," nor would prosecution "be wise." The UCSSA did not threaten American security and had been battling "the activities of the *Srbobran* crowd, activities which have been labeled as detrimental to the American war effort by the Department, the Office of War Information and the State Department." Like Sharp, he looked for an alternative, suggesting that in light of the change in government in Yugoslavia, and the UCSSA's complaint that it was not offered the exemption given to other groups supporting friendly governments, that it be offered such an exemption. If they refused "to file an exemption statement," more punitive options could still be considered.[107]

How much influence the United Committee had also remained an open question since support for Tito was not as strong within the Yugoslav-American community as it was within the UCSSA. By the fall of 1944, the FNB concluded that a stronger endorsement from those opposed to or uncertain of Tito depended upon his acceptance of an equal leadership position for the Serbs and his recognition of the Croatian Peasant Party. The role of the Soviet Union constituted another variable: support for Tito from the Russians had already eroded some Serb hostility toward him, (even *Amerikanski Srbobran* was printing accounts of the deeds of the Soviet army), but Tito's status as a Croat remained a liability. The majority of Croatian-Americans, "the descendants mostly of well-off peasants and themselves mostly happy participants in American life" had no sympathy for Communism. They supported Tito, whom they viewed as a successful fellow countryman, but that could change if Tito continued to attack Maček. Tito's willingness to work with Šubašić, Maček's "former lieutenant and disciple," appeared to be a positive sign, but some Croatian-Americans feared it was simply an expedient and that Tito eventually would repudiate Šubašić as well. If Tito ruled alone and as a Communist, support for him in the Yugoslav-American community "may well turn out to be a minority support."[108]

It soon appeared however, that the Yugoslav situation in the United States may, in the words of Poole, "be moving towards a new explosion," because of a pending attack by "the Tito-Moscow forces" on Šubašić and the YGIE. Adamic had been told that Tito had made his agreement with Šubašić only to obtain Western aid, but so little had materialized that Tito saw no point in continuing the collaboration. To Poole, this indicated that the Šubašić cabinet was divided between supporters of Tito, such as "our old friend Kosanovich" and supporters of Maček and a multiparty state. These same divisions were reflected in the United States. Croatian-Americans who were uncertain about Tito were moving toward the opposition; the ranks of the UCSSA, which Poole described as "completely and frankly the organ of Tito," were dividing. The UCSSA blamed Šubašić for this, since, before leaving America, he had instructed the Croatians to resist Tito if he continued to attack Maček. Poole had spoken to Adamic about this "new Yugoslav civil war in the United States" but Adamic appeared unconcerned and predicted that the vast majority of Croats would support Tito. Poole, echoing some of the more negative views of Adamic, speculated that the Slovene "yearns" to be sent to Yugoslavia as a peacemaker.[109]

The Bulletin confirmed Poole's analysis by printing a statement issued by the Partisans detailing how little assistance had been received since the agreement with Šubašić in June. While Tito's forces expressed their appreciation for what they had gotten, they considered it "only a drop in the ocean."[110] *The Bulletin* itself had become more moderate in tone, either in a deliberate contrast to the extreme rhetoric of the Serbs, or in recognition of Tito's more official status—or as a protection against registration under FARA. While the paper continued to support the Partisans and usually contained accounts by American and British offices rescued by or stationed with them, it also printed war news from other parts of the Balkans. In September, for example, *The Bulletin* published the text of the agreement reached in June between the Royal Government and Tito's National Committee of Liberation, but it also placed the Partisans and the struggle in Yugoslavia within the wider context of the Allied war effort. The issue featured a photograph of Tito meeting with Under Secretary of War Robert Patterson; an account of Tito's talks with Churchill, OSS head William Donovan, and other Allied leaders; and an announcement of Tito's intention to send New York Mayor Fiorella LaGuardia, who had made broadcasts in Serbo-Croatian for the OWI, the pistol he had carried throughout the war "as a token of his esteem."[111]

In any case, it was the Serbs who made the rhetorical strike that Poole dreaded. The SNF and the SNDC held a joint conference on October 1, 1944, and decided to initiate "a new and vigorous campaign" in opposition to the Partisans and the Šubašić regime. The themes to be followed included the charge that support for both Tito and Šubašić was "British-engineered, imperialistic, and Catholic" and constituted "an anti-Soviet defense bloc." The Soviets were certain to back Mihailović eventually and break with Tito as an agent of British policies.[112] In mid-October 1944, *Amerikanski Srbobran* published a front-page welcome for the "victorious Russian Army" entering Belgrade and appealed for consideration for the sacrifices made by the Serbs in the country's defense.[113] *The American Serb* announced that Belgrade had been liberated "by the mighty Soviet Army and units of the Army of Gen. Draza Mihailovich."[114]

These ethnic quarrels may have troubled American policymakers but they did not affect the outcome of the U. S. presidential election, despite the predictions of Adamic and Baloković. An FNB report on the role of ethnics in the presidential campaign of 1944 concluded that the election illustrated "anew the important position which the foreign nationality groups have come to occupy in American political life." The data Poole presented, gathered by the Office of Public Opinion Research at Princeton, showed that "nearly everybody seems to have voted 'American' rather than 'European,'" and the predicted "large-scale disaffections" from traditional voting patterns did not occur. Yet "minor gradations" appeared with the Yugoslavs in Chicago and Detroit either voting against the president, whom they had supported in 1940, or remaining neutral.[115]

Soviet support for Mihailović also did not materialize, and by the end of 1944, Šubašić and Tito had agreed that a new united government would be composed of six representatives from the Yugoslav-Government-in-Exile and twelve from Tito's National Committee of Liberation. Elections would be held at some future date to determine the status of the monarchy; in the interim, the king could not return to Yugoslavia, but a Regency Council appointed by him, in consultation with Tito and Šubašić, would exercise royal power.[116]

In the meantime, Baloković continued to use his contacts to assist the Yugoslavs. As the humanitarian needs of the people in Yugoslavia increased, the UC mounted their campaign to fill and dispatch a relief vessel to Yugoslavia. When the "American Committee for Yugoslav Relief Ship" project stalled, the Balokovićs sent Mrs. Roosevelt a packet detailing their efforts.[117] The First Lady again interceded with government officials on their behalf. In her uncompleted and posthumously published memoir, Joyce Borden Baloković recorded that "with the help of Adlai Stevenson (nephew by marriage) we stormed Washington in November 1944, demanding shipment of medical supplies to the partisans in Yugoslavia. We see Mrs. Roosevelt, Vice President Wallace, Secretary of State Stettinius, Assistant Secretary of War John J. McCloy and Admiral Land, all in one day. The medical supplies reached their destination."[118] Mrs. Roosevelt also mentioned the relief issue, although rather obliquely, in her newspaper column the following day, where she wrote of the strength and courage of the Yugoslav people and of her hope that "some relief can be brought to them."[119] Mrs. Baloković "cabled that part of it, word for word," to Sava Kosanović, Acting Foreign Minister, in London. The First Lady however declined, as part of a general policy, the Balokovićs request to be honorary chair of the relief ship's fund raising event.[120]

The FBI was quick to notice the Baloković-Roosevelt relationship. In early December, Assistant Director D. M. Ladd wrote to Hoover concerning "a utilization of Mrs. Eleanor Roosevelt by the leftist Yugoslavian violinist, Zlatko Balokovic," who was the president of the UCSSA, a "Communist-infiltrated" group once led by Louis Adamic, which has continued to follow "the same pro-Russian and pro-Tito propaganda" policy under Baloković. After encountering obstacles in the UCSSA's attempt to fill a relief ship to take materials to Yugoslavia, Baloković claimed he would intercede with "his friends, Mrs. R. and Wallace" when he was in Washington. At a UCSSA rally in early December, Baloković "boasted that he had conferred during the preceding week with Eleanor Roosevelt and Secretary of State Stettinius" and he "gave the impression that Mrs. Roosevelt will wholeheartedly support" the UCSSA and that Stettinius "had made definite promises" as well. The FBI had yet to receive information as to whether he actually saw these individuals but it would be provided to Hoover when available.[121]

*   *   *

Despite the twists and turns of Allied policy toward Yugoslavia, the FNB continued to provide thoughtful and useful analyses of the political fissures within the Yugoslav-American community. The FARA section by contrast seemed adrift, as it attempted to control ethnic activities that had less relevance to the war effort. The FBI uncovered little of use in its probes of either the SNDC or the United Committee, but here again postwar considerations seemed to take center stage. The left wing affiliations of the UC and its connections to the Soviet Union appeared to interest the agency far more than the anti-Communist posture of the Serbs. Both ethnic groups also became skilled in outlasting the FARA section's ineffectual attempts to police their activities, and the United Committee made the kind of political contacts that would provide it with a shield against registration.

Conclusion
To Achieve Propagandistic Control

At the end of 1944, DeWitt Clinton Poole gave high marks to the intelligence output of the Foreign Nationalities Branch (FNB), with Yugoslavia cited as a case in point. Contacts among Yugoslav factions in the United States and the information gleaned, Poole asserted, had "contributed, reliably as it proved, to an understanding of political potentials in Yugoslavia itself." The State Department could not maintain such contacts, "without putting an official cachet on the individuals in question and inviting criticism from politically hostile quarters." Yet the task was essential in a democracy because "foreign nationality groups are parts of the electorate" whose "aroused concern" and "influence as voters" rightly "command the attention of those who shape policy at both ends of Pennsylvania Avenue." The citizens the FNB studied were "American citizens first of all," whose Old World ties had been stimulated by the war. The freedom of expression allowed in the United States had enabled the FNB's "clientele" to be "fully vocal"; that, in turn, had facilitated its intelligence gathering. The end of the war did not, however, signal the end of FNB's usefulness. Poole predicted that America's traditional role of "host to political underdogs" would "grow still more multifarious and turbulent" with the postwar increase in American power. The presence of the United Nations headquarters in the United States would, he said, insure the continued activity of "unofficial claimants" as well as "official delegations." It remained essential "to have regular contact, other than crass police surveillance, with movements-in-opposition, which may some day be governments." He believed the FNB could best execute this task.[1]

* * *

The FNB continued to analyze Yugoslav events, but the new year brought little change within the Yugoslav-American community. Attacks on Vladko Maček continued as the Communist press published reprints of articles from Yugoslavia charging him with collaboration with the Ustasha.[2] The allegiance of the Serbian Orthodox Church also remained an issue, with pro-Partisan Serbs attempting to influence Bishop Dionisije while Serb nationalists sought to oust him.[3] When Poole met with the bishop, Louis Christopher, and Michael Dučić in late January 1945, it was clear to him that Serb nationalists had won the battle for the cleric's support. All three emphasized that they "regarded Tito as out-and-out Communist and therefore their enemy and the enemy of all they stood for." Their attitude toward King Peter was uncertain and dependent on the stance he took regarding the Tito-Šubašić agreement. Whether they would join with like-minded anti-Tito Croats or Slovenes in the United States also seemed unclear.[4]

King Peter, seeing his throne in jeopardy, refused to endorse the Tito-Šubašić accord. The British and the Soviets urged him to accept the agreement, but the State Department expressed caution. The three Allies could not "act on anything like an equal basis in Yugoslavia." Neither Great Britain nor the Soviet Union evidenced any genuine interest in Yugoslavia itself, but instead found the country "to be the ground where their respective policies for Southeastern Europe are being played out." The Soviets had not asked for a common policy for the three to follow and would continue to implement their own plans for the area. The British in turn were merely "trying to keep even with the Russians" while attempting "to prepare a facade of 'Allied' action."[5]

Peter's stance compromised his support within the Yugoslav-American community. The FNB observed that liberals used his hesitancy in approving the Tito-Šubašić agreement as proof of what Yugoslavia did not need: the "arbitrary rule of a monarch." While Partisan attacks on Maček had cost Tito some support among Croatian-Americans, he "made slight gains among the Serbs and Slovenes," with the heaviest backing coming from "Communist and leftist-liberal elements." Tito's support for Slovene territorial acquisitions also had caused Slovene opinion to shift in favor of the Partisans. Serb nationalists remained the "most vocal opposition to Tito in the United States," with the British most often cited by them as responsible for Tito's rise to power. Konstantin Fotić continued to offer the nationalists advice and to urge Peter to resist the Tito-Šubašić agreement, implying that the United States would support him if he did so.[6]

At the Yalta Conference in February, 1945, President Roosevelt overruled his State Department and supported his allies in calling on Tito and Šubašić to implement their agreement without further delay, or, as Stalin said, "irrespective of what fantasies there may be in the head of King Peter."[7] The three also agreed to hold free elections in the areas freed from Nazi control. In a meeting with the FNB, the leaders of the Serb National Federation (SNF) vowed that they would never accept Tito and that a civil war was inevitable in Yugoslavia. Only an American intervention, designed to guarantee the free elections called for at Yalta, could prevent this and they intended to emphasize that in their publications.[8] Fotić agreed that the "promised election" was the key to the future; if the West did not act to ensure the elections were fair, he told Poole, the people "would despair of any encouragement or further support from the West and conclude that they must ineluctably cast their lot with the Soviet Russian world."[9]

However, the king yielded to the Allies and in early March, a unified Yugoslav government, with Tito as prime minister and Ivan Šubašić as minister of foreign affairs, began to govern in Belgrade. The FNB observed that this brought a measure of unity to the Yugoslav-American community with most Yugoslav-Americans welcoming the establishment of a coalition government as the fruition of the Yalta accords. Croatians and Slovenes of moderate political views hoped that the government could follow a middle course "between Communism and capitalism." Conservatives who had long criticized Tito did not agree that the regime was anything but Communist, and Serb nationalists, seeking allies, claimed that all three ethnic groups should oppose the new regime because it did not represent the wishes of the peoples of Yugoslavia, but only those of the "Ustashi-Partisan scum of Josip Broz Tito." Although two Serbs were in the government, the Serbs in the United States charged that Tito was using them as "camouflage" and that the men themselves were traitors because of their willingness to be exploited by him.[10]

Draža Mihailović soon joined the discussion, via a statement printed in *Amerikanski Srbobran* of "unalterable opposition" to the regime now in Belgrade.[11] The new American representative in Belgrade, Richard C. Patterson, was no more sympathetic. Using information acquired from dissidents within the regime, Patterson advised Washington that Šubašić was powerless and that more and more Communists were being brought into the government. Opposition to the regime was growing, but it had "insufficient leadership and arms for a revolt." Patterson characterized the country as being under almost complete Soviet control; the "only chance for democracy is pressure from Washington and London on Moscow to make spirit of Yalta Declaration effective."[12]

Šubašić had a different view. After talks with the Soviets, Šubašić believed they were not as supportive of Tito as he had previously thought and he remained certain that the people of Yugoslavia would not accept Communism "even out of love or sentiment for Russia." A civil war would result from any Communist attempt to seize power, but Šubašić had hopes of preventing this war by securing economic assistance from the United States that would allow his people to recover the strength necessary to resist a Communist takeover. He told the FNB that conditions were too unsettled for elections to be held; his own return to Yugoslavia had prevented a "purge," but he believed the Partisans were willing to kill as many as necessary to secure their control of the country. The main task for him was to "outsit Tito," even though residence in Yugoslavia involved personal "insults and degradations" such as being under surveillance by the secret police.[13]

Tito, as if seeking to confirm the West's negative view of his regime, decided to test his strength against the Allies by insisting that the Yugoslav-liberated Italian province of Venezia Giulia, known to Yugoslavia as Julijska Krajina and to the United States as the Julian Region, be ceded to Yugoslavia after the war. The area had a mixed population of Italians, Croats, and Slovenes, and it had been the scene of international rivalries for decades. Claimed by both the Italians and the South Slavs, but controlled by the Hapsburgs until the end of World War I, the Julian Region passed to Italy in 1920. Although Yugoslavia agreed to this, it continued to claim that it had the right to at least part of the region.[14]

In 1941, to stiffen Yugoslavia's resistance to the Axis, the British had hinted that the Julian Region's disposition could be reopened after the war and the Yugoslav claim more sympathetically heard. Throughout the war, this territorial dispute had been one of the few issues uniting the Yugoslav-American community. The United States was noncommittal, and Roosevelt's successor Harry Truman, who believed that the "nationalistic ambitions of the partisan leader" Tito propelled Yugoslav policy, had no desire to "get us mixed up in a Balkan turmoil." The Americans suggested that the province be placed under the control of an Allied military government until a final settlement of the claims of Italy and Yugoslavia could be reached. The British, now concerned about what they saw as a Soviet military presence in the Balkans, supported the American position. In the spring of 1945, both Allies instructed the Partisans to withdraw from the area and to place their forces under an Allied command.[15]

The United States also applied economic and diplomatic pressure to Yugoslavia. Secretary of State Edward R. Stettinius talked with Šubašić at the

United Nations meeting in San Francisco in May and informed him that the two countries "could not discuss questions such as Lend-Lease until the Venezia Giulia . . . situation had been cleared up."[16] At a second meeting a week later, when Šubašić again raised the question of economic aid for Yugoslavia, Stettinius replied that such assistance would require congressional approval and that congressional opinion was deeply affected by the situation in Venezia Giulia. Šubašić warned Stettinius that "if assistance were denied from the United States, they might tend to resort to the only door open to them."[17]

As the Americans and the British opposed Tito's move toward Trieste and the surrounding areas, the ethnic groups, now more divided by politics, lined up on opposite sides. For the most part, Serb nationalists, while they supported Yugoslavia's claims for Trieste on the grounds that the Chetniks had liberated it, blamed the crisis over the territory on Tito and his supporters in Moscow. The rest of the Yugoslav-American community simply supported Tito and expressed astonishment at what they viewed as Anglo-American sympathy for Italy. The FNB estimated that "Tito's stock has taken a sharp rise among Slovene-Americans" as a result of the Trieste crisis, although the more conservative Slovenes continued to ally with the Serb nationalists in their opposition to Tito.[18]

The Partisans ultimately agreed to accept the Allied command in the Julian Region and the "May Crisis" passed, with the area divided into an Allied Zone A and a Yugoslav Zone B. A lack of Soviet support, coupled with Anglo-American pressure, probably caused Tito's change in policy.[19] State Department analysts had correctly surmised that the Soviets would support Tito "far enough to anchor Yugoslavia securely in the Soviet sphere of influence, but not far enough to bring on a capital crisis between the USSR and the Western Allies."[20]

As this dispute indicated, ethnic concerns moved more openly into the international arena during the United Nations meetings. According to the Common Council for American Unity (CCAU), a poll of the foreign-language press in April 1945 revealed that no segment of the public was more interested in the success of the UN meeting than "these millions of Americans of foreign birth and parentage." Virtually all supported the entry of the United States into the UN and hoped that America's commitment to democracy and human rights would characterize the new organization and be extended to their former homelands. Most of the papers polled also supported giving the UN even more power over member states than called for in the charter. The CCAU concluded that the "loyalty" of the foreign-born, "coupled with their special knowledge of and ties with other peoples throughout the world," provided the United States with "a special asset" as it assumed the mantle of leadership.[21] To the Yugoslav delegates in San Francisco, the ethnics were little more than an irritant. Šubašić continued to complain of surveillance, believing that visitors to the Communist delegates' hotel suites were "spying" on him and that his own visitors were being watched. He seemed uncomfortable with the Yugoslav-Americans who "besieged" the delegates, most of whom represented leftist organizations such as the UCSSA. The Communist delegates from Yugoslavia, who were at first more welcoming to the UCSSA and other such groups, soon became dismayed by the lack of unity that persisted within the Yugoslav-American community and the "meager" amount of money collected for Yugoslav relief. When the editor of *Slobodna Reč* and other leftists protested a particular government policy to the deputy chief of the Yugoslav delegation, he retorted that Yugoslavia's policies were made by its ministers and not by "you fellows from Pittsburgh who cannot even obtain 2,000 subscriptions for your newspaper."[22]

Serb-Americans also attended the UN conference, armed with documents supporting Mihailović and depicting the Tito-Šubašić regime as unrepresentative. Fotić, registered as a foreign agent under FARA, joined in these activities, and through press conferences and other demonstrations the Serb nationalists demanded Allied intervention in Yugoslavia to secure free elections in accordance with the Atlantic Charter and the Yalta accords.[23] Louis Christopher, attending as president of the SNF, held a press conference in which he claimed that Tito had killed thousands of Serbs and that Yugoslavia would remain "a powder keg" unless the government issue was solved. He also denied that Mihailović had collaborated with the enemy.[24]

Adamic took little part in United Committee affairs in the spring of 1945 due to a leg injury and pressing financial concerns, but he tried to influence both Yugoslav and American behavior. He warned Zlatko Baloković of various plots against the UCSSA, emanating from John Butkovich on the one hand and Šubašić on the other. Maček was the catalyst for Butkovich, whose aim, Adamic claimed, was to secure control of the Committee and "get you and me out of the way." Šubašić too had a "well-conceived plan to cripple" the organization "or even put it out of business." Adamic named no motive for Šubašić but said the Croat would try to "offer interesting and worthwhile jobs in Yugoslavia's government service to some of the best people now working" for the UCSSA.[25]

Adamic also met with the Yugoslav delegates in New York. He briefed them on the "importance of the change of Presidents" and assured them of the "friendship" that one of the officials of the UCSSA, Nick Bez, had with Harry Truman. He suggested to Bez, the founder of Air West and treasurer of the Democratic Party who had been born as South Slav Nikola Bezmalinovic, that he accompany the new Yugoslav ambassador, Stanoye Simić, when he presented his credentials to "your friend Harry" at the White House. He also urged Bez to travel to the conference to meet with the delegates himself and advised him to remember that Šubašić "is a snake."[26]

*   *   *

As the Foreign Nationalities Branch analyzed developments in Yugoslavia, its own future remained clouded. Poole's previous attempts to celebrate the branch's achievements had not produced any demands within the State Department to make the FNB permanent, and Poole personally appealed to Berle, before his departure to serve as ambassador in Brazil, to argue that the FNB would be of great use after the war. Reiterating a favorite theme, Poole observed that political intelligence took two forms: the "official . . . political reporting" of diplomats, which was best confined to "the legitimate political life of the country of residence"; and the "unofficial" which centers on "the illicit-or underground and revolutionary." Such work would best be performed by a "secondary political intelligence service" that can also report on dissident movements, which are themselves more likely to be based within the United States. The FNB, "an already going concern" could, with some expansion of its existing operations, perform these tasks well. He would "not go in for stealing letters, for dictaphones or the like," but "discretion" would best be served by having the FNB work for State while remaining attached to (under the "convenient cloak" of) the Office of Strategic Services (OSS) or its successor.[27]

Poole's importuning on behalf of the FNB failed, and he moved on to a variety of OSS and State Department assignments by the spring of 1945. Bjarne Braatoy, who had served as the Deputy Chief of the FNB since the previous fall, succeeded him and continued his predecessor's campaign to save the branch, but without success.[28] When President Truman disbanded the OSS in September 1945, a number of FNB personnel moved to the State Department, but the branch itself did not survive.

As Poole had predicted, the end of the war in Europe did not lead to the end of ethnic strife in America. In the Yugoslav-American community, the UCSSA continued to raise funds to support its political activity on behalf of Tito, and the Serbs remained active in their opposition.[29] With the FNB's decline, only the FARA section at Justice and the FBI seemed interested in the ethnics, but that too was about to change.

After several months of investigation, the War Division decided late in 1944 that a case against Ruth Mitchell could not be made under FARA and closed its investigation of her, but probes of the major Serb organizations and of the UCSSA continued. In early March 1945, Biddle sent the most recent copy of *The American Serb* to FARA chief Knapp with the request that he keep "an eye on this." The articles in the paper denounced the Allied approval of the Tito-Šubašić agreement, referring to that government as a "dictatorship" and to the Allied action as one that "intensified the tragedy of Yugoslavia." The paper carried several pictures of Allied airmen who had been rescued by the Chetniks, refuting Partisan claims that it was their forces who had been responsible for saving the airmen.[30]

Knapp quickly returned *The American Serb* to Herbert Wechsler, the assistant attorney general in the War Division, offering his view that there was "nothing that can be done under FARA about this Serb-at-any-cost publication." The section had tried for many months to have the Serbian National Defense Council (SNDC) register on the grounds that it combined "relief with 'political' activities," only to have the council create the "dummy group" called the American-Serbian Cultural Association. The section "then ceased firing on this front, which has since been further quieted by the decline in the Council's relief activities." Both the federation and the council continued to be under the "closest scrutiny [of] the FBI" to detect contacts with Fotić or others like him; the section had "mountains of reports" already generated by that agency and by Charlotte Slavitt, who had worked on the case "almost exclusively for a year." Although "everybody knows that this whole Serb set-up was Fotić's tool," sufficient proof "of a foreign principle . . . was never uncovered." The "clamor" of *Amerikanski Srbobran* continued to be "violent and extreme" with attacks on everyone (including the president) who was not in accord with their pan-Serb position. However, Knapp believed that "the FARA can never be effectively applied to the nativist foreign-language organizations on any broad basis or to achieve propagandistic control." Hundreds of organizations like that of the Serbs existed, but a "mere handful [had] registered, and then only because of open and extensive financial contributions to or propaganda dissemination for foreign governments." To Knapp, those were the only circumstances that warranted registration. In the other cases, "satisfactory evidence of real connections with a foreign government or political party . . . could never be obtained." Because of this, the office had resorted to "strained concepts" such as the "assuming and purporting clause" of the act, which was both "unwise" and "unconstitutional." (This clause required the registration of "any person who assumes or purports to act within the United States as an agent of a foreign principle in any of the respects" defined in the act.) Knapp had always suspected that "this clause was designed by Berle and others in the hope that it might cover propagandizing nativist organizations where no real foreign connection could be established," and his suspicion had recently been confirmed.[31]

Nonetheless, the case remained open. After Fotić registered under FARA as an agent of the Central National Committee in April 1945, J. Edgar Hoover instructed his agents to be on the alert for any "indications that Fotitch is exercising control or furnishing funds" to the SNDC, which would make the organizations liable to registration.[32] However, with Tito in power, the activities of the Serbs carried fewer diplomatic repercussions than they had when the United States had been committed to the YGIE. The Justice Department ended its probe of the Serbs in 1947; Hoover instructed his field agents to discontinue active investigation of the Defense Council and related organizations but to send occasional reports to headquarters of Serb activities.[33]

Both the Federation and the Defense Council continued to exist. Their Web pages today contain articles on their history, celebrating the contributions that Serbs have made to America. These include the rescue of American airmen during World War II, the donation of "two bombers" to the war effort, and the more recent heroic deeds of Serb-Americans on 9/11. Yet these pages also support the Bosnian Serbs and castigate media who circulate what the federation calls the "myths" of atrocities committed at Srebrenica and elsewhere.[34] The resolutions passed by the Serbian National Defense Council during its conventions in the late 1990s, in opposition to both the Serbian regime and the policy of the United States and its NATO partners, bear a remarkable resemblance to the rhetoric of the World War II era.[35] King Peter never returned to Yugoslavia and died in the United States in 1970. He was buried in the Saint Sava Serbian Orthodox Monastery in Libertyville, Illinois, the site of the 1942 Vidovdan celebration that had caused such concern among American officials. Peter's son, Crown Prince Alexander, returned to Serbia in 2001, after the dissolution of the former Yugoslavia, to advocate a restoration of the monarchy within Serbia's new parliamentary system. Alexander's request, in the spring of 2007, that his father be reburied in the royal family plot near Belgrade met a cool reception among American Serbs, who claimed that the king had requested that he be laid to rest in the monastery, in an area that was home to both a large Serbian population and the legacy of Abraham Lincoln.[36]

*　*　*

The American government's attention remained on the UCSSA for a bit longer, with the postwar Red Scare and Hoover's penchant for pursuing "fish ... hardly worth catching" a contributing factor.[37] Throughout 1945 and into the immediate postwar period, the United Committee, through the renamed American Committee for Yugoslav Relief, solicited funds for Yugoslavia with the support of prominent Americans. A fund-raising "Tribute to Yugoslavia" held in New York City in February 1945 featured Mayor La-Guardia, two United States senators, and members of the city's cultural community. Secretary of Commerce Henry Wallace and Vice President Truman sent messages of support, as did a host of labor leaders and foreign officials; Marshall Tito sent a message of thanks. In March, the committee organized a series of receptions around the country commemorating the anniversary of Yugoslav resistance to the Axis, and those too were attended by a variety of political officials—and in the case of Los Angeles, "by many Hollywood notables." At a luncheon for American aviators who had been saved by the Partisans in August 1945, Yugoslav Ambassador Simić assured the assembly that "the new government of Yugoslavia is a true democracy," and he asked for "understanding and sympathy for the grave problems confronting the Yugoslav people."[38]

Investigations of the United Committee continued as these events took place—but with doubts as to the efficacy of the probe. The UCSSA, in a sense, came to occupy the position that the Serbs had held during the war: a foreign entity existed, in this case Tito's government, and the United Committee had a connection to it. In February 1945, Wechsler informed Hoover that the Justice Department did not believe that the UCSSA could be made to register as an agent for the South-Slavic people. However, registration could be required if the group were "serving as a publicity agent for Marshal Tito or the political or governmental groups associated with him in Yugoslavia." Information furnished by the FBI, such as a letter of thanks sent by Tito to Adamic and published in *The Bulletin,* seemed to indicate that was the case. In order to develop this approach, Wechsler asked for a list of any other such materials published or distributed by the UCSSA; information on how the material was solicited or received; and if the Committee used the mail or any other channel of interstate commerce to distribute the material. He suggested that the FBI obtain all of this from the committee itself and had no objection if the FBI explained that the request involved the "possible application" of FARA.[39] Nothing occurred for several months as Hoover questioned the strategy, suggesting that the United Committee's members were not likely to willingly furnish material that would prove them in violation of the law, and might instead destroy their records. He advised that a subpoena for the records be issued first, and that FBI agents contact the United Committee, ready to use the subpoena if the records were not relinquished.[40]

The Justice Department also sought the assistance of Theodore J. Hohenthal of the Yugoslav desk in the Department of State to ascertain if the UCSSA was acting "for or on behalf of a foreign principle." Hohenthal furnished a press release issued by the United Committee containing the text of the Tito-Šubašić agreement, which the Committee said it had received by cable from the Yugoslav government in London. To Hohenthal's knowledge, "the terms of the Tito-Šubašić agreement were sent by the Yugoslav Government in London direct to the United Committee, who in turn made the text available to the Yugoslav Embassy in Washington, and that it was through this channel that the Embassy learned of the agreement."[41]

In March 1945, the Philadelphia FBI office forwarded copies of *The Bulletin* to Washington, and the information they contained complicated the government's case. One of the issues recounted the November visit of Zlatko Baloković to the White House, reporting that he "called on" Mrs. Roosevelt and "left with the First Lady a memorandum." The account also quoted Mrs. Roosevelt's newspaper column, in which she alluded to conditions in Yugoslavia, praised "the strength which these mountain people have shown in defense of their liberty" and hoped "the day will come soon when some relief can be brought to them."[42]

While Justice pondered the implications of this information, the FBI investigation went forward, but with the bureau shifting its emphasis, which had centered on the political beliefs of the United Committee's members, to be in accord with that of the rest of the Justice Department. In June 1945, the New York Office sent Hoover the text of a cable that Šubašić had sent to the UCSSA on January 25, 1945, denouncing the king for rejecting the Tito-Šubašić agreement. The agent noted that two days after receiving this cable, the UCSSA issued a statement that "set out information identical to that contained in the above message from Subasic." The agent also said that per Washington's request, he was not including this information in the "forthcoming report under the character of INTERNAL SECURITY-C" as usual but sending it in letter form "inasmuch as it is believed that this will be of considerable assistance in establishing the necessity for the UNITED COMMITTEE OF SOUTH-SLAVIC AMERICANS and individuals identified with it to register as agents of a foreign principle." Hoover sent the material to Wechsler.[43]

The New York FBI field office report issued in early July 1945 served both old and new concerns by stating that the UCSSA continued "to exert pro-Tito influence among American Yugoslavs." The dinner held in New York in February to raise funds for Yugoslav relief took on the color of a Communist meeting, with the field office emphasizing that "several persons prominent in Communist Party of America and Communist front organizations" had attended, although Mayor LaGuardia, along with a number of prominent politicians and airmen rescued by the Partisans, had been there as well. The New York office affirmed that it would continue to investigate whether the UCSSA or its officers were "receiving instructions from the Yugoslav Government pertaining to dissemination of information for that government," but most of the "undeveloped leads" listed concerned additional information on Communist influence within the organization.[44]

In July 1945, the War Division authorized a review of the United Committee's "books, records and papers," and in accordance with Hoover's suggestion approved the issuance of subpoenas in New York if the United Committee did not surrender the records voluntarily for inspection.[45] Hoover instructed the New York office to give this matter "continuous, preferred and expeditious attention."[46] A long argument then ensued between the FBI, the War Division, and the rest of the Justice Department about whether the subpoenas should be issued by the authorities in Washington or by those in New York, where the UCSSA was headquartered, and whether they should be issued to the committee as a group or to each of its officers.[47] By the time the case was finally referred to the United States Attorney in New York, the war had ended.

The FBI continued to gather information but the results did not advance the Justice Department's case. In October 1945, the New York field office obtained a package of UCSSA file materials from an informant. These materials were allegedly from a "Department of Justice" file maintained by the UCSSA for correspondence with the department concerning registration under FARA, and included Baloković's report to the executive committee that the UCSSA had received "an indefinite extension of time" for filing. In his covering memo, special agent in charge E. E. Conroy referenced an earlier informant's report that Biddle had written to Baloković on May 21, 1944, saying that Mrs. Roosevelt had suggested that Biddle see Baloković and extending an invitation for Baloković to come to Washington. The file also contained the memorandum from the UCSSA to Mrs. Roosevelt, dated May 31, 1944, requesting that she look into the manner in which FARA was being applied against American citizens. In another document from the packet, an August 1944 report to the executive committee of the UCSSA, Executive Secretary Rev. Strahinja Maletich claimed that Fotić was behind the Justice Department's pressure on the UCSSA to register and that he had convinced the authorities that the United Committee consisted of "subversive elements." Since the registration question was impeding the UCSSA's attempts to obtain a permit to collect relief, the Committee "considered as our first duty putting the registration of the United Committee in abeyance." However, Maletich recorded, after a conversation between Baloković and Biddle, "the question was put in abeyance for an indefinite period." Even with that, according to Maletich, Fotić had managed to continue to delay their relief license, which was only then about to be granted.[48]

Adamic also tried to establish a White House connection, but with less success. Fulfilling his earlier pledges to carry on his work in support of Tito, Adamic met with President Truman in early December, in an appointment arranged by Nick Bez, to plead for relief for Yugoslavia and for a more positive American policy toward Tito's government. Adamic told the president that the UCSSA represented "85 to 90 percent of the Americans who came to or who stem from various South-Slavic countries." He spoke of the loyalty of these people to America and their concern for their homeland and the losses it had sustained in the war. Truman appeared sympathetic, "a good, well-meaning man," as Adamic described him, until the conversation turned to Tito. The president interrupted Adamic to ask what he "really" thought of "Tito's police government," adding that such a regime was "all right with me if that's what the Yugoslav people want." When Adamic told Truman that a revolution was occurring in Yugoslavia and that "the people reporting to you . . . are unable to accept the change" and were distorting the information they sent, Truman countered that Richard Patterson, "who likes Tito," had told him that if "a man disagrees with his government, they shoot him." Once back on the more neutral ground of relief, the president again appeared moved by Adamic's accounts of the people's hardships, but was less willing to agree to Adamic's suggestion that the United States provide credits to Yugoslavia and stimulate trade. Although they parted cordially, Adamic left concerned that Truman remained "uninformed and misinformed about Yugoslavia . . . at the mercy of the clique in charge of Balkan affairs in the State Department."[49]

The United States extended recognition to Tito's regime shortly after Adamic's meeting with Truman, but it did so with the caveat that recognition did not indicate approval of Tito's policies. Patterson remained in Yugoslavia, accredited as the American ambassador, even though he was so openly critical of the regime that in a December issue of *The Bulletin*, Adamic referred to him as being "none too bright."[50] While continuing to write for *The Bulletin*, Adamic also established a new publication, *Today and Tomorrow*, whose "point of view is fluid." He intended to use this outlet to look at American foreign policy, minority issues, Russian relations, Slavs, and the Vatican. Hoover sent a copy of the first issue to the Foreign Activity Correlation Division at State.[51]

Despite his continued support for Tito, Adamic's personal relationships and those among the members of the UCSSA underwent increasing strain. In 1946, Stoyan Pribichevich complained to Adamic of his displeasure with the UCSSA and the drain their constant pleas for assistance exerted on his time and expertise. He had no desire to "become a United Committee employee ... a counterpart of some *Srbobran* editor." He believed it essential for his own career that he remain aloof from "any Yugoslav-American organizations" and target his writing to "the American, not the hyphenated-American audience." The committee's work on behalf of Tito had become increasingly disorganized and ineffective, and Pribichevich advised Adamic that they "do a little less banqueting and a little more work for the cause."[52] Adamic himself stepped down from his position as co-chairman of the United Committee in the spring of 1946, although he remained on the board. He later told a colleague in the Slovene community that he had never been "entirely satisfied" with the work of the United Committee; it had not adequately explained its operating procedures to its contributors, and the money spent on expenses "was rather high." He had also come to believe that "relief was not half so necessary as political work," and he simply "could not do both." He urged his correspondent to complete the fund drives currently underway, but he believed that the relief campaigns run by the United Committee should end.[53]

Frano Petrinović also resigned from the committee in the spring of 1946, expressing his distress to Adamic that the organization had become a "group which violently criticized the American government and sees no good anywhere in the world except in the Soviet Union and Soviet-controlled areas." He was "not a Communist" and had pledged his support to Tito believing that he "promised to the people of Yugoslavia political and economic freedom and respect for private property." While he was willing to give Tito time to fulfill that commitment, he could not remain in a United Committee "dominated by its Communist members." The group "had outlived its usefulness," and, he "as a guest of the United States," could not risk association with it.[54] He was also upset because the regime had confiscated his family's property in Yugoslavia. Adamic, while critical of Petrinović for being "quite unreasonable and impulsive," conceded that Yugoslavia was "going pretty far to the Left." However, in the absence of American aid for reconstruction, he thought there was little the leadership could do "but reconstruct things the

Russian way—with work brigades, by confiscating things, etc."[55] The condi-tions Petrinović and Adamic described caused the United States to become even more critical of Tito, and as the Cold War deepened, the Americans came to see Yugoslavia as just another of Stalin's satellite regimes.

As these events unfolded, the stalemate at Justice caused by the Balokovic/Biddle question continued. Hoover complained repeatedly to the Criminal Division, to which the administration of FARA had been moved in 1946, about the delay in what appeared to him to be an obvious case of "utter dis-regard and apparent contempt for the provisions of the Registration Act."[56] Although the Justice Department as yet had no proof of Balokovic's assertion of a meeting with Biddle, John F. X. McGohey, the United States Attorney implied "he would be hesitant to start legal action until he determines what commitment former attorney general Biddle made as to whether subject organization should register." He believed that the UCSSA probably had violated FARA, but if Biddle had granted them an extension, that "would be a valid defense" against any action the government might now undertake.[57]

By August 1947, the United States Attorney had ascertained that Biddle's diary contained no reference to a meeting with Balokovic, nor did his sec-retary have any memory of such a meeting. The United States Attorney asked for Biddle to be interviewed to determine, finally, if any discussions had taken place.[58] However, the Justice Department decided that Balokovic should be interviewed before Biddle and instructed the FBI to do so, only to have the FBI object since the matter was already in the hands of the United States Attorney's office.[59] The FBI believed the UCSSA was "a Communist medium" that "had had powerful interests supporting it," but "since this phase of the case is purely administrative in character" suggested it should pass out of the FBI's hands.[60] The Justice Department eventually interviewed Biddle "about the alleged conference, but he did not recall any such confer-ence and indicated that it had been his practice to refer such matters to the section concerned." The Justice Department decided, in the spring of 1948, that it was "fruitless" to continue that aspect of the investigation.[61] As this study has shown, the meeting in question did occur; the informant's packet provided to the FBI contained proof of this, but Biddle's recollection, or lack of it, carried more weight than the word of the United Committee.

In 1948 the United Committee ceased its activities. In 1949, it closed its offices and under the very gaze of the FBI (surveilling agents described the truck and the filing cabinets and crates in detail) moved and then secreted or destroyed its files.[62] Hoover confided to his staff that any prosecution of the United Committee would involve "considerable publicity" since Adamic was well known among Washington's "liberal" classes (he included Eleanor Roosevelt in this category); Baloković, who was married to an heiress, was "likewise intimate with many influential "left-wingers" both in and out of government."[63]

Ironically, the Committee's demise occurred just as its cause reached fruition. In 1948, to the surprise of the Americans who viewed Tito as Stalin's most loyal follower, the Cominform expelled Tito from the international Communist movement and called on the Yugoslav people to overthrow him. The rift between Tito and Stalin actually had been long in coming, as Tito, who saw himself as a leader in his own region, resisted Stalin's attempts at control. By 1949, the Truman administration, seeing an opportunity to drive a wedge in the Soviet camp, began to assist Tito to demonstrate that Communist states, if they rejected Soviet imperialism and did not threaten the interests of the West, would be welcomed by the United States and its allies.[64]

This policy had repercussions at home. In 1950, Irving Saypol, the United States Attorney in New York in charge of the continuing investigation of the United Committee, advised that no prosecution be undertaken and requested that the case be closed. The committee no longer existed; its records could not be found; and the department's investigation had uncovered "no conclusive proof of any actual communication" between the United Committee "and a foreign government." In a statement indicative of the continuing political dimensions of the registration issue, Saypol concluded by stating his belief "that a decision in these matters should be predicated on the basis of present international conditions and, therefore, consideration should be given to the new situation which has developed as a result of the Marshall Tito–Cominform split." Adamic and Baloković were supporting Tito in his break with the Soviet Union and "are at odds with the Communist Party in this country and the Cominform." Although his superiors in Washington thought the last factor irrelevant (a handwritten note on that part of his text reads "NO! Has nothing to do with the case!"), they agreed to close the case because of the passage of time and the lack of evidence, and instructed the FBI to do so as well.[65]

Yet both Adamic and Baloković remained the subject of FBI investigations, as the bureau continued to view support for Tito as a negative attribute. The Balokovićs had gone to Yugoslavia in 1946 as representatives of the American Committee for Yugoslav Relief, and despite the deterioration in American-Yugoslav relations, they continued to support aid for the Tito regime. They were targeted as subversives by the House Un-American Activities Committee in 1949 for this stance but eventually were able to clear their names. They returned to Yugoslavia to be honored by Tito for their relief efforts; Zlatko Baloković, who died in 1965, was buried in his native Croatia.[66]

Adamic did not fare as well. Increasingly disturbed by both the anti-Communism of America's postwar policy and the harshness of the Tito regime, Adamic's writing became more "sharp, his voice shrill, his logic faulty." Opposed to Truman's foreign policy, Adamic served as an advisor to Henry Wallace during his 1948 Progressive Party campaign. After the Tito-Stalin split, he visited Yugoslavia but was distressed to find that Tito and his government, while polite, had no interest in Adamic's advice.[67] Adamic also became a target of the House Un-American Activities Committee after being named a spy by "Red Spy Queen" Elizabeth Bentley. The FBI could not substantiate Bentley's charges but entered Adamic's name into its "Security Index" file in 1951 because he remained "one of the foremost exponents of Tito communism in the United States today."[68] The Bureau canceled this listing after Adamic's apparent suicide in September.[69]

*　*　*

Louis Adamic and those Americans who, as he said, happened to be born in another country, were symbols of the ambiguities of the administration's foreign nationalities policy. In *Dinner at the White House*, Adamic detailed the "funny moments" caused by the "schizophrenic character of the United States Government, particularly in wartime," when "its Right often does not know what its Left is doing, and the other way about." While the Justice Department was attempting to secure Adamic's registration "as a foreign agent," he was "helping with scripts for a morale-building radio show sponsored by the Immigration and Naturalization Service, and the Treasury Department was sending [him] on tours to persuade people to buy war bonds and writing [him] appreciative letters of thanks."[70]

In that same work, Adamic also wrote of his hope, in the early days of America's participation in the war, that Roosevelt would develop an "aggressive foreign policy favoring democracy abroad and striving for ideological compromise." Had the president done so, "he could have evoked much support in new-immigrant groups as well as in sections of old-line American elements." However, Adamic believed the December 1941 statement on "free movements" by the State Department had "precluded" that because "behind its cleverly ambiguous verbiage," it "sharply warned the new-immigrant groups. To preserve the unity of the country in order that we might wage war successfully," he continued, "they were to refrain from starting movements concerning their old countries such as had troubled the government during World War I. This, naturally, had a depressing effect."[71]

The Foreign Nationalities Branch sinned as well. To Adamic, the purpose of the FNB was "negative, in line with Berle's: to treat the new-immigrant groups not as integral parts of America with unique qualities which could be used to advantage, but with suspicion as including potential subversive elements, and thereby indirectly keeping them from developing positive movements with regard to postwar political setups in Europe." Ultimately, the FNB, which Adamic, like Alan Cranston, persisted in seeing as an arm of Berle, "functioned with extremely unfortunate results. Clever and subtle, it was perhaps more damaging to the American spirit than were the brutal anti-German hysteria and Palmer persecutions of the foreign-born during and after World War I. The general public who might have objected, as some individuals did to putting Japanese Americans in concentration camps, knew noting about it." Congress aided Berle's purpose when it passed a law "requiring anyone actively interested in the form of government of any foreign country to register with the Department of Justice as a "foreign agent." Although "sent the registration forms a number of times," Adamic "refused to fill them out, maintaining that [he] was not an isolationist and that, believing the United States should participate in world affairs, [he] was logically concerned with governmental forms in other countries; that [his] interest in European reconstruction was motivated by what [he] considered the national interest of the United States."[72]

Yet this was indeed the issue: Adamic perceived that he was acting in the "national interest"; the agencies charged with safeguarding that interest and developing a foreign policy to serve it did not. The ultimate intent of all of the government initiatives that Adamic described was the same: to control the political activities of ethnics and to limit their foreign contacts. Yet Berle was not the villain. Nativism had been a characteristic of America since the earliest days of the republic, and the unique strength and success of Axis propaganda made even liberals fear that liberty and security were not compatible. The strategy of Alan Cranston and Archibald MacLeish, which sought to encourage the "right kind" of ethnic activity, was based in the end on the fear that ethics would naturally gravitate to the wrong kind of behavior. The Office of War Information's functions were curtailed because of political quarrels that had more to do with redbaiting and anti–New Deal sentiment than with Cranston, but his work with groups such as the UCSSA made his agency vulnerable. It was also impossible, in a faction-ridden community such as that of the Yugoslavs, to control the direction that ethnic political activity would take. Berle's resolve simply to stop that activity seemed the wisest course of action to a nation at war.

DeWitt Clinton Poole had a better understanding of the ties that immigrants felt for their homelands, but his task was to use them as a resource, not to comfort them. Of all of the agencies involved in this study, the FNB enjoyed the most success in pursuing its primary mission as Poole defined it. The branch existed to provide intelligence on the activities of foreign nationalities and on conditions in their former homelands, to both protect and advance the war effort. Poole and his agency fulfilled their mandate and, despite Adamic's criticism and Poole's increasing preoccupation with the growth of Soviet influence, brought a measure of sensitivity to their task.

At the time of its passage, liberals took care to depict the Foreign Agents Registration Act as a measure based on disclosure and persuasion rather than coercion. Chester Lane, for example, joined the FARA section because he had "very little patience with the doctrines of suppression." He said, "I thought I could have what I would regard as a healthy influence in tempering the possible wave of hysteria." He was confident that "the record as a whole [would] show that our governmental attitude towards unpopular minorities and towards unpopular forms of expression was much less repressive in the course of World War II than it was in the course of World War I."[73]

Historians, in contrasting Franklin Roosevelt with Woodrow Wilson, probably would agree that the "dozens victimized for their utterances and associations during World War II did not approach the thousands prosecuted for sedition during World War I."[74] However, the record also shows "a president little concerned about civil liberties,"[75] who sanctioned wiretaps and mail interceptions for persons "suspected of subversive activities"[76] and whose administration witnessed the persistent triumph of national security concerns over liberal principles.[77] Most of the foreign nationalities community were not aware of these violations of their civil liberties but they were aware that the government viewed them as something other than "100% American," a designation that they craved during this particular conflict.

When Yugoslav-Americans joined together to aid their former homeland, they did so as Americans. When FARA targeted them and other members of America's foreign nationalities community as "agents of a foreign principle," they resented it. Like Knapp, they suspected that the real intent was to limit their activities and curb their liberties. Yet unity was essential to the war effort; Yugoslav-Americans were contentious, and the areas they sought to influence were also in dispute among the members of the Grand Alliance. The Serbs had an almost tribal commitment to a land that no longer existed;

the United Committee embraced a movement founded on an ideology that many Americans—and especially many American diplomats—found objectionable. All of this made Yugoslav-Americans appear to be a danger to the American officials who made foreign policy and who equated divided loyalties with a lack of patriotism. The battles that ensued were unnecessary, divisive, and fruitless, and coupled with the FBI surveillance that accompanied them, they represent the single best example of the government's antipathy toward ethnic political activity during World War II.

The nativism at work had two components: the racial factor, which identified hyphenated Americans as suspect, and the anti-radical impetus, which targeted foreign ideologies. Because of Nazi propaganda and fifth-column fears, anti-radicalism in the early war years had both right- and left-wing components. However, the fear of communist influence in America's ethnic communities, and the growth of Soviet power in Europe, brought leftists to the forefront again, and this influenced the administration's approach to foreign nationalities issues. Although Adolf Berle would have opposed any "race movements," he was particularly alarmed by those with leftist sympathies. The FBI also continually emphasized information that pointed to communist influence within groups like the American Slav Congress and the United Committee and ignored or discredited reports that minimized that danger. The FARA unit at the Justice Department pursued cases against ethnic organizations in a relatively apolitical fashion, but the information it received from the FBI undermined this stance. Poole's approach was more balanced and his understanding of the divided loyalties of the ethnics more pronounced, but he turned his attention more and more to sounding the alarm about the increase in Soviet power that the course of war seemed to promise. The postwar Red Scare actually "solved" the ethnic problem in that the vast majority of the now old "new" immigrants denounced the Communist regimes that had come to their homelands, and they became fervent supporters of American Cold War policies. This support for American foreign policy, rather than the criticism that immigrants such as Adamic engaged in, made ethnics an object of interest once again, but as exhibits of the virtues of the American system.

Notes

Introduction

1. Throughout this study I will use the term foreign nationalities as it was used by the Roosevelt Administration during World War II, to designate inhabitants of the United States who were born abroad, or born in the United States of foreign parents, with ethnic groups as an alternative.

2. John Higham, *Strangers in the Land: Patterns of American Nativism, 1860–1925,* 2nd ed. (New York: Atheneum, 1973), 4–5; Alan M. Kraut, "Nativism," in *Encyclopedia of American Political History: Studies of the Principle Movements and Ideas,* ed. Jack P. Greene (New York: Scribner's, 1984), 2:863.

3. Philip Gleason, "Americans All: World War II and the Shaping of American Identity," in *Americanization, Social Control, and Philanthropy,* ed. George Pozzetta, 113–49 (New York: Garland, 1991).

4. Higham, *Strangers,* 116–23, 236–37.

5. Higham, *Strangers,* 204–13.

6. Higham, *Strangers,* 215–16, 242–44; David M. Kennedy, *Over There: The First World War and American Society* (New York: Oxford University Press, 1980), 65.

7. Higham, *Strangers,* 213, 215, 217, 219.

8. Higham, *Strangers,* 202; Kraut, "Nativism," 870.

9. Higham, *Strangers,* 224–27.

10. Higham, *Strangers,* 262–63, 301–2, 329.

11. John Bodnar, *Remaking America: Public Memory, Commemoration, and Patriotism in the Twentieth Century* (Princeton, N.J.: Princeton University Press, 1992), 72; Russell A. Kazal, "Revisiting Assimilation: The Rise, Fall, and Reappraisal of a Concept in American Ethnic History," *American Historical Review* 100 (April 1995): 442, 464.

12. Nicholas V. Montalto, *A History of the Intercultural Education Movement 1924–1941* (New York: Garland, 1982), 17–18.

13. Richard Weiss, "Ethnicity and Reform: Minorities and the Ambience of the Depression Years," *Journal of American History* 66 (December 1979): 573.

14. Weiss, "Ethnicity," 578–79.

15. Montalto, *Intercultural Education,* 19–20, 50–52; Weiss, "Ethnicity," 579.

16. Montalto, *Intercultural Education,* 123, 146–47.

17. Foreign Nationalities Branch (FNB), with a foreword by DeWitt Clinton Poole, *Foreign Nationality Groups in the United States: A Handbook,* 2nd ed. (Washington, D.C., 1945), vii.

18. FNB, *Handbook,* viii.

19. Franklin D. Roosevelt to J. Edgar Hoover, April 3, 1942, Franklin D. Roosevelt Papers, Papers as President (PAP), President's Secretary's Files (PSF), Hoover Justice file, box 77, Franklin D. Roosevelt Library, Hyde Park, New York (hereinafter Roosevelt Papers, FDRL).

20. Timothy Holian, *The German-Americans and World War II: An Ethnic Experience* (New York: Peter Lang, 1996), 130–31; Roger Daniels, *Guarding the Golden Door: American Immigration Policy and Immigrants Since 1882* (New York: Hill and Wang, 2004), 87.

21. John Christgau, *World War II Alien Internment* (Ames: Iowa State University Press, 1985), viii.

22. Holian, *German-Americans,* 135–36.

23. Stephen Fox, *America's Invisible Gulag: A Biography of German-American Internment and Exclusion in World War II* (New York: Peter Lang, 2000), xvi.

24. Louis Gerson, *The Hyphenate in Recent American Politics and Diplomacy* (Lawrence: University of Kansas Press, 1964), 6.

25. Gerson, *Hyphenate,* 34.

26. Barbara Jelavich, *History of the Balkans: Twentieth Century,* 2 vols. (Cambridge, Eng.: Cambridge University Press, 1983), 2:143–51.

27. Jozo Tomasevich, *The Chetniks: War and Revolution in Yugoslavia, 1941–1945* (Stanford, Calif.: Stanford University Press, 1975), 262.

28. Cordell Hull to Konstantin Fotić, May 28, 1941, *Foreign Relations of the United States Diplomatic Papers, 1941* (Washington, D.C.: GPO, 1959), 2:980–81 (hereinafter *FRUS,* with year and volume number or title).

29. Stephen Clissold, ed., *A Short History of Yugoslavia* (Cambridge, Eng.: Cambridge University Press, 1966), 216–17; Matteo J. Milazzo, *The Chetnik Movement and the Yugoslav Resistance* (Baltimore, Md.: Johns Hopkins University Press, 1975), 104.

30. Tomasevich, *Chetniks,* 262–75.

31. FNB, *Handbook,* vii.

Chapter 1: About Aliens and the Fifth Column

1. Francis Biddle, *The Fear of Freedom* (New York: Doubleday, 1952; New York: De Capo, 1971), 1–2.

2. Senate Select Committee to Study Governmental Operations with Respect to Intelligence Activities, [hereinafter Select Committee], *Final Report,* Book 2, *Intelligence Activities and the Rights of Americans,* 94th Cong., 2d sess., 1976, S. Rep. 755, Serial 13133–4:22.

3. Select Committee, *Final Report,* Book 3, *Supplementary Detailed Staff Reports on Intelligence Activities and the Rights of Americans,* 94th Cong., 2d sess., 1976, S. Rep. 755, Serial 13133–5:393–94.

4. Rhodri Jeffreys-Jones, *American Espionage: From Secret Service to CIA* (New York: Free Press, 1977), 42–43.

5. Athan Theoharis, *The FBI and American Democracy: A Brief Critical History* (Lawrence: University of Kansas Press, 2004), 22.

6. Theoharis, *FBI,* 45–46.

7. Richard Gid Powers, *Secrecy and Power: The Life of J. Edgar Hoover* (New York: Free Press, 1987), 9–53.

8. Powers, *Secrecy and Power,* 64.

9. Theoharis, *FBI,* 24.

10. Kenneth O'Reilly, *Hoover and the Un-Americans: The FBI, HUAC, and the Red Menace* (Philadelphia, Pa.: Temple University Press, 1983), 5, 13–18, 22; Powers, *Secrecy and Power,* 33, 55, 64, 147; Theoharis, *FBI,* 31–36.

11. U.S. Senate, Select Committee, *Final Report,* Book 3, 94th Cong., 2d. sess., 1976, S. Rep. 755, Serial 13133–5:396.

12. Powers, *Secrecy and Power,* 230.

13. Kenneth O'Reilly, "A New Deal for the FBI: The Roosevelt Administration, Crime Control, and National Security," *Journal of American History* 69 (December 1982): 651–53.

14. Theoharis, *FBI,* 1–2.

15. Brett Gary, *The Nervous Liberals: Propaganda Anxieties From World War I to the Cold War* (New York: Columbia University Press, 1999), 194.

16. Foreign Official Status Notification, with attached Instructions, n.d., General Records of the Department of Justice, 1790–1989, Record Group (RG) 60, Records of the War Division, 1940–1946, entry SWPU, box 5, FARA Correspondence, Memoranda, etc. file, National Archives of the United States, College Park, Md. (NA II).

17. Reed Ueda, "Naturalization and Citizenship," in *Harvard Encyclopedia of Ethnic Groups,* ed. Stephan Thernstrom, Ann Orlov, and Oscar Handlin, 744–45 (Cambridge, Mass.: Harvard University Press, 1980).

18. Office of Education, minutes, September 28, 1938, Records of the Office of Education, RG 12, Radio Program Series (RPS), entry 174, box 221, Americans All—Planning file, National Archives of the United States, Washington, D.C. (NA I).

19. Service Bureau for Intercultural Education, news release, December 23, 1938, RG 12, RPS, entry 174, box 221, Correspondence with Service Bureau for Intercultural Education file.

20. Montalto, *Intercultural Education,* 150–58.

21. Weiss, "Ethnicity," 582; Louis Adamic, "Thirty Million New Americans," *Harper's*, November 2, 1934, 685.

22. Montalto, *Intercultural Education*, 160–62.

23. Rachel Davis-Dubois, announcement with attachments, November 26, 1938, RG 12, RPS, entry 174, box 221, Americans All—Correspondence with Service Bureau for Intercultural Education file.

24. Service Bureau for Intercultural Education, news release, February 7, 1939, RG 12, RPS, entry 174, box 221, Americans All—Promotion and Follow-Up file.

25. "Americans All—Immigrants All, Series Outline," n.d., RG 12, RPS, entry 174, box 221, Prospectus, Americans All—Immigrants All file.

26. "Americans All—Immigrants All," n. d., RG 12, RPS, entry 174, box 221, Americans All, Promotion and Follow-up file.

27. "Americans All—Immigrants All, Script #1," n.d., RG 12, RPS, entry 174, box 221, Prospectus, Americans All—Immigrants All file.

28. Office of Education, news release, "Slavs in America II," February 6, 1939, Rachel Davis-Dubois Papers, General, Box 3, Slavs file, Immigration History Research Center (IHRC), University of Minnesota.

29. Montalto, *Intercultural Education*, 166–69.

30. Roosevelt Presidential Press Conference, Number 577, September 8, 1939, *Complete Presidential Press Conferences of Franklin D. Roosevelt* (New York: De Capo, 1972), 14:153–55 (hereinafter *Roosevelt Presidential Press Conferences* with number, date, volume, and page).

31. Theoharis, *FBI*, 48.

32. Jordan A. Schwarz, *Liberal: Adolf A. Berle and the Vision of an American Life* (New York: Free Press, 1987), 169.

33. Francis Biddle, *In Brief Authority* (New York: Doubleday, 1962), 107–9.

34. Adolf A. Berle diary, April 25, 1940, Adolf A. Berle Papers, FDRL (hereinafter Berle diary with date).

35. Richard M. Fried, *The Russians Are Coming! The Russians Are Coming!* (New York: Oxford University Press, 1998), 6, 14–15.

36. "I'm an American," announcement, May 1, 1940, with script attachments, 25/2 Radio, Immigration and Naturalization Service (INS), Norfolk, Va.

37. Script No. 1, May 4, 1940, 25/2 Radio, Immigration and Naturalization Service (INS), Norfolk, Va.

38. "I'm an American," announcement, May 1, 1940, with script attachments. Mann and other German exiles were under FBI surveillance at the time; see Alexander Stephan, *"Communazis,"* trans. Jan van Heurck (New Haven, Conn.: Yale University Press, 2000).

39. "I'm an American," Script No. 8, June 22, 1940, 25/2 Radio, INS.

40. "I'm an American," Script No. 15, August 10, 1940, 25/2 Radio, INS.

41. "I'm an American," Script No. 6, June 8, 1940, 25/2 Radio, INS.

42. Richard Steele, *Free Speech in the Good War* (New York: St. Martin's, 1999), 74–79.

43. Special War Policies Unit (SWPU), annual report, November 30, 1942, RG 60, Subject Files, entry SWPU, Reports-Annual-Quarterly file.

44. "Report of the Chief of the Special Defense Unit, Lawrence M. C. Smith," *Annual Report of the Attorney General of the United States for the Fiscal Year Ended 30 June 1941*, January 3, 1942, 77th Cong., 2d. sess., 1942, H. Doc. 509, Serial 10713:266–67; Steele, *Free Speech*, 60–61.

45. Gary, *Nervous Liberals*, 176.

46. Steele, *Free Speech*, 60–61.

47. Chester T. Lane, "Reminiscences of Chester T. Lane," 1972, Oral History Research Office, Columbia University (New York: 1972), 604, 610, 630, 632, 638 (hereinafter Lane, Oral History with page).

48. Steele, *Free Speech*, 81; for a discussion of the origins of the law, see Michael R. Belknap, *Cold War Political Justice: The Smith Act, the Communist Party, and American Civil Liberties* (Westport, Conn.: Greenwood, 1977), 16, 22–25.

49. Gary, *Nervous Liberals*, 195–96.

50. "Report of the Chief of the Special Defense Unit, Lawrence M. C. Smith," *Annual Report of the Attorney General*, January 3, 1942, 266–69.

51. Robert Reynolds, "The Alien Problem," *Asheville North Carolina Citizen*, June 22, 1940, *Congressional Record* appendix, 76th Cong., 3d sess., 1940, 86 (16): 4171.

52. Alan Cranston to Jimmie [?], August 17, 1945, Alan Cranston Papers, box 4, Redbaiting 1943–1944 file, Bancroft Library, University of California—Berkeley; Daniel E. Weinberg, "The Foreign Language Information Service and the Foreign Born, 1918–1939" (PhD diss., University of Minnesota, 1973), 21–25.

53. FNB, "Common Council for American Unity," June 3, 1943, Records of the Office of Strategic Services (OSS), RG 226, Records of the FNB, entry 100, box 28, EU 221–230 file, NA II; Common Council for American Unity (CCAU), "Legislative News-Letter," February 10, 1941, Cranston Papers, box 3, Legislative Newsletters, 1940–41 file; Richard Steele, "War on Intolerance," *Journal of American Ethnic History* 9 (Fall 1999): 114–16, 22.

54. Alan Cranston, "Congress and the Alien," *Contemporary Jewish Record* 3 (May-June 1940): 245–52, Cranston Papers, box 3, Cranston's Published Articles, 1940–1944 file.

55. Read Lewis to James L. Houghteling, May 14, 1940, Cranston Papers, box 3, Correspondence January-June 1940 file.

56. Cranston to Lewis, May 24, 1940, Cranston Papers, box 3, Correspondence January-June 1940 file.

57. Foreign Language Information Service, "Legislative News-Letter," June 3, 1940, Cranston Papers, box 3, Legislative Newsletters, 1940–1941 file.

58. Berle diary, May 8, 1940; Biddle, *In Brief Authority*, 120; George Martin, *Madam Secretary: Frances Perkins* (Boston: Houghton, 1976), 406, 419.

59. Sumner Welles to Robert H. Jackson, and Jackson to Welles, May 15, 1940, with enclosures; Welles to Roosevelt, May 18, 1940 and Welles to FDR, *Supervision over Aliens Entering, Residing In, and Departing From the United States,* Robert H. Jack-

son Papers, box 90, Attorney General Immigration and Naturalization Transfer file, Library of Congress (LC), Washington, D.C.

60. Robert H. Jackson, *That Man: An Insider's Portrait of FDR,* ed. John Q. Barrett (New York: Oxford University Press, 2003), 60–61.

61. Jackson to Welles, May 15, 1940, Jackson Papers, box 90, Immigration and Naturalization Transfer file.

62. Memorandum, May 21, 1940, with attached Department of Justice press release, May 23, 1940, Jackson Papers, box 90, Attorney General Immigration and Naturalization Transfer file; Jackson, *That Man,* 61–62.

63. Martin, *Madam Secretary,* 442.

64. Roosevelt Presidential Press Conference, Number 645, May 21, 1940, 15:352–53.

65. Biddle, *In Brief Authority,* 108.

66. Biddle, *In Brief Authority,* 106.

67. Jackson, *That Man,* 62; "Sharp Limit Is Set on Entry of Aliens," *New York Times,* June 15, 1940, 9.

68. Biddle, *In Brief Authority,* 108.

69. Lewis to Cranston, May 22, 1940, Cranston Papers, Correspondence January-June 1940 file.

70. Donald Perry, "Aliens in the United States," *The Annuals of the American Academy of Political and Social Sciences, Minority Peoples in a Nation at War* 223 (September 1942): 1–9.

71. "Roosevelt Signs Bill to List Aliens," *New York Times,* June 29, 1940, L5.

72. Biddle, *In Brief Authority,* 110.

73. Maurice Isserman, *Which Side Were You On? The American Communist Party during the Second World War* (Middletown, Conn.: Wesleyan University Press, 1982), 68.

74. Biddle, *In Brief Authority,* 107.

75. Biddle, *Fear of Freedom,* 106.

76. CCAU, "Legislative News-Letter," July 1, 1940, Cranston Papers, box 3, Legislative Newsletters, 1940–1941 file.

77. Steele, *Free Speech,* 119.

78. Biddle, *In Brief Authority,* 112–17.

79. Earl G. Harrison, "The Alien Registration Act of 1940," August 7, 1940, American Council of Nationalities Services (ACNS), shipment 2, box 1, Alien registration, 1940, 2 files, IHRC.

80. "Good Guests of America," No. 1, September 17, 1940, ACNS, shipment 2, box 1, Alien Registration 1940 file.

81. Biddle, *In Brief Authority,* 112–17.

82. Robert Lewis Taylor, "Aliens All," *New Yorker,* November 9, 1940, 36.

83. Beulah Amidon, "Aliens in America," *Survey Graphic* 2 (February 1941): 26. The *Christian Century* in early January provided a more critical perspective on one aspect of the procedure. The receipts that were to be mailed to those who had

registered had not been sent out in a timely fashion, and aliens therefore could not prove that they had complied with the law. The magazine saw this as a violation of the government's pledge that aliens would not be treated with anything but tolerance and forbearance. "Little Alien, What Now?" *Christian Century* 57 (January 1941): 45–46.

84. Alan Cranston, "Alien Registration Accomplished—What Now?" *Common Ground* 1 (Spring 1941): 98.

85. Bernard G. Richards to Roosevelt, October 2, 1940, with attachment Adamic to Richards, September 29, 1940, Roosevelt Papers, Adamic file; Gerson, *Hyphenate,* 121–23.

86. M. E. Gilfond to Allen, February 10, 1941, with enclosure, Jackson Papers, box 90, Legal File, Attorney General Immigration and Naturalization Alien Registration file. According to the source text, the quote was actually fabricated by Gilfond.

87. R. Keith Kane to Thomas D. Quinn, October 22, 1940, RG 60, entry SWPU, box 14, Nationalities Section Program and Reports file.

88. L. M. C. Smith to the Solicitor General, November 19, 1940, RG 60, entry SWPU, box 14, Nationalities Section Program and Reports file.

89. Kane to the Solicitor General, December 20, 1940, RG 60, entry SWPU, box 14, Nationalities Section Program and Reports file.

90. Lane, Oral History, 606, 635.

91. Berle diary, July 19, 1941.

92. Berle diary, July 23, 1941.

93. Smith to the Acting Attorney General, June 19, 1941, with enclosure, RG 60, entry SWPU, box 4, FARA file.

94. Biddle to Frederick Van Nuys, November 24, 1941, 77th Congress, 1st sess., December 16, 1941, S. Rep. 913, 10–11.

95. Steele, *Free Speech,* 119–25; Biddle, *In Brief Authority,* 164–66.

96. CCAU, "Legislative News-Letter," October 1, 1941, Cranston Papers, box 3, Legislative Newsletters 1940–1941 file.

97. Biddle, *In Brief Authority,* 257–61; Steele, *Free Speech,* 125.

98. "The President Vetoes a Bill Proposing to Restrict Representatives of Friendly Countries in the United States," February 9, 1942, *The Public Papers and Addresses of Franklin D. Roosevelt,* ed. Samuel I. Rosenman (New York: Random House: 1938), 11:91–92.

99. Berle to Biddle, February 27, 1942, Berle Papers, State Department Correspondence 1938–1945, box 29, Francis Biddle file. Berle, after extensive discussions with British diplomats, thought that their complaint was solvable but complained that British intelligence simply "want the Act killed" because they did not want to disclose the "very considerable espionage" they practiced in the United States. Berle diary, February 1, 1942.

100. Biddle to Van Nuys, March 19, 1942, with enclosure "Proposed Amendment . . . ," February 27, 1942, RG 60, entry SWPU, box 5, FARA file.

101. James R. Sharp to Smith, March 26, 1942, RG 60, entry SWPU, box 4, FARA file.

102. FARA PL 532, April 29, 1942, *Statutes at Large*, 56: 248–58.

103. "War Division, Foreign Agents Registration Section, 1944–45 Justification," undated, RG 60, entry SWPU, box 6, FARA to Fascist Organizations file.

104. Department of Justice, press release, June 25, 1942, RG 60, entry SWPU, box 5, FARA Correspondence, Memoranda, etc. file.

105. Lane, Oral History, 637. The unit already had a group of translators who read and analyzed the foreign-language press; at the request of other agencies, such as the War Department, Navy, and the OWI, the unit had expanded this staff.

106. Gary, *Nervous Liberals*, 198–99; Harold L. Ickes, *The Secret Diary of Harold L. Ickes*, vol. 3, *The Lowering Clouds, 1939–1941* (New York: Simon, 1954), 368.

107. Gary, *Nervous Liberals*, 198–99.

108. Ickes, *Secret Diary*, 368.

109. Ickes to Clarence A. Dykstra, November 12, 1940, Harold L. Ickes Papers, Secretary of Interior File (SIF), LC, box 379, War—National Morale Committee (1) 1940 file.

110. Second Conference, Committee on Propaganda, November 18, 1940, Ickes Papers, SIF, box 247, Propaganda Committee, 1940 file.

111. Second Conference, Committee on Propaganda, November 18, 1940, Ickes Papers, SIF, box 247, Propaganda Committee, 1940 file.

112. Ickes to Lowell Mellett, November 26, 1940, with enclosure, "Tentative Draft: Report of Subcommittee," November 20, 1940, Ickes Papers, SIF, box 379, War—National Morale Committee (1) 1940 file.

113. Ickes to John McCloy, December 7, 1940, Ickes Papers, SIF, box 379, War—National Morale Committee (1) 1940 file.

114. John Morton Blum, *"V" Was for Victory: Politics and American Culture during World War II* (New York: Harcourt, 1976), 8–9.

115. Ickes to Mellett, March 18, 1941, Ickes Papers, SIF, box 379, War—National Morale Committee (3) 1941 March file.

116. Bradley F. Smith, *The Shadow Warriors: OSS and the Origins of the CIA* (New York: Basic Books, 1983), 27–34.

117. William J. Donovan and Edgar Mowrer, *Fifth Column Lessons for America*, with an introduction by Frank Knox (Washington, D.C.: American Council on Public Affairs, 1941).

118. Smith, *Shadow Warriors*, 26.

119. Douglas M. Charles, "'Before the Colonel Arrived': Hoover, Donovan, Roosevelt, and the Origins of American Central Intelligence, 1940–41," *Intelligence and National Security* 20 (June 2005): 232–35.

120. Schwarz, *Liberal*, 169–71.

121. Thomas F. Troy, *Donovan and the CIA* (Frederick, Md.: University of America, 1981), 419.

122. "White House Statement Announcing the President's Appointment Of William J. Donovan as Coordinator of Information," July 11, 1941, *Public Papers of Franklin D. Roosevelt*, 10:264.

123. Troy, *Donovan*, 93.

124. Ickes to Roosevelt, September 17, 1941, Ickes Papers, SIF, box 379, War—National Morale Committee (4) 1941 April-October file.

125. "The President Establishes the Office of Facts and Figures, Executive Order No. 8922," 24 October 1941, *Public Papers*, 10:425–27.

126. James Reston, "Federal Agency Set Up to Unify Data on Defense," *New York Times*, October 8, 1941, 1, 11.

127. Scott Donaldson in collaboration with R. H. Winnick, *Archibald MacLeish: An American Life* (Boston: Houghton 1992), 333; David Barber, "Archibald MacLeish's Life and Career," *American National Biography*, ed. John A. Garraty and Mark C. Canes (New York: Oxford University Press, 1999), 14:269–71.

128. Allan M. Winkler, *The Politics of Propaganda: The Office of War Information, 1942–1945* (New Haven, Conn.: Yale University Press, 1978), 11, 13, 32–38, 41.

129. Frank A. Warren, *Noble Abstractions: American Liberal Intellectuals and World War II* (Columbus: Ohio State University Press, 1999), xiv, 1, 3–7.

130. Jerre Mangione, *An Ethnic At Large: A Memoir of America in the Thirties and Forties* (New York: Putnam's, 1978), 304.

131. Memorandum, undated, Records of the Office of War Information, RG 208, entry 232, box 1115, NA II. Internal evidence indicates 1942 because 1942 fiscal year request is included.

132. Eleanor Fowle, *Cranston: The Senator from California* (California: Presidio, 1980) 31–38, 42, 47–48, 53; Cranston to R. J. Blakely, September 21, 1942, Cranston Papers, box 3, Hiring Papers file. In 1945, Cranston published a history of the "little group of powerful men" who "isolated America" by causing the country to reject membership in the League of Nations. The book, *The Killing of the Peace*, was written to "make it more difficult for any little cabal to do the same thing again." Alan Cranston, *The Killing of the Peace* (New York: Viking, 1945), ix-x.

133. Fowle, *Cranston*, 48–50.

134. Fowle, *Cranston*, 56–57.

135. Cranston to George A. Barnes, December 31, 1941, RG 208, entry 222, box 1080, Memos file.

136. Fowle, *Cranston*, 56–57.

137. Cranston to Lee Falk, January 29, 1942, Cranston Papers, box 3, Correspondence-outgoing—12–23–41 to 10–29–43 file.

138. Schwarz, *Liberal*, 24, 196.

139. Beatrice Bishop Berle and Travis Jacobs, eds., *Navigating the Rapids 1918–1971* (New York: Harcourt, 1973), June 4, 1940 (320–21); October 10, 1940 (340–41); Berle diary, 1 June 1940.

140. B. B. Berle and T. Jacobs, *Navigating the Rapids*, September 26, 1940, 336–37.

141. A. M. Wilson, "Foreign Nationalities Branch," undated, RG 226, entry 100, box 1, N.Y.-FNB-Ad-1 file (hereinafter Wilson, "Foreign Nationalities Branch," with page number).

142. Graham H. Stuart, *The Department of State: A History of Its Organization, Procedure and Personnel* (New York: Macmillan, 1949), 348. The division had originally been formed in the fall of 1940 to deal with intelligence issues.

143. J. P. Warburg to R. E. Sherwood, October 23, 1941, Tab B, "Exhibits Illustrating the History of the OSS-Foreign Nationalities," RG 226, entry 99, box 74, file 28 (hereinafter "Exhibits OSS"). These exhibits were an appendage to the Wilson history cited in note 137 but were not attached in the file.

144. Berle diary, October 16, 1941.

145. Wilson, "Foreign Nationalities Branch," 2–5.

146. Wilson, "Foreign Nationalities Branch," 2–5.

147. Wilson, "Foreign Nationalities Branch," 10.

148. Wilson, "Foreign Nationalities Branch," 10–13.

149. Wilson, "Foreign Nationalities Branch," 10–13. William J. Donovan to Roosevelt, December 20, 1941, Roosevelt Papers, PSF Subject, PSF-OSS, box 163, Donovan Reports December 1942, Folder 2 file. The source text reads "OK, FDR."

150. Wilson, "Foreign Nationalities Branch," 10–16; Donovan to Hull, January 12, 1942, Roosevelt Papers, PSF Subject, PSF-OSS, box 164, Donovan Reports, Folder 4 file.

151. General statement, undated, unsigned, RG 226, entry 100, box 2, Budget estimates, 1942–1942, New York-FNB-Ad-2 file; Wilson, "Foreign Nationalities Branch," 7.

152. General statement, undated, unsigned, RG 226, entry 100, box 2, Budget estimates, 1942–1942, New York-FNB-Ad-2 file.

153. Wilson, "Foreign Nationalities Branch," 1.

154. DeWitt Clinton Poole, "The Study of Foreign Political Developments in the United States: A New Field of Political Intelligence," December 31, 1944, RG 226, entry 100, box 121, FNB-INT-34 file (hereinafter Poole, "Foreign Political Developments").

155. Poole to Wallace R. Deuel, April 27, 1944, Tab E, "Exhibits OSS."

156. Poole to John C. Wiley, February 2, 1942, RG 226, entry 100, box 129, Wiley, JC originals file.

157. Poole, office memorandum, March 10, 1942, Tab M, "Exhibits OSS."

158. Poole to L. M. C. Smith, March 29, 1943, RG 226, entry 86, Foreign Nationalities Branch Miscellaneous Papers July 1942–August 1945 file.

159. Wilson, "Foreign Nationalities Branch," 71, 79–83.

160. U.S. State Department, "Policy Regarding 'Free Movements' in the United States," *Department of State Bulletin*, December 10, 1941, 5:519–20 (hereinafter *DSB* with date, volume, and page).

161. Berle diary, January 9, 1942.

162. Berle, memorandum, January 21, 1942, Tab R, "Exhibits OSS."

163. Berle diary, January 21, 1942.

164. Berle to Hull, January 26, 1942, Berle Papers, box 58, Hull Memo, January-August 1942 file.

165. Fowle, *Cranston,* 71–72.

166. Schwarz, *Liberal,* 201–4; "Adolf Augustus Berle," *American National Biography,* 2:657–59.

167. Cranston to MacLeish, January 26, 1942, Cranston Papers, box 4, Berle file.

168. Poole, office memorandum, January 28, 1942, attachment to John C. Wiley to Colonel G. Edward Buxton, June 19, 1942, RG 226, entry 100, box 129, State Department—Interdepartment New York-FNB-Op-2 file; Harold B. Hoskins, memorandum, February 6, 1942, with attachments, RG 226, entry 100, box 129, State Department—Interdepartment New York-FNB-Op-2 file.

169. MacLeish to Donovan, January 28, 1942, RG 226, entry 100, box 129, State Department—Interdepartment New York-FNB-Op-2 file.

170. Wiley, memorandum for the Files, January 28, 1942, RG 226, entry 100, box 129, State Department—Interdepartment New York-FNB-OP-2 file.

171. Hoskins, memorandum, February 2, 1942, RG 226, entry 100, box 129, Op-2-82 file. The Committee on War Information, chaired by MacLeish, dealt with information policy and included representatives from the Departments of State, Navy, War, and Justice.

172. Poole to Wiley, February 6, 1942, with attachment, Hoskins memo on Interdepartmental Committee for Psychological Warfare, February 2, 1942, RG 226, entry 100, box 129, State Department file.

173. Wiley to Donovan, February 10, 1942, RG 226, entry 100, box 129, State Department—Interdepartment New York-FNB-Op-2 file; Wilson, "Foreign Nationalities Branch," 30–31.

174. Hoskins, Minutes of the Third Meeting—Interdepartmental Committee for Foreign Nationality Problems, February 1942, dated February 16, 1942, RG 226, entry 100, box 129, State Department—Interdepartment New York-FNB-Op-2 file.

175. Poole to Donovan, March 20, 1942, RG 226, entry 100, box 129, State Department—Interdepartment New York-FNB-Op-2 file.

Chapter 2: A Feud Entirely European in Origin

1. FNB, *Handbook,* 232.

2. Jozo Tomasevich, *War and Revolution in Yugoslavia, 1941–1945: The Chetniks* (Stanford, Calif.: Stanford University Press, 1975), 8.

3. Tomasevich, *Chetniks,* 8–12; Jelavich, *History of the Balkans,* 2:143–51, 157, 200–202.

4. Tomasevich, *Chetniks,* 22–25; Jelavich, *History of the Balkans,* 2:204.

5. Arthur Bliss Lane to Hull, for Welles, March 6, 1941, *FRUS,* 1941, 2:949.

6. Welles to Roosevelt, March 27, 1941, Sumner Welles Papers, box 166, Europe Files, file 15.

7. Lane to Hull, March 31, 1941, *FRUS*, 1941, 2:973.

8. Walter R. Roberts, *Tito, Mihailović and the Allies 1941–1945* (New Brunswick, N.J.: Rutgers University Press, 1973) 19; Robert L. Wolff, *The Balkans in Our Time* (Cambridge, Eng.: Cambridge University Press, 1956), 201–3; Simon Trew, *Britain, Mihailović and the Chetniks, 1941–1942* (New York: St. Martin's, 1998), 4; Tomasevich, *Chetniks,* 39–43; King Peter II of Yugoslavia, *A King's Heritage* (New York: Putnam's, 1954), 17.

9. John R. Lampe, *Yugoslavia as History: Twice There Was a Country* (Cambridge, Eng.: Cambridge University Press, 1996), 200–203; Jelavich, *History of the Balkans,* 2:266.

10. FNB, *Handbook,* ix-xiii, 221–22.

11. Welles to Jackson, May 24, 1940, with enclosure, "Observations on, and Recommendations for, the Control of Aliens within the United States as a Measure of Prevention of Sabotage, Espionage, and Other Forms of Subversive Activity," Jackson Papers, box 90, Attorney General Immigration and Naturalization, Transfer of Immigration and Naturalization to Department of Justice file.

12. "The Yugoslav-Language Press in the United States and Canada," September, 2, 1944, FNB No. 210, Records of the War Department General and Special Staff, RG 165, entry 79, box 1958, War Department General and Special Staff file, NA II.

13. FNB, *Handbook,* 224–26; "Slovenian Politics in the United States," FNB No. 163, December 2, 1943, RG 226, entry 100, box 109, FNB Reports, volume 2, 151–90, New York-FNB-Int.-31 file.

14. John D. Butkovich to Roosevelt, April 9, 1941, General Records of the Department of State, RG 59, 860H.01/295–1/2, NA II; Gerson, *Hyphenate,* 124.

15. Williamson, memorandum of conversation, April 25, 1941, RG 59, 860H.01/330–1/2.

16. Williamson, memorandum, April 30, 1941, RG 59, 860H.01/423.

17. Wells to Hull, April 23, 1941, Welles Papers, box 166, Europe Files, file 15.

18. Constantin Fotitch, *The War We Lost; Yugoslavia's Tragedy and the Failure of the West* (New York: Viking, 1948), 109–11.

19. Welles to Berle, May 12, 1941, with attachment, RG 59, 860H.01/297 1/2.

20. Welles to Berle, April 28, 1941, and May 7, 1941, Welles Papers, box 166, Europe Files, file 15.

21. Berle, memorandum, June 2, 1941, RG 59, 860H.01/295 1/2.

22. Lampe, *Yugoslavia as History,* 210–13; Trew, *Britain,* 7–9, 37; Jelavich, *History of the Balkans,* 2: 267–68.

23. Trew, *Britain,* 16.

24. Tomasevich, *Chetniks,* 265–67.

25. Welles to Donovan, 26 October 1941, with enclosure, Welles Papers, box 166, Europe Files, file 15.

26. Lampe, *Yugoslavia as History,* 215; Tomasevich, *Chetniks,* 268–71.

27. Tomasevich, *Chetniks,* 275–76, 265–67. The three ministers had been sent to North America in the spring of 1941 to generate support for Yugoslavia among Slavic immigrants in the United States and Canada.

28. Poole to L. M. C. Smith, March 29, 1943, RG 226, entry 86, FNB Miscellaneous Papers July 1942–August 1945 file.

29. "Foreign Politics in the United States: The Serb Anti-Croat Campaign," FNB No. 15, April 13, 1942, RG 226, entry 100, box 108, FNB-Report 1–100 New York-FNB-Int. 31 file.

30. "Foreign Politics in the United States: The Serb Anti-Croat Campaign," FNB No. 15, April 13, 1942, RG 226, entry 100, box 108, FNB-Report 1–100 New York-FNB-Int. 31 file; "Foreign Politics in the United States: The Serb Anti-Croat Campaign: II," No. 26, 7 May 1942, RG 226, entry 100, box 108, FNB-Report 1–100 New York-FNB-Int. file.

31. "Foreign Politics in the United States: The Serb Anti-Croat Campaign: II," No. 26, 7 May 1942, RG 226, entry 100, box 108, FNB-Report 1–100 New York-FNB-Int. file. The American government referred to the bishop as Bishop Dionisije, and this study will follow their example henceforth for clarity.

32. Poole to Hoskins, May 13, 1942, with enclosure Poole to Alan Cranston, May 13, 1942, RG 208, entry 222, box 1022, Serbs file.

33. Poole to Cranston, May 13, 1942 with attachments, Poole to Hoskins, May 13, 1942, and Poole to Hoskins, May 13, 1942, with Serbian National Defense article, *American Srbobran,* April 28, 1942, RG 208, entry 222, box 1082, Serbs file.

34. Poole to Wiley, April 14, 1942, RG 226, entry 100, box 129, Wiley, J. C. originals file.

35. Hugh R. Wilson to Wiley, April 14, 1942, with enclosures Re: Serb National Federation, April 8, 1942, and Re: Croatian Affairs, April 7, 1942, by S. K., RG 226, entry 100, box 98, YU 41–50 file.

36. Nicholas Mirkovich to Adamic, April 22, 1942, Louis Adamic Papers, box 51, file 7, Manuscripts Division, Department of Rare Books and Special Collections, Princeton University Library, Princeton, NJ.

37. Poole to Wiley, April 14, 1942, RG 226, entry 100, box 129, Wiley, J.C. originals file.

38. Mladen Trbuhovich, "Analytical Report to the Facts and Figures Office on the Downfall of Yugoslavia, Its Interior Controversies, the Croatian Betrayal and Their Activities Here and Abroad," undated, RG 208, entry 222, box 1075, Hungarian file. Internal evidence indicates this was written in April 1942.

39. Trbuhovich, "Analytical Report," 18.

40. Special agent in charge (SAC) Pittsburgh to Hoover, September 7, 1942, with enclosures, FOIA/FBI SNDC file 97–1340–9.

41. Michael S. Sweeney, *Secrets of Victory: The Office of Censorship and the American Press and Radio in World War II* (Chapel Hill: University of North Carolina Press, 2001), 76–77.

42. Cranston to Ulrich Bell, April 2, 1942, RG 208, entry 221, box 1073, Katherine Blackburn file.

43. "Hint Curb on Press in Foreign Tongue," *New York Times,* April 13, 1942, Cranston Papers, box 4, Office Files, 1942–1943.

44. Lewis to the editor of the *New York Times,* April 17, 1942, ACNS, shipment 4, box 7, Foreign-Language Press file.

45. Summary of meeting of April 13, 1942, RG 208, Records of the Historian—Subject File 1941–1946, entry 6E, box 11, minutes of the Committee on War Information, December 1941–May 1942 file; Hoskins, minutes of the ninth meeting of the Interdepartmental Committee on Foreign Nationality Problems, April 15, 1942, RG 226, entry 100, box 129, Op-2-82 file.

46. Sweeney, *Secrets of Victory,* 78–79.

47. Department of Justice, press release, April 28, 1942, RG 208, entry 222, box 1081, Press Control file.

48. *New York Times,* May 22, 1942, 42.

49. Henry A. Christian, *Louis Adamic: A Checklist* (Kent, Ohio: Kent State University Press, 1971), xxi, xxvii; William C. Beyer, "Creating 'Common Ground' on the Home Front: Race, Class, and Ethnicity in a 1940s Quarterly," in *The Home Front War: World War II and American Society,* ed. Kenneth Paul O'Brien and Lynn Hudson Parsons (Westport, Conn.: Greenwood, 1995), 41–44.

50. Carey McWilliams, *Louis Adamic and Shadow-America* (Los Angeles: Whipple, 1935), 13, 20–21, 39, 53.

51. Louis Adamic, address to the Common Council for American Unity, April 3, 1941, Adamic Papers, box 37, file 8.

52. Louis Adamic, *Two-Way Passage* (New York: Harper, 1941), 10.

53. Adamic, *Two-Way Passage,* 14, 225+.

54. Adamic, *Two-Way Passage,* 268–70.

55. Eleanor Roosevelt to Adamic, October 18, 1941, and Adamic to Eleanor Roosevelt, October 30, 1941, #1587, Eleanor Roosevelt Papers, FDRL (hereinafter ER Papers).

56. Eleanor Roosevelt to Adamic, December 29, 1941, #1587, ER Papers.

57. Eleanor Roosevelt to Adamic, undated, #1629, ER Papers.

58. Louis Adamic, *Dinner at the White House* (New York: Harper, 1946).

59. Adamic, *Dinner,* 8–39.

60. Adamic, *Dinner,* 66, 64.

61. Adamic to Eleanor Roosevelt, January 25, 1942, #1629, attachment to Eleanor Roosevelt to Adamic, January 30, 1942, ER Papers.

62. Adamic, "Memorandum for Mrs. Roosevelt," January 25, 1942, #10, Anna Roosevelt Halstead Papers, FDRL (hereinafter Halstead Papers).

63. Adamic, "Memorandum for Mrs. Roosevelt."

64. Adamic, "Memorandum for Mrs. Roosevelt."

65. Adamic, "Memorandum for Mrs. Roosevelt."

66. Eleanor Roosevelt to Adamic, January 30, 1942, #1629, ER Papers.

67. Adamic, *Dinner,* 140.

68. Biddle to W. Colston Leigh, February 5, 1942; "Louis Adamic Drafted by the Government," Harper news release, undated; press clipping, February 17, 1942, Adamic Papers, box 47, file L.

69. Clayton Koppes, "Hollywood and the Politics of Representation: Women, Workers, and African-Americans in World War II Movies," in O'Brien and Hudson, *Home Front War,* 36.

70. John LaTouche, "Treasury Star Parade," "Two Way Passage," June 7, 1942, Adamic Papers, box 39, file 4.

71. Poole to Hoskins, May 27, 1942, RG 226, entry 100, box 98, Yu 81–90 file. On May 28, 1942, Hoskins sent Dunn, Atherton, Cannon, and Welles a copy of the report Poole had made of his conversation with Šubašić. Poole to Hoskins, May 27, 1942, with Hoskins attachment, RG 59, 860H.01/449.

72. Wiley to Donovan, June 3, 1942, with attachment Poole to Wiley, May 30, 1942, RG 226, entry 100, box 98, YU 71–80 file.

73. Wiley to Donovan, May 27, 1942, RG 226, entry 100, box 98, YU 81–90 file.

74. Wiley to Donovan, May 27, 1942, RG 226, entry 100, box 98, YU 81–90 file; Hoskins, "Minutes of the Twelfth Meeting of the Interdepartmental Committee for Foreign Nationality Problems," May 27, 1942, RG 208, entry 232, box 1115, State Department file. Wiley later told Donovan that "the State Department is alive to the situation in consequence of the information" FNB had supplied.

75. Daniel Leab, *I Was a Communist for the FBI: The Unhappy Life and Times of Matt Cvetic* (University Park: Pennsylvania State University Press, 2000), 37.

76. As quoted in Jeffrey Ryan, "The Conspiracy That Never Was: United States Government Surveillance of Eastern European American Leftists, 1942–1959," (PhD diss., Boston College, 1990), 44.

77. FBI, General Intelligence Survey, August 1944, Harry Hopkins Papers, box 146, FDRL.

78. J. P. Warburg to Hoskins, November 8, 1941, with attachments, RG 59, 860H.01/371; Stephen Zeman to Stephen A. Early, November 15, 1941, with attached statement by American Slav Congress Committee, RG 59, 860H.01/364.

79. Warburg to Hoskins, November 18, 1941 with attachment, Hoskins to Warburg, November 19, 1941, RG 59, 860H.01/365.

80. Leab, *I Was a Communist,* 36; Mary Cygan, "American Slav Congress," in *Encyclopedia of the American Left,* ed. Mari Jo Buhle, Paul Buhle, Dan Georgakas (Urbana and Chicago: University of Illinois Press, 1992), 28–29.

81. MacLeish to Berle, April 2, 1942, with attachment, Cranston to MacLeish, April 2, 1942 and Berle to MacLeish, April 4, 1942, Berle Papers, State Department Correspondence, 1938–1945, box 43, MacLeish, Archibald file.

82. Poole to Wiley, April 7, 1942, RG 226, entry 100, box 129, Wiley, J. C. originals file.

83. Hoskins, "Minutes of the Ninth Meeting of the Interdepartmental Committee

for Foreign Nationality Problems," April 15, 1942, RG 226, entry 100, box 129, State Department, Interdepartment file.

84. Lee Falk to Station Manager, April 15, 1942, RG 208, entry 232, box 1114, American Slav Congress file.

85. Cranston to Ulrich Bell, April 20, 1942, RG 208, entry 221, box 1073, Ulrich Bell file.

86. Roosevelt to the American Slav Congress, April 25, 1942, with attachments, Roosevelt Papers, PPF 8032, American Slav Congress, American Slav Congress file.

87. Ryan, "Conspiracy," 22.

88. Poole to Hoskins, May 27, 1942, with attachments, RG 59, 860H.01/383 _.

89. Hoskins, "Minutes of Tenth Meeting of the Interdepartmental Committee for Foreign Nationality Problems," April 29, 1942, RG 226, entry 100, box 129, Op-2-82 file.

90. "The American Slav Congress," FNB No. 25, May 2, 1942, RG 226, entry 100, box 108, FNB Report 1–100 New York-FNB Int-31 file.

91. "American Slav Congress," FNB No. 25, May 2, 1942.

92. Cranston to Poole, April 30, 1942, RG 208, entry 222, box 1074, Central European file.

93. "Foreign Politics in the United States, National Slav Day: June 21, 1942," FNB No. 49, July 10, 1942, RG 208, entry 232, box 1116, Slavs file.

94. Tomasevich, Chetniks, 270–72.

95. Fotitch, War We Lost, 115.

96. Welles to Roosevelt, July 21, 1941, and FDR to Welles, July 23, 1941, RG 59, 860H.001 Peter 11/21 1/2.

97. Welles to Fotić, April 11, 1942, Welles Papers, box 166, Europe Files, file 16.

98. Oscar Brown, "King Peter's Visit," July 3, 1942, with attachments, RG 226, entry 100, box 99, YU 131–140 file.

99. "Yugoslav Activities in the United States," FNB No. 55, July 21, 1942, RG 226, entry 100, box 108, FNB Report 1–100 New York-FNB-Int. 31 file.

100. Cannon to Hoskins, June 6, 1942, with attached Cannon to Hoskins, undated, RG 59, 860H.01/452.

101. Cannon to Atherton and Dunn, June 8, 1942, RG 59, 860H.01/138 1/2. Handwritten notations on the source text indicate that Dunn approved and Atherton agreed.

102. "Yugoslav Activities in the United States," FNB No. 55, July 21, 1942, RG 226, entry 100, box 108, FNB Report 1–100, New York-FNB-Int. 31 file.

103. Poole to Wiley, June 25, 1942, RG 226, entry 100, box 129, Wiley, J. C. originals file.

104. Poole to Cranston, June 9, 1942, RG 208, entry 222, box 1074, Central European file.

105. Poole to Hoskins, June 11, 1942, with attachment, RG 59, 860H.01/451; SAC Pittsburgh to Hoover, November 2, 1942, with attachments, FOIA/FBI SNDC file 97–1340–4 and 24 June 1942 with attachments, FOIA/FBI SNDC file 97–1340–5.

106. Berle diary, memorandum of conversation, June 12, 1942.

107. Poole to Wiley, June 16, 1942, RG 226, entry 100, box 129, Wiley, J. C. originals file; Nicholas Mirkovich to Cranston, May 26, 1942, RG 208, entry 221, box 1071, M-Foreign Language file.

108. Stoyan Pribichevich, "The Yugoslav-Government-In-Exile and the Serb Anti-Croat Campaign," FNB No. 41, June 25, 1942, RG 226, entry 100, box 108, FNB Report 1–100 New York-FNB-Int. 31 file.

109. King Peter, *King's Heritage,* 131–36.

110. Berle diary, memorandum, June 27, 1942, and July 4, 1942.

111. King Peter, *King's Heritage,* 156–57.

112. King Peter, *King's Heritage,* 143.

113. King Peter, *King's Heritage,* 152.

114. Brown, "King Peter's Visit," July 3, 1942, with attachments, RG 226, entry 100, box 99, YU 131–140 file.

115. "Foreign Politics in the United States, FNB Intelligence Report," No. 56: Subject: The Visit of King Peter II in Retrospect, July 25, 1942, RG 226, entry 100, box 108, FNB Reports 1–100 New York-FNB-Int 31 file.

116. Foreign Politics in the United States, "Croatian-American Congress," FNB B-3, September 14, 1942, RG 226, entry 100, box 110, FNB Report (B) Series No. 1–100 New York-FNB-Int. 32 file.

117. "Foreign Politics in the United States, Intelligence Report," FNB No. 56, 25 July 1942.

118. Andre Visson to Wiley, undated, with attachment, Visson to James P. Warburg, July 14, 1942, RG 226, entry 100, box 99, YU 151–160 file.

119. Fotitch, *War We Lost,* 179.

120. Roosevelt to Peter II, August 3, 1942, RG 59, 860H.001 Peter II.

121. "Yugoslav Activities in the United States," FNB No. 55, July 21, 1942, RG 226, entry 100, box 108, FNB Report 1–100, New York-FNB-Int. 31 file.

122. Cranston to Davis, July 15, 1942, RG 208, entry 221, box 1073, Elmer Davis file.

123. *The Vidovdan Dan Conference,* RG 208, entry 222, box 1081, Vidovdan Dan Conference file. This memo is undated and unsigned, but internal evidence indicates it was written by Cranston.

124. "Yugoslav Activities in the United States," FNB No. 55, July 21, 1942.

125. "Message from Attorney General Francis Biddle to Vidovdan Dan Conference, July 4, 1942," and "Message from Assistant Secretary of State Adolph Berle Jr. to Vidovdan Dan Conference, July 4, 1942," RG 208, entry 222, box 1081, Vidovdan Dan Conference file.

126. "Foreign Politics in the United States, Intelligence Report," FNB No. 56, 25 July 1942.

127. Fotitch, *War We Lost,* 165.

128. "Yugoslavs Claim 1,500 Axis Troops," *New York Times,* June 18, 1942, 13.

129. "King Peter Will Wed Alexandra of Greece," *New York Times,* June 18, 1942, 14.

130. "Reverses Form Grim Backdrop for Roosevelt-Churchill Talks," *Newsweek,* June 29, 1942, 28.

131. See for example, *New York Times,* June, 25, 1942, 25; *New York Times,* July, 2, 1942, 12; *New York Times,* July 4, 1942, 12.

132. *New York Times,* June 27, 1942, 12.

133. "Popular King," *Newsweek,* July 6, 1942, 36.

134. OWI, *The Unconquered People* (Washington, D.C.: GPO, 1942).

135. "The Twenty-Second Letter," script, August 12, 1942, RG 226, entry 100, box 99, YU 161–170 file.

Chapter 3: A Question of Public Order

1. Berle diary, memorandum to Hull, June 18, 1942.

2. Wilson, "Foreign Nationalities Branch," 50–52.

3. Wilson, "Foreign Nationalities Branch," 53.

4. William J. Donovan to Brig. Gen. W. B. Smith, August 17, 1942, RG 226, Exhibit D, Documentation, Entry 99, Box 73, 15.

5. Wilson, "Foreign Nationalities Branch," 50–55.

6. Smith, *Shadow Warriors,* 97.

7. Wilson, "Foreign Nationalities Branch," 59–64.

8. Bernard A. Drabeck and Helen E. Willis, eds., *Archibald MacLeish: Reflections* (Amherst: University of Massachusetts Press, 1986), 147–48.

9. Drabeck and Willis, *Archibald MacLeish,* 147–48. MacLeish also had constant battles with Hoover and the FBI, who raised questions about the political reliability of a number of MacLeish's appointees. MacLeish himself was the target of an FBI probe, and according to one biographer, his file eventually totaled more than six hundred pages. Scott Donaldson, *Archibald MacLeish: An American Life* (Boston: Houghton, 1992), 353–56.

10. Drabeck and Willis, *Archibald MacLeish,* 151.

11. Donaldson, *Archibald MacLeish,* 360–62.

12. "The President Establishes the Office of War Information, Executive Order No. 9182," June 13, 1942, *Public Papers of Franklin D. Roosevelt,* 11:274–78.

13. The OWI incorporated not only the OFF, but the Office of Government Reports, the Division of Information from the Office of Emergency Management, the Foreign Information Service of COI, and some of the psychological warfare components of COI. Winkler, *Politics of Propaganda,* 33; Charles David Lloyd, "American Society and Values in World War II From the Publications of The Office of War Information," (PhD diss., Georgetown University: 1975), 279.

14. Winkler, *Politics of Propaganda,* 31–32; Matthew Gordon, with an introduction by Elmer Davis, Book Section OWI, Book Digest No. 4, *News Is a Weapon,* November 9, 1942, RG 208, box 4, Office Files, 1942–43; Elmer Davis and Byron Price, *War Information and Censorship* (Washington, D.C.: American Council on Public Affairs, 1943), 10, 13.

15. George Creel to Elmer Davis, August 4, 1942, Elmer Davis Papers, LC, box 1, Elmer Davis Correspondence 1940–1942 file.

16. Office of War Information, *American Handbook* (Washington, D.C.: Public Affairs Press, 1945), 217–23.

17. Lloyd, "American Society," 280–81.

18. FNB, *Handbook,* vii.

19. "Address by Mr. Alan Cranston, Chief of the Foreign Language Division of the Office of Facts and Figures, Before the New England Foreign Language Newspapers Association, May 3, 1942," American Council for Nationalities Services, shipment 4, box 7, Foreign Language Press, Cranston file.

20. *Foreign Language Division,* undated, unsigned, RG 208, entry 232, box 1115, OWI-Foreign Language Division file. A slightly different version of this, with the heading *Report on the Foreign Language Division,* and dated June 30, 1942, is in RG 208, Records of the Office of the Director, 1942–1945, entry 1, box 3, Organization 1–3 New Bureau 1942–1945 file. Internal evidence indicates the author is Cranston.

21. Berle diary, memorandum of conversation, July 6, 1942.

22. Berle to MacLeish, July 17, 1942, RG 208, Office of the Director, entry 1, box 1, Committees (Interdepartmental, etc.) 1942–1945 file.

23. As quoted in Martin Weil, *A Pretty Good Club: The Founding Fathers of the US Foreign Service* (New York: Norton, 1978), 170.

24. Richard Rohman to Poole, July 8, 1942, RG 226, entry 100, box 91, SL 31–40 file.

25. Rohman to Poole, August 20, 1942, RG 226, entry 100, box 91, SL 51–60 file.

26. Rohman to John C. Wiley, July 24, 1942, with attachment, "American Slav Congress," 1942, RG 226, entry 100, box 91, SL 21–30.

27. Rebecca Wellington, "Minutes of the Fourteenth Meeting of the Interdepartmental Committee for Foreign Nationality Problems," July 22, 1942, RG 226, entry 86, Foreign Nationalities Branch, Misc. Papers, July 1942 through August 1945 file.

28. Berle to Davis, July 30, 1942, Berle Papers, State Department Correspondence, 1938–1945, box 32, DA file.

29. Wellington, "Minutes of the Fifteenth Meeting of the Interdepartmental Committee for Foreign Nationality Problems," August 12, 1942, RG 208, entry 232, box 1115, State Department file.

30. Berle to Davis, August 26, 1942, RG 59, 860H.01/400A.

31. Cranston to Davis, September 4, 1942, Cranston Papers, box 4, Berle file.

32. Davis to Berle, September 7, 1942, RG 208, entry 221, box 1073, Tracy Phillips file.

33. Berle to Davis, September 9, 1942, Berle Papers, State Department Correspondence, 1938–1945, box 32, DA file.

34. Cranston to Davis, July 15, 1942, RG 208, entry 221, box 1073, Elmer Davis file.

35. Cannon to Hoskins, June 6, 1942, with attached Cannon to Hoskins, undated, RG 59, 860H.01/452.

36. See for example, Welles, memorandum of conversation, August 11/August 19/ September 3, 1942, Welles Papers, box 166, Europe Files, file 16.

37. Foreign Politics in the United States, "Yugoslav Politics in the United States," FNB B-1, 11 September 1942, RG 226, entry 100, box 110, FNB Report (B) Series No. 1–100 New York-FNB-Int. 32 file.

38. Adamic to Cranston, September 4, 1942, Cranston Papers, box 4, Serbian Division 1942–1943 file. Adamic also sent a telegram to Eleanor Roosevelt on this issue. Eleanor Roosevelt to Adamic, September 7, 1942, Cranston Papers, box 4, Serbian Division 1942–1943 file.

39. Adamic to Eleanor Roosevelt, September 6, 1942, Adamic Papers, box 49, file 4.

40. Blair Bolles to Adamic, September 11, 1942, telegram, Adamic Papers, box 45, file 7.

41. Rohman to Wiley, August 24, 1942, RG 226, entry 100, box 99, YU 181–190 file.

42. Welles, memorandum of conversation, August 5, 1942, *FRUS*, 1942, 3:806–7.

43. FBI, Pittsburgh field report, April 13, 1944, with enclosures, FOIA/FBI SNDC File 97–1340–140.

44. Wellington, "Minutes of the Fifteenth Meeting," August 12, 1942.

45. Wellington, "Minutes of the Seventeenth Meeting of the Interdepartmental Committee for Foreign Nationality Problems," September 9, 1942, RG 208, entry 232, box 1115, State Department file.

46. "General Draza Michailovich and the Slavic Press in the United States," FNB No. 68, September 12, 1942, RG 226, entry 100, box 108, FNB Report 1–100 New York-FNB-Int. 31 file. The non-Communist Slavic press had either ignored this controversy or called on the Soviets to cease the attacks.

47. Poole to Wiley, September 17, 1942, RG 226, entry 100, box 105, YU 1321–1330 file.

48. Cranston to Davis, September 17, 1942, Cranston Papers, box 4, Serbian Division 1942–1943 file.

49. Poole to Wiley, September 18, 1942, RG 226, entry 100, box 105, YU 1321–1330 file.

50. Poole to Wiley, September 18, 1942.

51. Berle to Hull, September 18, 1942, *FRUS*, 1942, 3:815.

52. M. W. Beckleman, "Memorandum to Mr. DeWitt C. Poole, Summary of Proceedings," September 23, 1942, RG 226, entry 100, box 99, YU 251–260 file.

53. Cranston to Davis, September 21, 1942, RG 208, entry 221, box 1073, Elmer Davis file.

54. Wellington, "Minutes of the Eighteenth Meeting of the Interdepartmental Committee for Foreign Nationality Problems," September 30, 1942, RG 208, entry 232, box 1115, State Department file.

55. Cranston to Robert Blakely, "Activities of the Foreign Language Division (September 1 to September 30, 1942)," October 9, 1942, Cranston Papers, box 3, Monthly Reports 2/42–1/43 file.

56. B. D. Merritt to Cranston, October 3, 1942, and Poole to Berle, October 6, 1942, with enclosure, "From a Conference in Washington, The *American Srbobran*—September 28, 1942," October 3, 1942, RG 226, entry 100, box 100, YU 301–330 file.

57. William M. Boyd to Cranston, October 17, 1942, with attachment from October 5, 1942, RG 208, entry 221, box 1070, Foreign Language B file.

58. Cranston to Davis, September 23, 1942, with handwritten "OK E. D." and attachment "Draft of Statement on Internecine Disputes of Foreign Countries Carried on in the United States by Foreign Interest Groups," RG 208, entry 221, box 1073, Elmer Davis file. In his memo to Davis, Cranston pronounced the document "sound" and advised Davis to approve it.

59. Wellington, Minutes of the Eighteenth Meeting of the Interdepartmental Committee for Foreign Nationality Problems, September 30, 1942, RG 208, entry 232, box 1115, State Department file.

60. F. L. Belin to Wiley, October 9, 1942, with attachments "The Yugoslav Situation: Brief Resume," September 23, 1942, and Poole to Belin, October 8, 1942, RG 226, entry 100, box 100, YU 301–310 file.

61. Biddle to Hull, October 19, 1942, *FRUS,* 1942, 3:827–30.

62. Ivan Ivanovitch, "Ban Dr. Subasic Severs his Ties with the Yugoslav Government in London," FNB No. 59, 25 October 1942, RG 226, box 100, YU 240–281 file.

63. Foreign Politics in the United States, "Yugoslav Politics in the United States," FNB B-12, 29 October 1942, RG 226, entry 100, box 110, FNB Reports (B) Series No. 1–100, New York-FNB-Int. 32 file.

64. Poole, memorandum for Colonel Donovan, November 10, 1942, with attachment, B. C. to H. G. Thomas, November 2, 1942, RG 226, entry 100, box 100, YU 291–300 file.

65. Wellington, minutes of the Twentieth Meeting of the Interdepartmental Committee for Foreign Nationality Problems, October 28, 1942, RG 208, entry 232, box 1115, State Department file.

66. Peter P. Klassen to Poole, November 17, 1942, RG 226, entry 100, box 100, YU 341–350 file.

67. Ivan Ivanovitch to Poole, December 2, 1942, rep. no. 95, "Official and Private Reaction to Ruth Mitchell's Letter to New York Herald Tribune," with attachment, RG 226, entry 100, box 100, YU 311–320 file; *New York Times,* October 26, 1969, 82.

68. Klassen, memorandum of conversation, December 9, 1942, with handwritten notations on the source text by Poole and Klassen, RG 226, entry 100, box 100, YU 441–450 file.

69. Biddle to Hull, December 2, 1942, no. 35, with enclosure, RG 59, 860H.01/428.

70. Wellington, minutes of the Twenty-Third Meeting of the Interdepartmental Committee for Foreign Nationality Problems, December 2, 1942, RG 208, entry 232, box 1115, State Department file.

71. Bell to Cranston, December 14, 1942, RG 208, entry 221, box 1070, Foreign Language B file.

72. Cranston to Bell, December 18, 1942, RG 208, entry 221, box 1070, Foreign Language B file.

73. Office of War Information (OWI), "Information Guide for Foreign Language Press and Radio, No. 1," December 1, 1942, entry 222, box 1081, Foreign Language Press file.

74. OWI, *The Thousand Million,* (Washington, D.C.: U.S. GPO, 1942).

75. Beckleman to Poole, December 11, 1942, RG 226, entry 100, box 100, YU 281–290 file.

76. Fotić to editor of the *March of Time,* December 12, 1942, enclosure to Welles, memorandum of conversation, December 14, 1942, Welles Papers, box 166, Europe Files, file 16.

77. Berle diary, December 14, 1942.

78. "Slovenian Politics in the United States," FNB No. 163, December 2, 1943, RG 226, entry 100, box 109 FNB Reports, volume 2, 151–190, New York-FNB-INT.-31 file. Matjaz Klemencic, "Slovenian Americans," in *Encyclopedia of the American Left,* 704–5.

79. S. L., interview with Louis Adamic, report #140, November 27, 1942, RG 226, entry 100, box 101, YU 651–660 file.

80. Louis Adamic, "Mikhailovitch: Balkan Mystery Man," *Saturday Evening Post,* December 19, 1942, 20–21, 84, 86.

81. S. R. to Adamic, November 13, 1942, Adamic Papers, box 49, file 5.

82. Poole, memorandum for Colonel Donovan, and Poole to Berle, December 30, 1942, RG 226, entry 100, box 101, YU 491–500 file.

83. D. Ladd to Hoover, December 1, 1941, FBI, Department of Justice, Washington, D.C., FOIA/FBI Adamic file 100–63760–1 and Newark Field Office Report, December 2, 1942, FOIA/FBI Adamic file 100–63670–8.

84. F. L. Welch to Ladd, December 22, 1942, FOIA/FBI Adamic file 100–63670–17.

85. R. W. Black to Welch, December 21, 1942, FOIA/FBI Adamic file 100–63670–11.

86. Adamic to Berle, December 16, 1942, with attachment, Vincent Cainkar, "A Declaration by Sloven-Americans," December 5, 1942, Berle Papers.

87. Wellington, minutes of the Twenty-Fifth Meeting of the Interdepartmental Committee for Foreign Nationality Problems, January 13, 1943, RG 208, entry 232, box 1115, State Department file.

88. Welles, memorandum of conversation, January 15, 1943, with attachments, 860H.01/528.

89. Poole, memorandum of conversation with Cannon, January 21, 1943, RG 226, entry 100, box 121, YU 611–620.

90. Poole to Cranston, January 21, 1943, with attachment memorandum for Colonel Donovan, January 20, 1943, Cranston Papers, box 4, Serbian Division 1942–1943 file.

91. Biddle to Hull, December 28, 1942, *FRUS,* 1942, 3:836–38; Hull (Cannon) to Biddle, December 30, 1942, no. 4, RG 59, 860H.01/430.

92. Hull to Stimson, December 30, 1942, and Welles to Fotić, December 31, 1942, *FRUS,* 1942, 3:840–41.

93. Biddle to Hull, January 2, 1943, no. 38, *FRUS,* 1943, 2:962–64.

94. Ilija Jukić, *The Fall of Yugoslavia* (New York: Harcourt, 1974), 142.

95. Biddle to Hull, January 4, 1943, RG 59, no. 1, 860h.01/431.

96. Biddle to Hull, January 4, 1943, RG 59, no. 2, 860h.01/432.

97. Biddle to Hull, January 5, 1943, no. 40, *FRUS*, 1943 2:966–68.

98. Philip C. Horton, memorandum of conversation with Sava N. Kosanović, January 6, 1943, RG 226, entry 100, box 101, YU 531–530 file.

99. Welles, memorandum of conversation, January 7, 1943, RG 59, 860H.002/233.

100. Welles, memorandum of conversation, January 7, 1943, RG 59, 860H.01/441.

101. Biddle to Hull, January 12, 1943, no. 12, with attachment, 860H.01/439.

102. Biddle to Hull, February 1, 1943, no. 45, 860H.01/444.

103. Poole to Donovan, January 13, 1943, RG 226, entry 100, box 105, YU 1321–1330 file, with attachment "Re: Milhalovitch," December 29, 1942.

104. "The Michailovich Controversy in the American Foreign Language Press," FNB No. 102, February 4, 1943, RG 226, entry 100, box 101, YU 621–630 file.

105. Cranston to Davis, January 7, 1943, with attachment *Disloyal Foreign Language Newspapers Published in the U.S.*, January 7, 1943, RG 208, Office of the Director, entry 1, box 7, Publications 3–1 Foreign Press, 1942–1944 file.

106. Adamic to Cranston, January 31, 1943, RG 208, entry 221, box 1070, Memoranda General file.

107. Cranston to Adamic, February 2, 1943, RG 208, entry 221, box 1070, Memoranda General file.

108. Cranston to Arthur Sweetser, February 11, 1943, Cranston Papers, box 3, Correspondence—outgoing—12–23–41 to 10–27–43 file.

109. Advance Release, Department of Justice, December 6, 1942, Biddle Papers, box 3, Saboteurs file.

110. Poole to Donovan, December 22, 1942, RG 226, entry 100, box 101, YU 481–490 file.

111. Poole to Donovan, December 22, 1942, RG 226, entry 100, box 101, YU 481–490 file.

112. Detroit Field Office to Hoover, February 3, 1943, #25, and October 13, 1943, #42, FBI/FOIA SNDC file 97–1340; Hoover to Smith, March 4, 1943, #25, and June 5, 1943, #29, and September 4, 1943, #39, FBI/FOIA SNDC file 97–1340.

113. Wellington, minutes of the Twenty-Sixth Meeting of the Interdepartmental Committee for Foreign Nationality Problems, January 27, 1943, RG 226, entry 100, box 129, State Department—Interdepartment—New York FNB-Op-2 file.

114. Wellington, minutes of the Twenty-Fifth Meeting of the Interdepartmental Committee for Foreign Nationality Problems, January 13, 1943, RG 208, entry 232, box 1115, State Department file.

115. Cranston to Zarko Butkovich, February 3, 1943, RG 208, entry 221, box 1070, Foreign Language B file.

116. Boyd-Boich to Cranston, February 8, 1943, with attachment, Croatian Catholic Union and the "Croatian Congress," RG 208, entry 221, box 1070, Foreign Language-B file.

117. Boyd-Boich to Cranston, February 8, 1943, with enclosure "Croatian Catholic Union and the Croatian Congress," RG 208, entry 221, box 1070, Foreign Language-B file.

118. Cranston to Boyd-Boich, February 11, 1943, RG 208, entry 221, box 1070, Foreign Language-B file.

119. Wellington, minutes of the Twenty-Seventh Meeting of the Interdepartmental Committee for Foreign Nationality Problems, February 10, 1943, RG 208, entry 232, box 1115, State Department file. The group also agreed to keep a more abbreviated set of minutes, simply recording "the decisions taken and action recommended."

120. Poole to Berle, February 11, 1943, with attachment Poole, *Memorandum to the Director of Strategic Services* 2–11–43, Berle Papers, box 45, "Po" file; Poole, Memorandum to Director of Strategic Services, February 11, 1943, Tab QQ, "Exhibits OSS."

121. Poole to Berle, February 11, 1943, with attachment Poole, *Memorandum to the Director of Strategic Services* 2–11–43, Berle Papers, box 45, "Po" file; Poole, Memorandum to Director of Strategic Services, February 11, 1943, Tab QQ, "Exhibits OSS."

122. Fowle, *Cranston*, 65–66.

123. Norman Thomas to Davis, January 12, 1943, with attachments of Memorandum on Assassination of Carlo Tresca and the Italian Situation; Davis to Thomas, January 15, 1943; Thomas to Davis, January 19, 1943; Cranston to Davis, January 21, 1943, RG 208, Office of the Director, entry 1, box 7, Propaganda 1943 file.

124. Adamic to Davis, January 25, 1943, Cranston Papers, box 3, Correspondence—incoming—a-z 1942–1944 file, and Davis to Adamic, January 23, 1943, Cranston Papers, box 4, OWI: anti-Communism, 1940 8–1–33 file.

125. Cranston to Adamic, January 28, 1943, RG 208, entry 221, box 1070, Memoranda General file.

126. Cranston to Davis, February 15, 1943, with attachments, Cranston Papers, box 4, Berle file.

127. Cranston to Berle, with attachment, February 17, 1943, Berle Papers, box 31,"Cra-Cru" file.

128. Berle to Poole and Cranston, February 18, 1943, Berle Papers, box 31, "Cra-Cru" file.

129. Poole to Cranston, February 23, 1943, with attachment, RG 208, entry 222, box 1074, Central European file.

130. "The American Croatian Congress: February 20 and 21," FNB No. B-28, 22 February 1943, RG 226, entry 100, box 1, unmarked black binder.

131. Albert Parry, "The Croat Congress: Behind the Scenes," FNB Report No. 38, February 23, 1943, RG 226, entry 100, box 102, YU 711–720 file.

132. "Current Yugoslav Politics in the United States," FNB No. 125, May 6, 1943, RG 226, entry 100, box 102, YU 871–880 file.

133. Wellington, minutes of the Twenty-Seventh Meeting of the Interdepartmental Committee for Foreign Nationality Problems, February 24, 1943, with attachments, RG 226, entry 100, box 129, Op-2–82 file.

134. Summary of telephone conversation, "DeWitt Poole by phone 2/24/43," attached to Poole to Cranston, February 23, 1943, with attachment, RG 208, entry 222, box 1074, Central European file.

135. Poole to Cranston, February 26, 1943, with attachments, Cranston Papers, box 4, Berle file.

136. Cranston to Berle, March 16, 1943, with attachments, Cranston Papers, box 4, Berle file.

137. Cranston to Berle, March 16, 1943, with attachments, Cranston Papers, box 4, Berle file.

138. Wellington, Minutes of the Twenty-Ninth Meeting of the Interdepartmental Committee for Foreign Nationality Problems, March 17, 1943, RG 226, entry 100, box 129, Op-2–82 file.

139. Poole to Smith, April 23, 1943, RG 226, INT-19MI-209 file.

140. Berle to All American Diplomatic and Consular Officers, March 23, 1943, 800.01/160A Supplement, FBI/FOIA ASC file 100–56674–76.

Chapter 4: To Bully a Conscientious Little Paper

1. J. W. Gallman to Hull, April 6, 1943, RG 59, no. 8509, 860H.001 (remainder is not legible in source text).

2. A. J. Drexel Biddle to Hull, April 20, 1943, RG 59, no. 57, 860H.01/474.

3. Berle diary, memorandum of conversation with attachment, March 24, 1943.

4. Poole, memorandum for the Director of OSS and the Department of State, S-3, April 24, 1943, RG 226, entry 100, box 119, Yugoslavia (30) #1 New York-FNB-Int. 33 file.

5. Poole, memorandum of conversation, April 15, 1943, RG 226, Int-19–MI-201 file.

6. Adamic to Poole, May 9, 1943, RG 226, entry 100, box 28, EU 211–220 file.

7. "The Mihailović Issue in the Yugoslav Press," FNB, May 10, 1943, RG 226 entry 100, box 102, YU 881–890 file.

8. Poole, memorandum to the Director of Strategic Services and the Department of State, June 9, 1943, RG 226, entry 100, box 103, YU 948 file.

9. Poole, memorandum for the Director of Strategic Services and the Department of State, S-26, June 9, 1943, RG 226, entry 100, box 103, YU 941–950 file.

10. Poole to Cannon and Poole to Smith, June 12, 1943, with attachment, Poole, memorandum to the Director of Strategic Services and the Department of State, S-28, June 11, 1943, RG 226, entry 100, box 103, YU 941–950 file. Poole also sent a copy to Cranston.

11. Tomasevich, *Chetniks,* 303–7; the Yugoslav Embassy to the Department of State, June 21, 1943, *FRUS,* 1943, 2:1012–14.

12. Biddle to Hull, July 2, 1943, *FRUS,* 1943, 2:1016–17.

13. Winant to Hull, June 30, 1943, *FRUS,* 1943 2:1015–16; Aide-Memoire British Embassy to Department of State, July 6, 1943, *FRUS,* 1943 2:1018.

14. Cannon, memorandum, August 6, 1943, and Hull to Biddle, no. 3, August 6, 1943, RG 59, 860H.01/508.

15. Tomasevich, *Chetniks,* 303–7; Welles, memorandum of conversation, August 11, 1943, RG 59, 860H.01/537.

16. Louis Adamic, *My Native Land* (New York: Harper, 1943), 14, 4–49, 52, 399–414.

17. Louis Adamic, "Mihailovitch: Balkan Mystery Man," *Saturday Evening Post,* December 19, 1942, 20–21, 84, 86; Atherton to Welles, May 1, 1943, RG 59, 860H.00/1473 1/2.

18. FNB Report, No. 104, February 9, 1943, enclosure to "Hungarian," February 11, 1943, RG 208, box 1075.

19. A. R., Foreign Nationalities Branch, "Yugoslav Committee," June 24, 1943, Pittsburgh #430, RG 226, entry 100, box 103, YU 971–980 file.

20. Poole, memorandum to the Director of OSS, Secretary of State, Department of Justice, Office of War Information, S-13, May 13, 1943 with attachments, *Zlatko Balokovich,* May 12, 1943, and Poole, memorandum for Mr. Gold, May 5, 1943, RG 226, entry 100, box 102, YU 871–880 file.

21. "United Committee of American Yugoslavs," FNB No. B-52, June 29, 1943, RG 226, entry 100, box 103, YU 981–990 file.

22. Poole to Berle, July 8, 1943, with attachment, Subasic to National Council of Americans of Croat Descent, undated, RG 208, entry 222, box 1074, Classified Material file.

23. UCSSA *Bulletin* 1, no. 1 (September 7, 1943): 3, 6, Adamic Papers, box 89, file 1. (There are two issues with this volume and issue number but with different dates.)

24. UCSSA *Bulletin* 1, no. 1 (September 7, 1943): 3, 6, Adamic Papers, box 89, file 1; UCSSA *Bulletin* 1, no. 1 (August 1943): 1, Department of Justice, United Committee of South-Slavic Americans File 149–1670.

25. UCSSA *Bulletin* 1, no. 1 (September 7, 1943): 6, Adamic Papers, box 89, file 1. The UCSSA also published what they claimed was first picture of Tito printed in the United States.

26. UCSSA *Bulletin* 1, no, 2 (October 1, 1943), "The Yugoslav Crisis," 1–2, Adamic Papers, box 89, file 1.

27. Cannon, memorandum, July 2, 1943, RG 59, 860H.01/524.

28. "A South-Slavic Popular Front," FNB No. B-66, August 12, 1943, RG 226, entry 100, box 103, YU 1041–1050 file.

29. S. J. Drayton, SAC Chicago to Hoover, June 21, 1943, FBI/FOIA SNDC file 97–1340–32.

30. Poole to Smith, May 8, 1943, with enclosure RG 226, entry 100, box 102, YU 871–880 file.

31. "The Greater Serbia Movement in the United States," FNB No. 130, June 3, 1943, entry 100, box 103, YU 931–940 file.

32. Charlotte Slavitt, memorandum for Sharp, May 26, 1943, DOJ/FOIA file

146–28–430; Alexander Dragnich, memorandum, May 26, 1943, DOJ/FOIA file 146–28–430.

33. Hoover to A. M. Thurston, June 1, 1943, with attachment, FBI/FOIA SNDC file 97–1340–30.

34. Sharp, memorandum for Lane, June 5, 1943, DOJ/FOIA file 146–28–430.

35. Slavitt, memorandum for Sharp, June 7, 1943, with attachment, Slavitt and Dragnich, memorandum for Sharp, May 1, 1943, DOJ/FOIA file 146–28–430.Only the memorandum of historical background, which Slavitt and Dragnich prepared, was in the file under that date and attached to the cover memo. What Slavitt wrote must be inferred from the Dragnich criticism that followed.

36. Dragnich, memorandum for Sharp, June 17, 1943, DOJ/FOIA file 146–28–430.

37. Office of War Information, Foreign Language Division, *OWI Director Denounces "American Srbobran" For Spreading Race Hate,* June 15, 1943, entry 226, box 1090, Special Releases-1943 file.

38. Davis to Berle, June 7, 1943, with attachment, and Berle to Davis, June 9, 1943, RG 59, 860H.01/493.

39. Ruth Mitchell to Davis, June 19, 1943, RG 208, Office of the Director, entry 1, box 7, Publications 3–1 Foreign Press 1942–44 file.

40. Davis to Mitchell, June 23, 1943, Mitchell to Davis, June 24, 1943, RG 208, Office of the Director, entry 1, box 7, Publications 3–1 Foreign Press 1942–44 file.

41. Smith to Davis, June 28, 1943, Markham to Davis, June 26, 1943, Davis to Mitchell, June 30, 1943, RG 208, Office of the Director, entry 1, box 7, Publications, 3–1 Foreign Press 1942–1944 file.

42. Berle diary, memorandum of conversation, June 22, 1943; Berle, memorandum of conversation, June 22, 1943, *FRUS,* 1943, 2:1014–15.

43. Poole to Bradford Smith, June 24, 1943 with attachment, Kosanović to Poole, June 22, 1943, RG 208, entry 222, box 1074, Classified Material file. Poole viewed the Kosanović letters as "worth consideration," and sent them to the other officials working on foreign nationalities issues. The second letter, also dated June 22 and concerning the book, is not attached to this file but can be found in the copy of the correspondence contained in DOJ/FOIA 146–28–430; Kosanović's name is censored from the copies released to the author.

44. Cannon, memorandum, July 6, 1943, with attachments, RG 59, 860H.01/490.

45. Albert Parry, "The Serbian National Defense Council," FNB Report No. 86, July 3, 1943, and "Serbian National Defense Council Congress," FNB No. B-54, July 8, 1943, RG 226, entry 100, box 103, YU 991–1000 file.

46. "The Greater Serbian Campaign and the Davis-Werlinich Exchange of Letters," FNB No. B-55, July 8, 1943, RG 226, entry 100, box 103, YU 981–990 file.

47. Sharp, memorandum for Messrs. Land and Smith, DOJ/FOIA file 146–28–430.

48. FBI, General Intelligence Survey, August 1943, Hopkins Papers, box 145, Yugoslav Activities 16–18 file.

49. Poole to Carl F. Butts, August 3, 1943, RG 226, entry 100, box 103, YU 1031–1040 file. Poole asked Butts to destroy this letter after he had read it.

50. Poole to Smith, August 12, 1943, with attachment, August 5, 1943, RG 226, entry 100, box 103, YU 1031–1040 file.

51. Poole to Berle, July 9, 1943, RG 59, 860H.01/541 (copies were also sent to Smith and Cannon); Lane, memorandum for Hoover, July 21, 1943, DOJ/FOIA file 146–28–430. The names are excised in the released copy.

52. Slavitt, memorandum for Sharp, August 3, 1943, DOJ/FOIA file 146–28–430.

53. Slavitt, memorandum for Sharp, August 3, 1943, DOJ/FOIA file 146–28–430.

54. Lane to Samuel Werlinich, July 21, 1943, DOJ/FOIA file 146–28–430.

55. Lane to Hoover, August 17, 1943, DOJ/FOIA file 146–28–430.

56. Dragnich to Sharp, August 19, 1943, DOJ/FOIA file 146–28–430.

57. Dragnich, memorandum for Sharp, August 23, 1943, with enclosure, conference with Sima Werlinich, August 18, 1943, DOJ/FOIA file 146–28–430.

58. Dragnich, memorandum for Sharp, August 30, 1943, DOJ/FOIA file 146–28–430.

59. J. P. Wolgemuth to Hoover, October 11, 1943, with enclosures, FBI/FOIA file 97–1340–49.

60. "Convention of the Serb National Federation," September 12–18, 1943, FNB B-86, September 29, 1943, RG 226, entry 100, box 104, YU 1091–1100 file; Poole to Sharp, September 29, 1943, DOJ/FOIA file 146–28–430.

61. Edward B. Hitchcock to B. M. Pekich, May 18, 1943, RG 208, Office of the Director, entry 1, box 7, Publications 3–1 Foreign Press 1942–1944 file.

62. Dragnich, memorandum, June 22, 1943, DOJ/FOIA file 146–28–430.

63. Lane identifies his contact at the War Services Staff of the Treasury Department as "J. H. Houghteling," but all indications are that he meant "J. L. [James L.] Houghteling," who indeed moved to the Treasury Department from the INS.

64. Lane, Memorandum for the File, June 25, 1943, DOJ/FOIA file 146–28–430.

65. Berle to Davis, July 7, 1943, Berle Papers, State Department Correspondence 1938–1945, box 32, DA file.

66. Cranston to Col. William Westlake, September 16, 1943, Cranston Papers, box 4, Serbian Division 1942–1943 file; "Convention of the Serb National Federation," September 12–18, 1943, FNB, No. B-86, RG 226, entry 100, box 104, YU 1091–1100 file.

67. Pekich to Davis, October 5, 1943, with attachment Pekich to Morgenthau, October 5, 1943, Davis to Pekich, October 12, 1943, RG 208, Office of the Director, entry 1, box 7, Publications 3–1 Foreign Press 1942–1944 file.

68. Lew Frank Jr. to S. O. Lesser, October 14, 1943, RG 208, box 1115, entry 232, Office Memoranda 1943 file.

69. Winkler, *Politics of Propaganda*, 63–71, 150; David Lloyd Jones, "The U.S. Office of War Information and American Public Opinion During World War II, 1939–1945," (PhD diss., SUNY Binghamton: 1976), 463–64, 468, 500–502.

70. Winkler, *Politics of Propaganda,* 63–71, 150; Jones, "The Office of War Information," 463–64, 468, 500–502. The House had originally eliminated the entire budget, but a conference committee restored some of the funding. Ninety percent of the appropriation was given to the Overseas Branch, which received thirty-four million dollars.

71. Congress, House, Remarks of Joe Starnes, The Work of the O.W.I., 78th Cong., 1st sess., 1943, CR, vol. 98, pt. 11 (July 1, 1943): A3351–52.

72. Excerpt from *Congressional Record,* remarks of Congressman Lesinski, June 17, 1943, Cranston Papers, box 4, OWI hearings 1943 file.

73. "Summary of Cox Committee Charges," n.d., RG 208, entry 222, box 1078, Cox Committee file.

74. "Draft of Statement on Cox Committee Charges against Foreign language Division of OWI," n.d., RG 208, entry 222, box 1078, Cox Committee file; Milton S. Eisenhower to Cranston, October 22, 1943, RG 208, Office of the Director 1, entry 1, box 1, clearance I file.

75. Cranston to Charles Allen, April 28, 1943, with attachments, RG 208, entry 222, box 1079, Foreign Language Division, Objectives, etc. file.

76. Cranston to Robert Blakely, October 9, 1942, Activities of the FLD (September 1 to September 30, 1942), Cranston Papers, box 3, Monthly Reports 2/42–1/43 file.

77. Cranston to Lewis, September 22, 1943, Cranston Papers, box 4, Redbaiting 1943–1946 file.

78. Lewis to Clarence Cannon, September 27, 1943, Cranston Papers, box 4, Redbaiting 1943–1944 file.

79. Lloyd, "American Society," 18; Cranston to Allen, October 15, 1943, Cranston Papers, box 4, Military Service, 1943 file; Cranston to Lewis, August 4, 1941, with attachment, Cranston Papers, box 3, Correspondence August-September 1941 file.

80. Lane, Oral History, 640–41.

81. Smith, memorandum for the Attorney General, July 6, 1943, Lawrence M. C. Smith Papers, accession number 6377, box 26, War Policies Unit file, American Heritage Center, University of Wyoming.

82. Smith, memorandum for the Attorney General, July 6, 1943, Lawrence M. C. Smith Papers, accession number 6377, box 26, War Policies Unit file, American Heritage Center, University of Wyoming.

83. Smith, memorandum for the Attorney General, July 6, 1943, Lawrence M. C. Smith Papers, accession number 6377, box 26, War Policies Unit file, American Heritage Center, University of Wyoming.

84. Smith, memorandum for the Attorney General, July 6, 1943, Lawrence M. C. Smith Papers, accession number 6377, box 26, War Policies Unit file, American Heritage Center, University of Wyoming.

85. Department of Justice, news release, August 28, 1943, Smith Papers, box 26, War Policies Unit file.

86. Wilson, "Foreign Nationalities Branch," 4:11–13 (page numbers in source text begin again at 1 in this chapter).

87. Poole, memorandum to the Director of Strategic Services and the Secretary of State, S-41, August 3, 1943, RG 226, entry 100, box 119, Yugoslavia (30) #1 file.

88. Poole, memorandum for the Director of Strategic Services and the Secretary of State, S-44, August 9, 1943, RG 226, entry 100, box 119, Yugoslavia (30) #1 file.

89. Poole, memorandum for the Director of Strategic Services and the Secretary of State, S-44, August 9, 1943, RG 226, entry 100, box 119, Yugoslavia (30) #1 file.

90. "Yugoslavia on the American Scene," FNB No. 152, September 23, 1943, and "Convention of the Serb National Federation," FNB No. B-86, September 29, 1943, RG 226, entry 100, box 104, YU 1091–1100 file.

91. Alexander Kirk to Hull, October 14, 1943, no. 1340, with enclosure, RG 59, 860H.001/Peter II/98.

92. Poole, "Notations for the Staff: No. 2," October 8, 1943, RG 226, entry 100, box 4, New York-FNB, AD 3 file.

93. Poole to Secretary of State, November 20, 1943, S-71, RG 165, entry 79, box 1962.

94. UCSSA, *Bulletin* 1, no. 2 (October 1, 1943), Adamic Papers, box 89, file 1.

95. Berle diary, memorandum of conversation, October 15, 1942.

96. OWI, FLD, news release, "U.S. Stamp Issue Honors Yugoslavia," October 26, 1943, RG 208, entry 227, box 1092, Oct. 1–Oct. 7 Material Released file; Jones, 190–91.

97. Roberts, *Tito, Mihailović and the Allies,* 152, 167, 170, 172; R. Harris Smith, *The OSS: The Secret History of America's First Central Intelligence Agency* (Berkeley: University of California Press, 1972), 140, 157.

98. "Tito's Partisans," *Newsweek,* October 18, 1943, 23.

99. "Bloody Balkans," *Newsweek,* November 8, 1943, 22–23.

100. "Guerrilla Warfare in Yugoslavia," *Life,* December 6, 1943, 47–51.

101. Jelavich, *History of the Balkans,* 2:270–71; Adam Ulam, *Titoism and the Cominform* (Westport, Conn.: 1971), 33–34; MacVeagh to Hull, December 18, 1943, *FRUS,* 1943, 2:1033.

102. Berle to Hull, November 25, 1943, Berle Papers, box 58, Hull memos, Aug-Dec 1943 file.

103. Hull to American Embassy London, for Bucknell, December 8, 1943, no. 7759, RG 59, 860H.01/578A.

104. Lincoln MacVeagh to Hull, December 8, 1943, *FRUS,* 1943, 2:1023–24. MacVeagh replaced Biddle in November and after the move to Cairo.

105. Harriman to Hull, December 14, 1943, *FRUS,* 1943 2:1025–26.

106. John Ehrman, *Grand Strategy* (Her majesty's stationary office, 1972), 270–73. MacVeagh to Hull, December 16, 1943, *FRUS,* 1943, 2:1028–29.

107. MacVeagh to Hull, December 16, 1943, *FRUS,* 1943, 2:1029–31.

108. Hull to MacVeagh, December 30, 1943, *FRUS,* 1943, 2:1038–39.

109. Poole, memorandum for the Director of Strategic Services and Secretary of State, Number S-77, December 7, 1943, RG 226, entry 100, box 119, Yugoslavia (30) #1 file.

110. Poole, memorandum for the Director of Strategic Services and Secretary of State, Number S-77, December 7, 1943, RG 226, entry 100, box 119, Yugoslavia (30)

#1 file; "Political Thinking among Yugoslavs in the United States," January 22, 1944, FNB B-150, RG 226, entry 100, box 104, Yu 1221–1230 file. Berle later told Poole that he had found this analysis "to be of value" and that "material of this kind was very helpful." Poole, memorandum of conversation, February 1, 1944, RG 226, entry 100, box 100, YU 331–340 file.

Chapter 5: A Wordy Civil War

1. Constantine Poulos to Dowsley Clark, March 6, 1944, RG 208, entry 178, box 972, Organizations 2–21 file.

2. Poulos to Clark, April 6, 1944, RG 208, entry 178, box 972, Organizations 2–21 file.

3. Poulos to Adamic, May 15, 1944, with enclosure Poulos to Neil Dalton, May 6, 1944, Adamic Papers, box 48, folder 8.

4. Dalton to Clark, May 31, 1944, with attachments, Achilles N. Sakell to Dalton, May 29, 1944, and Sakell, memorandum, May 18, 1944, RG 208, Records of the News Bureau, Office of the Chief, entry 178, box 972, Organizations 2–21 file.

5. "Tito's Government and the Yugoslav-American Press," FNB No. B-140, January 5, 1944, RG 226, entry 100, box 110, New York-FNB.-INT. 32 file.

6. *The American Serb,* FNB No. B-146, January 11, 1944, RG 226, entry 100, box 110, FNB Report (B) Series No. 101–180, volume 2, New York-FNB-Int. 32 file.

7. "Forthcoming Special Conference of the American Slav Congress," FNB No. B-145, January 10, 1943, RG 226, entry 100, box 110, FNB Reports B series volume 2 file.

8. "The American Slav Congress Moves Leftward," FNB No. B-158, February 18, 1944, RG 226, entry 100, box 110, FNB Reports (B) Series 101–180, volume 2, New York-FNB-Int. 32 file.

9. Louis Adamic, "What's Happening in Yugoslavia," *The Bulletin* 2, no. 1 (January 2, 1944): 3, Adamic Papers, box 89, file 1.

10. Sava Kosanović, "A Serbian Speaks Out," *The Bulletin* 2, no. 2 (January 15, 1944): 1, Adamic Papers, box 89, file 1.

11. Adamic to Stephen Early, January 28, 1944; Early to Hull, January 28, 1944, RG 59, 860H.01/721; Edward R. Stettinius, memorandum of conversation, February 3, 1944, RG 59, 860H.01/731.

12. "Tito's Government and the Yugoslav-American Press," January 5, 1944, FNB No. B-140, RG 226, entry 100, box 110, New York-FNB.-INT. 32 file; "Political Thinking among Yugoslavs in the United States," FNB No. B-150, January 22, 1944, RG 226, entry 100, box 104, Yu 1221–1230 file.

13. Fotitch, *War We Lost,* 241–42.

14. Fotitch, *War We Lost,* 243–44.

15. Butts, "General Reaction to the Churchill Speech," FNB #593, Serbian, March 1, 1944, RG 226, entry 100, box 105, YU 1281–1290 file.

16. "Yugoslav-American Reactions to Churchill's Speech," FNB No. B-171, March 15, 1944, RG 226, entry 100, box 105, YU 1291–1300 file.

17. Poole, memorandum to the Director of OSS and the Department of State, Number S-89, February 26, 1944, RG 226, entry 100, box 105, YU 1271–1280 file.

18. MacVeagh to Hull, March 28, 1944, RG 59, no. 72, 860H.001 Peter II/108.

19. Tomasevich, *Chetniks,* 304.

20. Peter II, *King's Heritage,* 130, 211, 246.

21. "Done with the Past," UCSSA, *The Bulletin* 2, no. 3 (March 10, 1944): 1, Adamic Papers, box 89, file 1.

22. Winant to Hull, April 15, 1944, *FRUS,* 1944, 4:1357.

23. "Notes on the Yugoslav Press in the United States," FNB, May 1, 1944, RG 226, entry 100, box 120, Yugoslavia (30) #2 file.

24. "Yugoslav Notes," FNB No. B-188, April 25, 1944, RG 226, entry 100, box 105, YU 1361–1370 file.

25. Lord Halifax to Hull, April 27, 1944, with enclosure Churchill to FDR, April 26, 1944, RG 59, 860H.01/4–2744.

26. Peter II to FDR, April 17, 1944, Fotić to FDR, April 17, 1944, FDR to Hull, April 26, 1944, FDR to Peter II, n.d., RG 59, 860H.01/866.

27. Tito to FDR, March 15, 1944, G. Edward Buxton to FDR, April 24, 1944, FDR to Buxton, April 26, 1944, Berle to Dunn and Cannon, April 28, 1944, Hull (Cannon) to FDR, May 17, 1944, with attachment, RG 59, 860H.01/867.

28. Poole, memorandum of conversation, April 25, 1944, RG 226, entry 100, box 122, State Department Conversations file.

29. "New Yugoslav Conflict Shows Itself Here," May 9, 1944, FNB No. 186, RG 226, entry 100, box 109, FNB Reports, Vol. 2, 151–190, N.Y.-FNB. Int. 31 file.

30. United States Department of Justice and Immigration and Naturalization Service, "A Handbook for 'I Am an American Day' Committees," 1944, RG 208, entry 232, box 1113, I Am an American Day file.

31. "Yugoslav Factionalism Deepens in the United States," FNB No. B-179, March 30, 1944, RG 165, entry 79, box 1959, B151–190 file; FNB, Public Meeting Report, No. 176, May 1, 1944, CIA/FOIA SNDC file 97–1340–145.

32. Frank Knox to Davis, undated, with enclosures, RG 208, Office of the Director, entry 1, box 7, Publications 1942–1944 file; Louis Adamic, *The Native's Return: An American Immigrant Visits Yugoslavia and Discovers His Old Country,* (New York: Harper, 1934), 358–65.

33. "Yugoslav Notes," FNB No. B-188, April 25, 1944, RG 226, entry 100, box 105, file: YU 1361–1370; Poole, Memorandum of Conversation, April 21, 1944, RG 226, entry 100, box 105, YU 1351–1360 file.

34. Butts, memorandum, April 28, 1944, no. 670, RG 226, entry 100, box 105, YU 1371–1380 file.

35. *The Bulletin* 2, no. 5 (May 10, 1944): 3, Adamic Papers, box 89, file 1.

36. Poole, memorandum of conversation, February 1, 1944, RG 226, entry 100, box 100, YU 331–340 file.

37. Poole to Berle, April 29, 1944, and Berle to Poole, May 8, 1944, RG 226, entry 100, box 122, A. A. Berle Jr., New York FNB Op 2 file.

38. Pittsburgh Field Office Report, February 2, 1944, FBI/FOIA SNDC file 97–1340–78; in early April 1943, the Dučić family had informed Hull of Dučić's death and thanked Hull for granting "a peaceful asylum in America" to the "greatest of Serbia's modern poets." Telegram to Hull, April 8, 1943, RG 59, 860H.01/461.

39. Biddle to Secretary of the Treasury, March 1, 1944, FBI/FOIA SNDC file 97–1340–67.

40. Sharp, memorandum for Hoover, March 3, 1944, DOJ/FOIA file 146–28–430. This was released by the Justice Department after an FBI/FOIA and has the h/w number 97–1340–110. The names were excised in the released copy.

41. Sharp, memorandum for Hoover, February 23, 1944, DOJ/FOIA file 146–28–430. The document was requested from the FBI but furnished by the Justice Department. It has the h/w number 97–1340–99.

42. Hoover to James P. McGranery, March 6, 1944, FBI/FOIA SNDC file 97–1340–94.

43. Herbert Wechsler to Hoover, August 5, 1944, with attachments, Dragnich, memorandum, July 14, 1943, and memorandum for Sharp, January 7, 1944, DOJ/FOIA file 146–28–430. Released by the Justice Department after being forwarded by FBI, with written file number of 97–1340–196.

44. "Issues of Foreign Politics Enter Field of War Relief," FNB No. 228, January 16, 1945, CIA Release 62–64427–3–368.

45. SAC Pittsburgh to DC, June 23, 1942, FBI/FOIA SNDC file 97–134–03.

46. Mitchell to Homer Fox, November 14, 1942, DOJ/FOIA file 146–28–430.

47. L. M. Peyovich to The President's War Relief Board, August 14, 1943, with enclosure, FOIA/DOJ file 146–28–430.

48. Adamic to Hull, October 14, 1943, Wellington to Norden, November 27, 1943, Poole to Berle, November 22, 1943, RG 226, entry 100, box 122, A. A. Berle Jr. New York FNB Op2 file; Poole to Berle, December 31, 1943, RG 226, entry 100, box 104, YU 1181–1190 file.

49. C. Belgen, memorandum of conversation, October 2, 1944, and Leon Q. Shoob, memorandum of conversation, October 4, 1944, RG 226, entry 100, box 106, YU 15511580 file; "Report to the Director," B911, January 23, 1945, RG 226, entry 100, box 106, YU 1641–1670 file.

50. "The American Committee for the Yugoslav Relief Ship," FNB No. 121, December 6, 1944, RG 226, entry 100, box 106, YU 1601–1640 file.

51. A. W. Schwartz, memorandum, May 8, 1943, RG 60, entry SWPU, box 5, FARA Correspondence, Memorandum, etc. file.

52. Shoob, memorandum of conversation, May 22, 1944, RG 226, entry 100, box 105, YU 1401–1410 file.

53. Slavitt, memorandum for Sharp, March 11, 1944, with attached letter from Richard S. Kaplan to the SNDC, February 10, 1944, DOJ/FOIA file 146–28–430.

54. Sharp to President's War Relief Control Board, March 16, 1944, DOJ/FOIA file 146–28–430.

55. Slavitt, memorandum for the file, March 23, 1944, DOJ/FOIA file 146–28–430.

56. SNDC to Sharp, March 20, 1944, DOJ/FOIA file 146–28–430.

57. Sharp, memorandum for Hoover, May 5, 1944, DOJ/FOIA file 146–28–430.

58. Pittsburgh Field Office Report, April 13, 1944, FBI/FOIA SNDC file 97–1340–140.

59. H. T. O'Connor, SAC Pittsburgh to Hoover, April 3, 1944, Hoover to SAC Pittsburgh, April 24, 1944, FBI/FOIA SNDC file 97–1340–136; O'Connor to Hoover, May 1, 1944, FBI/FOIA SNDC file 97–1340–142.

60. Shoob, memorandum of conversation, April 20, 1944, RG 226, entry 100, box 105, YU 1351–1360 file; Dragnich, memorandum for Sharp, April 22, 1944, DOJ/FOIA file 146–28–430.

61. Butts, memorandum, Serbian, #664, April 24, 1944, RG 226, entry 100, box 105, YU 1361–1370 file.

62. Hoover to SAC Pittsburgh, May 25, 1944, FBI/FOIA SNDC file 97–1340–153.

63. Kaplan to Sharp, May 16, 1944, DOJ/FOIA file 146–28–430. The paper already carried that disclaimer.

64. Dragnich, memorandum for Sharp, June 6, 1944, DOJ/FOIA file 146–28–430.

65. Slavitt, memorandum for the file, June 2, 1944, DOJ/FOIA file 146–28–430.

66. Pittsburgh Field Office report, June 28, 1944, FBI/FOIA SNDC file 97–1340–174.

67. Adamic to Sharp, January 14, 1944, DOJ/FOIA UCSSA file 149–1670.

68. Dragnich, memorandum for Sharp, February 16, 1944, DOJ/FOIA UCSSA file 149–1670.

69. Slavitt, memorandum of conference, February 19, 1944, and memorandum for Sharp, February 24, 1944, DOJ/FOIA UCSSA file 149–1670.

70. Slavitt, memorandum for Sharp, February 26, 1944, with attachments, DOJ/FOIA UCSSA file 149–1670.

71. Christy George Peters to Sharp, April 11, 1944, and Sharp to Peters, April 22, 1944, DOJ/FOIA UCSSA file 149–1670.

72. Zlatko Baloković and Rev. Strahinja Maletich to Sharp, May 3, 1944, DOJ/FOIA UCSSA file 149–1670.

73. Sharp to the UCSSA, May 10, 1944, DOJ/FOIA UCSSA file 149–1670.

74. Slavitt, memorandum for the file, May 23, 1944, DOJ/FOIA UCSSA file 149–1670.

75. Sharp to Edward J. Ennis, May 24, 1944, DOJ/FOIA UCSSA file 149–1670.

76. Report of the Attorney General, June 1, 1944, RG 60, entry SWPU, box 13, FARA file.

77. Winant to Hull, June 1, 1944, *FRUS*, 1944, 4:1376–77; Jelavich, *History of the Balkans*, 2:271.

78. MacVeagh to Hull, June 17, 1944, *FRUS*, 1944, 4:1379.

79. Berle diary, June 1, 1944.

80. The Democratic Yugoslavia News Agency Bulletin, July 25, 1944, RG 226, entry 100, box 120, Yugoslavia (30)—#2 file.

81. Cannon, memorandum of conversation, July 8, 1944, *FRUS,* 1944, 4:1388–89.

82. FBI, General Intelligence Survey, August 1944, Hopkins Papers, box 146, Yugoslavian Activities, 55–56 file.

83. "The Yugoslav-American Press Considers the Subasich Government and the Recall of Ambassador Fotić," FNB No. B-234, August 5, 1944, RG 165, entry 79, box 1960, B-226–240 file.

84. "Recent Moves in the Serb Nationalist Press," August 26, 1944, RG 226, entry 100, box 120, Yugoslavia (30) #2 file.

85. "Balkan Unity" and "A Radio Interview," *The Bulletin* 2, no. 7 (July 20, 1944), Adamic Papers, box 89, file 1.

86. Poole, memorandum of conversation, August 1, 1944, RG 226, entry 100, box 122, State Department Conversations file.

87. Poole, memorandum of conversation, August 4, 1944, No. S-109, RG 226, entry 100, box 106, YU 1480–1490 file.

88. Poole, memorandum of conversation, August 22, 1944, RG 226, entry 100, box 122, NY FNB Op 2 file.

89. Poole to Berle, August 31, 1944, with enclosure, memorandum of conversation, by Poole, August 30, 1944, RG 226, entry 100, box 106, YU 1511–1530 file.

90. "Opposition to Tito Actual and Potential," FNB No. 212, September 21, 1944, RG 165, entry 79, box 1958.

91. "A message from Marshall Tito," FNB No. N-37, September 23, 1944, RG 226, entry 100, box 106, YU 1531–1550 file.

92. Poole, memorandum of conversation, August 1, 1944, RG 226, entry 100, box 122, Weekly Conference with Mr. Berle, State Department Conversations file.

93. Slavitt, memorandum for Laurence A. Knapp, July 21, 1944, DOJ/FOIA file 146–28–430.

94. FBI Quarterly Intelligence Report, August 10, 1944, #229, FBI/FOIA SNDC 97–1430.

95. New York Field Office Report, April 11, 1944, FBI/FOIA UCSSA file 100–212169–44.

96. Hoover to New York Field Office, May 1, 1944, FBI/FOIA UCSSA file 100–212169–41.

97. Hoover to the Attorney General, May 24, 1944, FBI/FOIA UCSSA file 100–212169–59. The majority of the document is redacted.

98. Hoover to Berle, May 24, 1944, FBI/FOIA UCSSA file 100–212169–63. Much of the file is redacted.

99. Malvina Thompson to Joyce Baloković, May 21, 1944, with attachment, Esther Lape to Eleanor Roosevelt, May 16, 1944, ER Papers, White House Correspondence, Personal Letters, 1944, box 796, All-Ba file.

100. Eleanor Roosevelt to Francis Biddle, May 30, 1944, with attachment, Biddle to Eleanor Roosevelt, May 31, 1944, ER Papers, White House Correspondence, 1933–1945, 70 1944, box 402, Biddle, Francis file.

101. Eleanor Roosevelt to Joyce Baloković, June 3, 1944, with attachment, Joyce Baloković to Eleanor Roosevelt, May 31, 1944, ER Papers, White House Correspondence, 1933–1945, 70 Correspondence with Government Departments 1944, box 401, Bab-Ban file; memorandum by Sava Kosanović, n.d., ER Papers, White House Correspondence, 1933–1945, 70 Correspondence with Government Departments, 1944, box 104, Bab-Ban file.

102. United Committee of South Slavic Americans, Memorandum for Mrs. Franklin Roosevelt, Re: Application of Foreign Agents Registration Act by the United States Department of Justice, n.d., ER Papers, White House Correspondence, 1933–1945, Correspondence with Government Departments 1944, box 104, Bab-Ban file.

103. United Committee of South Slavic Americans, Memorandum for Mrs. Franklin Roosevelt, Re: Application of Foreign Agents Registration Act by the United States Department of Justice, n.d., ER Papers, White House Correspondence, 1933–1945, Correspondence with Government Departments 1944, box 104, Bab-Ban file.

104. Joyce Baloković to Eleanor Roosevelt, June 14, 1944, ER Papers, White House Correspondence, 1933–1945, 90 Congratulations and Greetings, 1943, W1 1944, box 528, BA file.

105. Boston Field Office to Hoover, June 26, 1944, with enclosure, Staff Sgt. Ralph G. Martin, Stoyan Pribichevich, John Talbot, Edd Johnson, "The Yugoslav Struggle through American Eyes," May 1944, UCSSA, New York, FBI/FOIA UCSSA file 100–212169–69.

106. Slavitt to Knapp, July 21, 1944, DOJ/FOIA UCSSA file 149–1670.

107. Dragnich, memorandum for Knapp, August 30, 1944, DOJ/FOIA UCSSA file 149–1670.

108. "Opposition to Tito Actual and Potential," FNB No. 212, September 21, 1944, RG 165, entry 79, box 1958.

109. Poole to Berle, October 10, 1944, RG 226, entry 100, box 106, YU 1551–1580 file.

110. "Leftist Slavic Americans Give Currency to Tito's Strictures on Anglo-American Aid," FNB No. 82, October 26, 1944, RG 226, entry 100, box 106, YU 1551–1580 file.

111. See *The Bulletin* 2, no. 9 (September 15, 1944), Adamic Papers, box 89, file 1.

112. "Conference and Assembly of Serbian National Council and Serb National Federation," FNB No. 241, October 18, 1944, RG 226, "Exhibits OSS," entry 99, box 74, file 28.

113. "*Amerikanski Srbobran* Welcomes the Red Army and Pleads for Consideration for the Serb Nation," FNB No. 86, October 31, 1944, RG 226, entry 100, box 106, YU 1551–1580 file.

114. SAC New York to Hoover, November 16, 1944, with attachment, *The American Serb* 1, no. 10 (October 1944), FOIA/FBI SNDC file 197–1340–246.

115. Poole, memorandum to the Director of Strategic Services and the Secretary of State, March 19, 1945, RG 226, entry 100, box 31, EU 541–550 file.

116. Yugoslavia: The Tito-Subasic Agreement, *FRUS*, Malta and Yalta, 1945: 250–54; Roberts, *Tito, Mihailović and the Allies*, 273; Herbert Feis, *Churchill, Roosevelt and Stalin: The War They Waged and the Peace They Sought* (Princeton, N.J.: Princeton University Press, 1967), 543.

117. Joyce Baloković to Eleanor Roosevelt, n.d., with attachments, ER Papers, White House Correspondence, 1933–1945, 100 Personal Letters, 1944, box 796, All-Ba file.

118. Joyce Borden Baloković, *Singing Wings* (Camden Herald Publishing, 1973), no page number.

119. *The Bulletin* 3, no. 1 (January/February 1945), Adamic Papers, box 89, file 1.

120. Thompson to Joyce Baloković, December 11, 1944, with attachment, Baloković to Thompson, December 5, 1944, ER Papers, White House Correspondence, 1933–1945, 20.2, Patroness Declined, 1944, box 28, AL file.

121. Ladd to Hoover, December 9, 1944, FBI/FOIA UCSSA file 100–212169–115.

Conclusion

1. Poole, "The Study of Foreign Political Developments," December 31, 1944, RG 226, entry 100, box 121, Int. 34 file.

2. "Dissension among Croatian Separatists Here and Resumption of Communist Attacks on Machek," FNB No. 159, January 8, 1945, RG 226, entry 100, box 106, YU 1641–1670 file.

3. "Bishop Dionisije's Dilemma," No. B-305, January 19, 1945, RG 226, entry 100, box 120, Yugoslavia (30) #2 file.

4. Poole, memorandum of conversation, January 24, 1945, RG 226, entry 100, box 122, State Department Conversations file.

5. Lord Halifax to Edward R. Stettinius, January 22, 1945, *FRUS*, 1945, 5:1183–84; Cannon, memorandum, January 29, 1945, *FRUS*, 1945, 5:1192–94.

6. "Crosscurrents from the Homeland Agitate Yugoslav-American Community," FNB No. 232, February 15, 1945, RG 226, entry 100, box 110, FNB Reports Volume 4, New York-FNB. Int. 31 file.

7. Matthews Minutes, n.d., *FRUS*, Malta-Yalta, 1945: 850–55; Trilateral Documents, Communique Issued at the End of the Conference, February 11, 1945, *FRUS*, Malta-Yalta, 1945: 968–75.

8. "Report to the Director," FNB B-947, March 7, 1945, RG 226, entry 100, box 107, YU 1701–1740 file.

9. Poole, memorandum for the Director of Strategic Services and Secretary of State, No. S-135, March 10, 1945, RG 226, entry 100, box 107, YU 1701–1740 file.

10. "Yugoslav-Americans and the Coalition Government in Belgrade," FNB No. B-347, April 16, 1945, RG 226, entry 100, box 107, YU 1741–1760 file.

11. "Serb Nationalists and Mihailovich," FNB No. 243, March 24, 1945, RG 226, entry 100, box 107, YU 1741–1760 file.

12. Richard C. Patterson to Stettinius, April 9, 1945, *FRUS*, 1945, 5:1218.

13. Bjarne Braatoy, memorandum for the Director of Strategic Services and the

Secretary of State, No. S-142, April 25, 1945, RG 226, entry 100, box 107, YU 1761–1770 file.

14. Roberto G. Rabel, *Between East and West: Trieste, the United States and the Cold War, 1941–1954* (Durham, N.C.: University of North Carolina Press: 1988), 2–16.

15. Harry S. Truman, *Memoirs,* vol. 1, *Year of Decisions* (New York: Doubleday, 1955), 245, 247, 249; Rabel, *Between East and West,* 18–51.

16. Stettinius to Joseph Grew, 18 May 1945, *FRUS,* 1945, 5:1229.

17. Llewellyn E. Thompson, Memorandum of Conversation, 25 May 1945, *FRUS,* 1945, 5:1233–34.

18. "Yugoslav-Americans Stunned by Anglo-American Stand on Trieste," FNB No. B-365, 26 May 1945, RG 226, entry 100, box 107, YU 1801–10 file.

19. Rabel, *Between East and West,* 67.

20. OSS Research and Analysis Branch, "Situation Report: USSR," May 19, 1945, RG 59, R & A 1785.44, OSS-INR Reports file.

21. CCAU, "Foreign Language Press on Dumbarton Oaks," n.d., ACNS, shipment 4, box 7, Foreign Language Press file.

22. "Yugoslav Delegation to San Francisco Reported Cool to Yugoslav-American Leftists," FNB No. 302, April 27, 1945, RG 226, entry 100, box 107, YU 1771–1780 file.

23. "Serb and Croat Nationalist Activities at San Francisco," FNB No. B-356, May 12, 1945, RG 226, entry 100, box 107, YU 1791–1800 file.

24. *New York Times,* May 1, 1945, 13:5.

25. Adamic to Baloković, March 26, 1945, Adamic Papers, box 3, file 3.

26. Adamic to Nick Bez, April 18, 1945, Adamic Papers, box 45, Bez file. In the letter, Adamic confided, "I'm damn near broke," and he said he had not been able to "work for pay" for more than a year.

27. Wilson, "Foreign Nationalities Branch," 108–9.

28. Wilson, "Foreign Nationalities Branch," 111–18.

29. "United Committee of South-Slavic Americans Plans to Augment Activities," FNB No. 361, June 20, 1945, CIA/OSS in FBI File, CIA release.

30. Herbert Wechsler to Hoover, December 4, 1944, DOJ/FOIA file 146–28–430; Biddle to Knapp, March 5, 1945, with attachment, *The American Serb* 2, no. 2 (February 1945), DOJ/FOIA file 146–28–430.

31. Knapp to Wechsler, March 8, 1945, Wechsler to Biddle, March 9, 1945, with attachment, *The American Serb* 2, no. 2 (February 1945), DOJ/FOIA file 146–28–430; *The Foreign Agents Registration Act of 1938, As Amended* (Washington, D.C.: GPO, 1942), 11.

32. Hoover to SAC Detroit, July 6, 1945, FBI/FOIA SNDC file 97–1340–295.

33. Hoover to Detroit Field Office, October 29, 1947, #348 and December 13, 1947, #351, FBI/FOIA SNDC file 97–1340.

34. http://www.serbnatlfed.org/Archives.WTCArticle.htm.

35. http://www.snd-us.com/Features/res_jun99.htm.

36. "Serbian King Buried in the U.S. May Be Returned Home," *New York Times,*

March 5, 2007, A17. The press releases for the Royal Family of Serbia may be found at http://www.royalfamily.org.

37. Biddle, *Brief Authority,* 257–61.

38. Letter, undated and unsigned, Baloković Papers, box 2, file 18.

39. Wechsler to Hoover, February 3, 1945, DOJ/FOIA UCSSA file 149–1670.

40. Hoover to Wechsler, March 8, 1954, FBI/FOIA UCSSA file 100–212–169.

41. Jesse MacKnight, memorandum to the files, March 1, 1945, DOJ/FOIA UCSSA file 149–1670. This material had also been published in *The Bulletin.*

42. SAC Philadelphia to Hoover, March 12, 1945, with enclosures, *Today and Tomorrow* 1, no. 1 (January-February 1945), and *The Bulletin* 3, no. 1 (January-February 1945), FBI/FOIA UCSSA file 100–212169–156.

43. E. E. Conroy, SAC New York to Hoover, June 23, 1945, with attachments, FBI/FOIA UCSSA file 100–212169–180.

44. New York Field Office Report, July 9, 1945, FBI/FOIA UCSSA file 100–212169–193. It was not until the late summer of 1945, after the war had ended in all theaters, that FBI reports on the UCSSA included the category of FARA after that of Internal Security; synopses and summaries usually listed the FARA first and Communist influence second as grounds for investigation.

45. Wechsler to Hoover, July 6, 1945, DOJ/FOIA UCSSA file 149–1670; Hoover to New York Field Office, July 20, 1945, #199, FBI/FOIA UCSSA file 100–212–169.

46. Hoover to SAC New York, August 11, 1945, FBI/FOIA UCSSA file 100–212169–217.

47. Hoover to New York Field Office, July 20, 1945, #199, and Hoover to Wechsler, date not legible, #231, FBI/FOIA UCSSA file 100–212–169.

48. E. E. Conroy, SAC New York to Hoover, October 25, 1945, with attachments, FBI/FOIA UCSSA file 100–212169–302.

49. Adamic to Bez, December 17, 1945, Adamic Papers, box 45, Bez file.

50. See for example, *The Bulletin* 3, no. 5 (December 1945), and 4, no. 1 (April 1946), Adamic Papers, box 89, file 1.

51. Hoover to Frederick B. Lyon, April 4, 1945, with attachment, *Today and Tomorrow,* January-February 1945, 1, no. 1, 100–212169–143.

52. Pribichevich to Adamic, March 29, 1946, Adamic Papers, box 48, file 9.

53. Adamic to Joseph Brljavac, August 6, 1946, Adamic Papers, box 45, file 7.

54. Petrinović to Adamic, April 3, 1946, Adamic Papers, box 48, file 8.

55. Adamic to Bez, June 24, 1946, Adamic Papers, box 45, Bez file.

56. Hoover to T. L. Caudle, February 11, 1946, #379, FBI/FOIA UCSSA file 100–212–169.

57. New York Field Office (Edward Scheidt) to Hoover, September 13, 1946, FBI/FOIA UCSSA file 100–212169–476 and September 20, 1946, FBI/FOIA UCSSA file 100–212169–483; James M. McInerney to Hoover, November 20, 1950, DOJ/FOIA UCSSA file 149–1670.

58. SAC New York (Scheidt) to Hoover, August 20, 1947, FBI/FOIA UCSSA file 100–212169–605.

59. T. Vincent Quinn to John F. X. McGohey, November 7, 1947, DOJ/FOIA UCSSA 149–1670.

60. xxxx to xxxx, January 31, 1948, FBI/FOIA UCSSA file 100–212169–630 (names are redacted in the source text).

61. Frank W. Schattschneider to William E. Foley, November 8, 1950, DOJ/FOIA UCSSA file 149–1670.

62. Hoover to Alexander M. Campbell, April 6, 1949, #661 and New York Field report, August 15, 1949, #672, FBI/FOIA UCSSA file 100–212–169. Although fragments exist in the papers of Baloković and Adamic and in a number of FBI files, the full files of the UCSSA have not been found.

63. Hoover to Ladd, July 12, 1949, #449, FBI/FOIA UCSSA file 100–212–169.

64. See Lorraine M. Lees, *Keeping Tito Afloat: The United States, Yugoslavia and the Cold War* (University Park, Penn.: Pennsylvania State University Press, 1997).

65. Irving H. Saypol to James M. McInerney, October 16, 1950, DOJ/FOIA UCSSA file 149–1670; McInerney to Hoover, November 2, 1950, FBI/FOIA file 149–1670. The previously referenced letter of November 8 to William Foley also contained a disclaimer that the Tito–Stalin split "has no relation to the matter."

66. Historical sketch, Finding Aid, Baloković Papers, IHRC.

67. Christian, *Checklist*, xli-xliv.

68. D. M. Ladd to Hoover, September 19, 1950, and March 15, 1951, FBI/FOIA Adamic file 100–63670–99.

69. Hoover to SAC Newark, September 8, 1951, FBI/FOIA Adamic file 100–63670–113.

70. Adamic, *Dinner*, 159.

71. Adamic, *Dinner*, 153–54.

72. Adamic, *Dinner*, 153–58.

73. Lane, Oral History, 616.

74. Steele, *Free Speech*, 1.

75. Leo P. Ribuffo, *The Old Christian Right: The Protestant Far Right from the Great Depression to the Cold War* (Philadelphia: Temple University Press, 1983), 215.

76. Geoffrey S. Smith, *To Save a Nation: American 'Extremism', the New Deal and the Coming of World War II*, rev. ed. (Chicago: Ivan R. Dee: 1992), 184.

77. Brett Gary, *Nervous Liberals*, 273.

Sources

American Heritage Center
Papers of:
Lawrence M. C. Smith

Bancroft Library, University of California–Berkeley
Papers of:
Alan Cranston

Columbia University Oral History
Chester T. Lane

Department of Justice/Federal Bureau of Investigation files on:
Louis Adamic
United Committee of South Slav Americans
American Slav Congress
Serbian National Defense Council/Serb National Federation

Franklin D. Roosevelt Library
Papers of:
Franklin D. Roosevelt
Eleanor Roosevelt
Adolf A. Berle
Francis Biddle
Harry Hopkins
Sumner Welles

Immigration and Naturalization Service
Records of "I'm an American" Program

Immigration History Research Center
Papers of:
American Council for Nationalities Services
Rachel Davis-Dubois
Zlatko Baloković

Library of Congress
Papers of:
Elmer Davis
Cordell Hull
Harold L. Ickes
Robert H. Jackson
Archibald MacLeish

National Archives
Record Group 12—Office of Education
Record Group 44—Office of Government Reports
Record Group 59—Department of State
Record Group 60—Department of Justice
Record Group 165—Records of the War Department
Record Group 208—Office of War Information
Record Group 226—Office of Strategic Services/Foreign Nationalities Branch

Princeton University Library
Papers of:
Louis Adamic

Index

Adamic, Louis: *Amerikanski Srbobran* attacks on, 116; anti-royalist, pro-U.S.S.R. position, 169–70; anti-Serbian position, 156–57, 178; background, 67; as Communist, 111–12; on Cranston, 121–22; Cranston and, 9; Eleanor Roosevelt and, 68–69, 71, 99, 178, 234n38; Federal Bureau of Investigation surveillance of, 111, 209–10; Foreign Language Information Service advisory board role, 23; on Fotić, 132; on immigrant alienation, 17; King Peter visit strategy meeting and, 81; on Mihailović, 132; as 1944 pro-Yugoslav spokesperson, 169; objections to United Committee of South-Slavic Americans registration under Foreign Agents Registration Act, 179–89; "passage back" concept, 68–71; Poole analysis of, 156; on postwar implications of Yugoslav ethnic dissent, 110–11; on postwar leftward movement of Yugoslavia, 207–8; predictions regarding future of U.S.A. and U.S.S.R., 170; propaganda value to Foreign Nationalities Branch, 63; as "propagandist" for immigrants, 67–68; protest against Fotić ambassadorship by, 98; radio broadcasts, 20, 21; on Roosevelt and Yugoslav-American community, 30; screenwriting project, 71; as Slovene and Partisan advocate, 72; on Tito, 132; on Tito-Ribar government, 163; Truman meeting regarding Yugoslavia relief and Tito support, 206; United Committee of South-Slavic Americans leadership, 8, 58; United Nations briefings, 199–200; on U.S. government policies regarding ethnic groups, 210–11; on victory and vision, 68; warnings to Baloković, 199; works of, 67–68

Adamic, Stella, 68, 69

Albania, 56

Alexander (crown prince of Yugoslavia), 202

Alexander I (King of Yugoslavia), 55

Alexandra (princess of Greece), 165–66

Alien and Sedition Acts of 1798, 28

Alien Enemy Bureau, 14

Alien Registration Act: administration of, 29; Bill of Rights v., 28; immigrant community reaction to, 36; passage of, 28; perceived limitations of, 31; provisions of, 22–23, 28; statistics related to implementation of, 31

All-Slav Movement, 94–95

American Civil Liberties Union, 23

"American Committee for Yugoslav Relief Ship," 192–93

American Friends of Yugoslavia, 107, 173

American Handbook (Office of War Information publication), 93

Americanization, 23, 72. *See also* "passage back" concept

American nativism: anti-radicalism of, 3, 213; characteristics of, 1; Cold War and,

of South-Slavic Americans registration under Foreign Agents Registration Act, 179–81; Poole on, 133–34; United Committee of South-Slavic Americans formation and, 133
Bell, Ulrich, 108
Berle, Adolf A.: on American Slav Congress (ASC) support, 76; background and vision of, 42–43; on Biddle, 32; on Central and Eastern European refugee agitation, 130; on Communism and American Slav Congress, 96–97; Cranston v., 51, 122; Croatian Fraternal Union of America meetings with, 60; on dangers inherent in foreign political disputes, 140; on Department of Justice/Department of State power struggles, 32; Department of State debate influence of, 49–53; disagreement with Cranston on Serb-Croat dispute, 93–97; on domestic functions of government agencies v. Department of State authority, 123; on espionage in Labor Department, 25–26; on ethnic/partisan war plane dedication policy, 146–47; exploration of guiding principles for U.S. citizens and foreign nationals by, 120–21; Federal Bureau of Investigation power struggle and, 1; on foreign-language groups, 48–49; foreign language press contact of, 44; on foreign nationality groups, 49–51; on Fotić recall, 157; on "free movements" policy of U.S. government, 126; on German immigrants, 43; on government agency function clarification need, 90, 124; on immigrants and loyalty, 43–44; liberal attitude of, 50–51; opposition to support of American Slav Congress, 96; on Pan-Slav Conference, 94; policy on ethnic activity summarized, 128; on pressure exerted on U.S. government by ethnic groups, 119; on propaganda and control, 43; on protecting allied agents and personnel, 221n99; recommendations to Hull regarding foreign nationals, 49–53; on role of Office of War Information in Serb-Croat dispute, 95; on security v. civil liberties, 19; on Serbian National Defense Council propaganda, 81; Slav organization research by, 75; on Tito and Subasić, 182–83; on U.S. policy regarding Serb-Croat

dispute, 102–3, 158; on Yugoslav-American v. American identity, 97
Bez, Nick, 200, 206
Biddle, Francis: alien registrants and, 30; on Alien Registration Act, 28; as alien sympathizer, 28–29; attorney general appointment by Roosevelt, 33; Baloković meetings about United Committee of South-Slavic Americans registration as foreign agents, 187–88; Berle on, 32; censorship policy of, 65–66; on containing factional and ethnic conflicts stirred by foreign-language newspapers, 114; on fifth column associations with aliens, 28; on Foreign Agents Registration Act and Department of Justice, 33, 34; on foreign propaganda material impact, 182; on freedom v. fear, 13; on Hoover, 33; Hoover and, 33; on Immigration and Naturalization Service transfer to Department of Justice, 27; Perkins and, 25; principles of, 7; on safeguarding U.S. and allied agents and personnel, 34
Boas, Frank, 4
Bolshevism, 2–3
bomber naming incident, 146–47
Bosnia-Herzogovina, 56. See also Partisan resistance movement; Ustasha
Boyd-Boich, William, 60
Braatoy, Braje, 200
Bridges, Harry, 25
British Broadcasting Corporation, 100
Brock, Ray, 169
Brown, Oscar, 79, 83
Brownlow, Louis, 37
Brunot, James, 175
Bulgaria, 56
Bulletins (Foreign Nationalities Branch publication), 48
Bulletin (United Committee of South-Slavic Americans publication), 58, 134, 156
Bureau of Intelligence, 146
Bureau of Investigation, 3
Bureau of Naturalization, 2
Butkovich, John, 12, 58–59, 61–62, 77, 84
Butts, Carl, 170

Cainkar, Vincent, 58, 77
Campbell, Ronald, 79
Cannon, Cavendish, 101, 108, 132, 141–42
censorship, 65–66. See also departments and

LORRAINE M. LEES is an associate professor of history at Old Dominion University in Virginia and the author of *Keeping Tito Afloat: The United States, Yugoslavia, and the Cold War.*

The University of Illinois Press
is a founding member of the
Association of American University Presses.

_____

Composed in 10.5/13 Adobe Minion
with Meta display
at the University of Illinois Press
Manufactured by Thomson-Shore, Inc.

University of Illinois Press
1325 South Oak Street
Champaign, IL 61820-6903
www.press.uillinois.edu